Repetition in Discourse

Library of Congress Cataloging-in-Publication Data

Repetition in discourse / edited by Barbara Johnstone.
        p.   cm. — (Advances in discourse processes)
     Includes bibliographical references and index.
     ISBN 0-89391-830-X (v. 1). — ISBN 0-89391-931-4 (pbk. : v. 1).—
ISBN 0-89391-831-8 (v. 2).—ISBN 0-89391-932-2 (pbk. : v. 2)
     1. Discourse analysis. 2. Repetition (Rhetoric) I. Johnstone,
Barbara.   II. Series.
P302.82.R47   1994
401'.41—dc20   92-42685
                                                                    CIP

Ablex Publishing Corporation
355 Chestnut Street
Norwood, New Jersey 07648

Repetition in Discourse Interdisciplinary Perspectives

Volume One

Barbara Johnstone, Editor
Texas A&M University

Volume XLVII in the Series
Advances in Discourse Processes
Roy O. Freedle, *Editor*

 Ablex Publishing Corporation
Norwood, New Jersey

Perhaps,
The man-hero is not the exceptional monster,
But he that of repetition is most master.

Wallace Stevens
"Notes Toward a Supreme Fiction"

Contents

Preface to the Series

Roy O. Freedle

Series Editor

This series of volumes provides a forum for the cross-fertilization of ideas from a diverse number of disciplines, all of which share a common interest in discourse—be it prose comprehension and recall, dialogue analysis, text grammar construction, computer simulation of natural language, cross-cultural comparisons of communicative competence or other related topics. The problems posed by multisentence contexts and the methods required to investigate them, while not always unique to discourse, are still sufficiently distinct as to benefit from the organized model of scientific interaction made possible by this series.

Scholars working in the discourse area from the perspective of sociolinguistics, psycholinguistics, ethnomethodology and the sociology of language, educational psychology (e.g., teacher–student interaction), the philosophy of language, computational linguistics, and related sub-areas are invited to submit manuscripts of monograph or book length to the series editor. Edited collections of original papers resulting from conferences will also be considered.

Volumes in the Series

Vol. I	Discourse Production and Comprehension. Roy O. Freedle (Ed.), 1977.
Vol. II	New Directions in Discourse Processing. Roy O. Freedle (Ed.), 1979.
Vol. III	The Pear Stories, Cognitive, Cultural, and Linguistic Aspects of Narrative Production. Wallace L. Chafe (Ed.), 1980.

Preface

In recent years, many humanists and social scientists have rejected the notion that understanding is a simple matter of encoding and decoding. Current theory in linguistic pragmatics, in rhetoric, in cultural anthropology, and in literary theory stresses the situated, interactive, rhetorical nature of understanding. Various approaches to the ways understanding is constructed in the process of inter-action—such as interactional sociolinguistics, epistemic rhetoric, ethnography of communication, functionalist poetics, and reader response theory—make reference to the crucial role of repetition in this process. Linguists have examined repetition in conversation and in language acquisition. Anthropologists and folklorists have studied the role of parallelism as a feature of performance and as a recurring characteristic of ritual forms of talk. Students of poetics discuss repetition as a key feature of artistic language. Literary theorists and rhetoricians discuss "intertextuality," or the ways in which the authors of new texts make use of old texts. Clearly, any-one interested in a comprehensive theory of understanding must pay close attention to the mechanisms and functions of repetition.

What is needed is a way of thinking about repetition that ties together the insights from various fields and perspectives and vari-ous texts and genres, a way of thinking that makes it clear that discoveries about the crucial structural, interactional, and semantic functions of repetition across a range of disciplines and approaches are more than simply coincidental. In these volumes, we attempt to approach such a synthesis by examining the functions of discourse repetition from a variety of perspectives. Some of us are primarily interested in textual functions of repetition: How does repetition function in the process by which people are able to distinguish a list of unrelated sentences from a paragraph or a conversation? Others study its rhetorical uses: How does repetition create knowledge?

The rhetorical strategy of "browbeating" depends on repetition, but so does the persuasive power of speakers like Martin Luther King, Jr., as well as the power of teachers and tutors and novelists to force their audiences to recategorize and reinterpret. What can be learned from the obvious utility of repetition in situations in which some speakers fail to control the information or the discourse rules at hand? Many of us are concerned with the interactional functions of repetition: the role of repetition in creating interpersonal engagement in conversation and in signalling how speakers are to understand their interlocutors' words. We all appreciate, and many of us explicitly study, aesthetic functions of repetition: Repetition is a salient feature of all verbal art, be it in flirtatious banter, dramatic representations of conflict and failure, traditional Southeast Asian poetry, or postmodern novelistic foregrounding of the mundane. We are also interested in referential functions of repetition: Repetition can be a semantic strategy, as when speakers use conventionalized patterns such as phonological reduplication and lexical couplets to convey elements of lexical and phrasal meaning. As syntacticians discover more iconic and more functional reasons for sentences having the forms they do, repetition emerges as a more basic semantic strategy than it has been thought to be.

This volume and its companion are results of an NEH-sponsored conference on Repetition in Discourse which was held at Texas A&M University in May 1990. With the exception of our introductory chapter, which is in fact a "record of things said and done," these are not conference proceedings; the chapters in these two books were written after the conference, under the influence, I hope, of what went on there. The unusual and very successful format of the conference, at which 10-minute summaries of work in progress were followed by intensive, broad-ranging small-group discussions, meant that those of us who chose to could really be influenced by one another—and most of us did choose to. The fact that the conferees came from a variety of disciplines and departments and academic ranks (from graduate student to professor emeritus), and that all had exactly the same role to play, meant that the influence could flow in all directions—and I think it did.

This volume begins with what might be called an introduction, if only because of its being at the beginning of the book. This chapter is an experimental form of discourse which is intended to represent the fact that the work reported on in these volumes is all jointly produced and many-voiced. It is currently popular to point out that all discourse has these characteristics, but ours does particularly. We talked intensively, and our contributions to our talk were clearly and obviously shaped by one another's. The first chapter weaves together some of our talk, which was tape-recorded with everyone's permission, and which is used, also with everyone's permission, without attribution to particular speakers. It is organized around the questions we discussed at the conference, some of which I suggested and some of which were suggested by other conferees.

The rest of Volume I foregrounds the foregrounded, the genres of discourse in which repetition has historically appeared most salient. Two chapters discuss broad methodological issues: how we notice repetition, and how it can be represented in transcription and translation. In turning then to literary discourse, the structure of the volume reflects the fact that repetition has far more frequently been noted in literature and other forms of verbal art than in other genres of discourse, perhaps because it is more noticeable there. Seven chapters on repetition in literature deal with drama, fictional and nonfictional prose, and poetry, in English, French, German, and Thai, examining, for example, how repetition creates parody, reflects the postmodern worldview, and characterizes authorial and generic style.

Repetition has often been noted, too, in teaching and learning, as when naughty pupils used to be forced to copy a sentence one hundred times, but also more subtly. Six chapters on repetition in learning discuss the role of repetition in first- and second-language acquisition and classroom talk among native speakers, in creole discourse, and in the discourse of elderly stroke and Alzheimer's victims. These chapters deal with pregrammatical functions of repetition and their grammaticalization; with repetition as a way of creating joint cognition; and with repetition as a strategy with which partially competent speakers can find room in interactions.

The companion volume to this one deals with repetition in less marked speech situations. Four chapters discuss repetition in spontaneous, everyday conversation, dealing with its roles in play and joking, in negotiating conflict, and in reflecting and perpetuating cultural aesthetics. Three chapters discuss institutional kinds of talk—communication between pilots and air traffic controllers, television interviews, and therapy sessions. Repetition is seen to serve crucial functions in all, preventing (and sometimes causing) air disasters, helping TV interviewees display rapport with their hosts, and aiding therapists in drawing their clients out and clients in demonstrating insight.

Three chapters in Volume II deal with visual discourse. Repetition of spatial configurations is a cohesive device in American Sign Language and a rhetorical device in graphic communication, and repeated visual images reinforce repeated verbal imagery in the perpetuation of authoritative values. The final two essays broaden the

focus again, suggesting that repetition is central to how we understand each other in all situations and crucial for understanding how
culture is transmitted. The volume ends with a 275-item annotated
bibliography on repetition in discourse.

Though these two volumes do not claim to provide a definitive
statement about repetition and its functions, they represent and attempt to recapture the most intensive interdisciplinary effort to date
to work toward an understanding of this crucial, ubiquitous discourse phenomenon.

Acknowledgments

This project was made possible by the National Endowment for the Humanities, which provided the major funding for the conference from which these volumes result and for the compilation of the volumes. Support for the conference was also provided by the Texas A&M Association of Former Students, the Department of English at Texas A&M University, and the College of Liberal Arts. I am very grateful to all.

My greatest personal debt, by far, is to Delma McLeod-Porter, who served as administrative assistant before, during, and after the conference, and as editorial assistant in the preparation of these books. I cannot imagine having done this, or ever doing such a thing again, without her calm efficiency and the marvelous Southern tact with which she made me feel that I was always in control of the situation, even when she really was. Many other people, at Texas A&M and elsewhere, also helped see the project through. Guy Bailey and Charles Johnson provided much-needed moral support in the frustrating process of grant writing and rewriting, as did Christine M. Kalke at the NEH. Abdel-Rahman Abu-Melhim, Laura Anderson, Guy Bailey, Valerie Balester, Robert and Lonnie Boenig, Suzanne Cherry, Kathleen Ferrara, Laurie Haynes, Kate Kelly, Annette Kirk, Diane Kirk, and Cindy Schnebly helped with transportation and hospitality and moderated and taped conference sessions. Larry Mitchell proved, as usual, to be an exemplary department head, getting the conference started with thoughtful introductory remarks and participating in most of the rest of it. I thank all of these people.

My interest in repetition owes its inception to A. L. Becker, who cryptically suggested more than 10 years ago that I look into the topic, knowing full well, I now see, that it would become an obsession. I owe him my largest intellectual debt. I am also grateful to everyone else who has worked on this topic and whose work I have read or heard, but most especially to the people whose work is represented in these volumes. What I have learned from them will continue to keep me busy for years.

Chapter 1
Repetition in Discourse: A Dialogue

Barbara Johnstone et al.*

Department of English
Texas A&M University

This chapter presents some of the discussion that occurred during the conference from which the selections in this volume and its companion volume result. This talk took place during times when we met in groups of seven or so to mull over general questions

* Co-authors are all the conference participants who took part in discussions, whether they talked or made others' talk possible by listening. All have agreed to let their voices be woven together. They are Abdel-Rahman Abu-Melhim, Laura Anderson, Valerie Balester, Martha Bean, A. L. Becker, Tina L. Bennett-Kastor, Jeutonne P. Brewer, Jill Brody, Suzanne Cherry, Steven Cushing, Masako Dorrill, Susan Ehrlich, Kathleen Ferrara, Phillip J. Glenn, Rebecca S. Gault, Laurie Haynes, Robert Hopper, Thomas John Hudak, Katherine E. Kelly, Annette Kirk, Diane Kirk, Laurie Knox, Michael Macovski, Bruce Mannheim, Delma McLeod-Porter, Marilyn Merritt, J. Lawrence Mitchell, Robert E. Nofsinger, Neal R. Norrick, G. Genevieve Patthey-Chavez, James E. Porter, B. Hannah Rockwell, Dennis Rygiel, Cynthia Schnebly, Susan C. Shepherd, Dina Sherzer, Joel Sherzer, JoEllen M. Simpson, Deborah Tannen, Russell S. Tomlin, Greg Urban, and Elizabeth A. Winston. Wolfram Bublitz did not attend the conference but did submit questions for discussion, and Delma McLeod-Porter prepared the transcriptions from which I have worked. After the conference, Jill Brody sent detailed and very useful notes about the discussions she attended, and Neal Norrick wrote with more thoughts. Robert Hopper, Neal Norrick, Larry Mitchell, Dina Sherzer, and Joel Sherzer helped edit a draft of this chapter.

suggested by the conference's organizer and other participants— or, on occasion, to critique the written questions or abandon them altogether. The questions were of the general heuristic sort: What forms of repetition in discourse can we distinguish? What are the functions of repetition in discourse? Are there functions universally served by repetition? What are differences across languages, social and cultural groups, modalities and genres of discourse? Some questions proved more useful than others; as they were meant only to spark discussion, the questions are not reproduced here. Twenty hours of discussion were taped, and the tapes transcribed. These "working sessions" formed the core of the conference; they were supplemented with brief summaries of individuals' projects.

My original thought was that the tapes would form the basis for a traditional introduction, in which I would summarize, in my words, what I thought had been accomplished at the conference, perhaps also reviewing, in my own words, what I took to be the most significant previous lines of research on linguistic repetition and fitting the chapters in these volumes into that scheme. Having already written such an introduction for a journal-issue collection of papers on repetition (Johnstone, 1987a), however, I didn't especially want to write another similar essay. A more significant objection to the job occurred to me during the conference. A traditional, single-authored, single-voiced summary would be the worst possible way of representing what the conference was expressly designed to do, namely, to make it possible for 43 people to produce, by talking together, new shared understandings of the phenomenon we were all interested in. I have tried, then, to find a way to weave our many voices together in this chapter, not by reproducing the transcriptions of our discussions (a format which is very hard to read; fluent writing is necessarily unlike speech), but instead by experimenting with a new way of composing. I have picked out the topics which we all seemed to talk about and come back to again and again—forms, functions, universals, differences—as well as topics that particularly sparked people's interest. For each, I have attempted to order bits of the transcriptions—sometimes whole speeches or sentences, sometimes phrases or words—into a text that would be both readable and many-voiced.

This has involved massive reorganizing. Actual conversations are sometimes represented here, but more often the voices of people who were not in the same rooms, or talking at the same times, speak together, finish one another's utterances, reinforce one another's claims. The style of this chapter, unlike that of the ones that follow, is conversational, though the conversation has been adapted to the medium of type. I have attempted to add cohesion to our text with headings, paragraphing, and transitional words and phrases; I have edited out some hesitation and hedging; and I have removed some spoken-like repetition and added some written-like repetition.

Though we are as individuals each authorities about the bits of repetition in discourse we have studied (and report on in other chapters in this volume and its companion), our tone as a group is tentative and questioning. Our collective authority rests only in our having thought about the topic, and talked about it, intensively. There is still much work to be done.

WHAT COUNTS AS REPETITION?

What are we trying to cover? How can we limit ourselves? Should we limit ourselves?

Most generally, repetition is pattern, and pattern is repetition. Why, then, do we label certain types of patterns repetition, and other types not? Perhaps because of a cultural bias: We think of certain patterns as repetition, and other patterns are something else. Alternatively, perhaps two things are the same if they produce a cognitive reflex, if they trigger a greater need for cognitive processing. How far apart can the model and the copy get before we don't call it a repetition? For traditional Thai poetry (Hudak, this volume), critics and poets list specific patterns of rhyme that appear in good poetry. But the analyst can find other patterns as well, such as reverse rhyme or para-rhyme. Are those also patterns of rhyme? Would a modern translation of Homer be a repetition? (Some theories of translation view translating as reproducing, making an exact copy, as much as possible.)

Part of the answer to the question, "What counts as repetition?" will have to do with how easily we can identify something as being "another one of those"; with audience perception. If I say "We deserve a break today," that will be a repetition for some people, who associate it with McDonald's, but not for others. A physicist at a press conference announced, "Read my lips: No new forces;" you don't understand that as a repetition, or really understand it at all, unless you know about the 1988 American presidential election. For people who are trained in a literate tradition, repetition of particular words is the easiest kind to identify, and there is more difference of opinion about whether to use term in cases of pragmatic repetition such as paraphrasing, in which there really is nothing palpable that's the same.

Do we want to call something repetition only if native speakers call it repetition? There is repetition at the phonetic level which, in Western cultures, we resist—and we'd still want to call it repetition. We are frequently touched off by sounds in our utterances. Such sound touchoffs include speech errors like, "*Fore*man stopped at the 40—no, the 30 yard line." But when people do that they take considerable steps to cover their tracks, to show themselves not to be merely repeating a sound pattern.

If I am cross-examining someone, firing questions at them, one after another, the questions all different, is that repetition? Is it parallelism? If I say "hello," is there any repetition there? When you say "hello" back, is that the first case of repetition? From one perspective, any instance of "hello/hello" is an identical repetition. But perhaps this isn't the sort of definition of repetition we want. (One could, on this criterion, count multiple uses of *the* in an English text as repetitions.) What about if you say "hello" and I say "hi"? Is that repetition, because in a larger sense we both know that they are instances of greeting?

One possible response is that neither "hello/hello" nor "hello/hi" involves repetition; while there is an element that is identical to a preceding element, from the perspective of the second speaker it is not a repetition. If I say "hello," and you say "hello?" with a questioning voice, that *is* a repetition, though, because it's a reframing of your *prior text* (Becker, Volume II). On the other hand, maybe to comprehend "hello" at all we need some prior text, prior text outside the immediate discourse.

If we can't agree on the answer to this question, it's because we don't have a theory with which to limit the field. Can we be theoretical? What, for example, is the Marxist approach to repetition? What is the poststructural approach? The postmodern approach? The generative-transformational approach? If we can't take the theories that we fight about and apply them to repetition, then we really don't know what repetition is.

Let's see how far we can go if we say that, in order to have repetition, there has to be a prior text. What will this work for, and what will it not work for? In one sense, prior text means "cultural memory," and that's involved with our understanding of any item. Would it be useful to limit ourselves to co-occurring prior texts? Some would use the term "repetition" only if the repetend and the repetition, the model and the copy, are both right there on the scene, often in adjacent items. Such a definition includes only prior texts that are local. At the other end of the continuum, others talk about global prior texts, things like retelling, allusions; in the middle might be quotation. In order to understand, for example, the repetition that is played with in the movie "Play it Again, Sam" one has to know "Casablanca," and this is a matter of recognizing not small items, but the whole setting and atmosphere, so it's a very different cognitive effort.

What about the idea of restricting ourselves to the more local? Once we get beyond that, almost anything could be said to count as a repetition; once we get into intertextuality, we begin to lose the focus. But how do we define the local in an oral tradition? If we only look at local repetition, we bias the analysis toward written forms; if we include global repetition in our purview, we're going to be more aware of what occurs in oral cultures. *Local* must be defined, and how do we define it in a village of people talking to each other constantly, or in a family?

Maybe we can talk about a continuum of localness. A next-turn repeat in a conversation would be extremely local, something said yesterday, less so. Could we not say that a local repetition is something that has happened in the scene, in the current strip of interaction? We need to create some boundaries in order to operate; it might be useful to imagine an intratextual/intertextual continuum and then focus on the intratextual end of that spectrum, for methodological convenience. When we're counting repetitions, when do we count, and where do we count? Don't we have to restrict ourselves?

But what would we gain? Discourse of any sort can be interpreted only in terms of the prior texts it evokes, many of which are not present at all. Every text has been constituted by other texts, so that it's inherently intertextual, and the text that's constituting the other text isn't going to be known as a text until it itself is later constituted intertextually. The hardest thing to know, in a foreign culture, is whether somebody is presenting a completely original thought, or whether what they're saying is a cliche. So global repetition is present in every utterance; it's not a feature only of some sorts of discourse. If this means that we find repetition in everything, maybe that's not a problem. The opening into the future may lie with including our memories into our languaging, and to include our memories bursts the frame of local repetition. It doesn't mean that local repetition isn't interesting any more, but it means that it might be reinterpreted in this larger framework.

WHAT ARE THE FUNCTIONS OF REPETITION?

Repetition functions didactically, playfully, emotionally, expressively, ritualistically; repetition can be used for emphasis or iteration, clarification, confirmation; it can incorporate foreign words into a language, in couplets, serving as a resource for enriching the language. People repeat to produce trance, as in mantras or the Lamaze method for overcoming pain. Actors repeat to learn their lines; academics copy out quotes when they read in a new area. Repetition can be a bridging device in conversation, a way of dealing with an interruption, or a way of validating what another speaker has said. Repetition is a persuasive device. It is one of the primary forms of play.

The infant is driven to repeat, perhaps partly because it's pleasurable, and caregivers repeat an infant's actions and behaviors in one way or another, even if not necessarily linguistically. Other uses of repetition grow out of that (Bennett-Kastor, this volume). People have studied repeating routines in parent–child dyads, across cultures (Briggs, 1984; Schieffelin, 1979; Watson-Gegeo & Gegeo, 1986; Demuth, 1986). In some cases, the caregivers are trying to teach the child exactly what to say in a particular context by actually eliciting an imitation or a repetition from the child. Some reduplications are characteristic of baby talk: *moo-moo, choo-choo, mama, papa*. Reduplication is an easy grammar, a way of practicing syllabification. And then there's the sort of repetition that goes on when one tries to teach a child how to talk about a topic, when the topic is what gets repeated. The caregiver says, "See the bird. Bird. Yeah. Bird. It's a bird." In one way, it is obvious that a child who knows only a hundred words will have to repeat more than an adult does, but caretakers also teach the child to repeat. Bill Cosby makes a joke about this: You never just say "no" to a child, it's "no no no no no no."

Adults also repeat when they expand children's utterances (Ferguson, 1979), as when the child says "Mommy ball," and Mommy says, "Yeah, give Mommy the ball." That's a technique for teaching sentence structure. In middle-class America, the first words that children parrot back to a parent are met with praise and applause. In school, children are asked to regurgitate information, and repetition can also become a form of punishment.

When someone has a dramatic experience, he or she is compelled to tell it again and again. Elderly adults tell self-defining stories over and over (Brewer, this volume). We have stories that we have to tell, such as, for women, pregnancy and childbirth stories. Retelling is pleasurable. We can prompt people to retell stories as a way of drawing them into conversation. And retelling or rehearing can become pathological, too, as with Lenny in Steinbeck's *Of Mice and Men*, who repeatedly asks to hear the story about the rabbits; this is part of what shows him to be simple-minded.

Repetition is a way to get the floor in conversation, to recycle until it's your turn. When you're thinking of something to say you repeat yourself, or when you realize the person you're talking to isn't ready to reply. Repetition always gives you more time in conversation, whether that's the intent or not, and it fills space in many cases. In Kenyan classrooms (Merritt, this volume), repetition ensures that something is being said every couple of minutes: "Air is everywhere. What I said is that air is everywhere. Class, repeat: 'Air is everywhere.' " The verbal channel must be filled. Other societies might not have that anticipation that the verbal channel has to be occupied continuously.

One function of repetition is to preface or to express disagreement. That is, if you take a position and I repeat your position, one function of my repetition is to preface that I am getting ready to disagree with you, or perhaps the repetition itself constitutes disagreement with you. The closer the repetition is to identical, the closer it often is to direct disagreement. There seem to be two general trends: Repetition is both collaborative, on the textual level of jointly creating cohesion, and conflictual, on the ideational level.

In service encounters, if the customer says, "I'd like a pack of Marlboros," the server will often say, "Pack of Marlboros." This "playback" (Merritt, 1977) seems to have multiple functions. It provides a chance for the customer to say, "Oh, no, I wanted Kents," or something. And it maintains the rhythm, tells the customer, "I heard what you said and I'm getting it; you have to see that what I'm doing, though nonverbal, is being responsive to your request."

When there are multiple reformulations between teacher and student, the last reformulation is by the student, and it's an acknowledgment of having understood, or of giving up. Exact or reduced repetition of the teacher by the student, with questioning intonation, is often used when the student is unhappy with where the teacher is going. As a student, one can't say, "I want to do something else." If the teacher said, "And that is a great example," though, the student could say, "Example?" as a way of politely stalling the teacher, a way of signaling trouble with a voice of authority (Bean & Patthey-Chavez, this volume). Exact repetition tends to stop interactions and make them loop back.

Two iterations can be "more than," plural or emphatic. A playful situation in which there are three, four, or five repetitions is often a funnier or more intensely playful situation. The repetition is hyping the play (Hopper & Glenn, Volume II).

Something that some repetitions do some of the time is metalinguistic work. Repetition calls attention to the prior. Repetition allows speakers to retrieve something that's now back in time and bring it forward again for further treatment (see Nofsinger, Volume II).

Repetition is a great aid to memory, and repeating a text evokes associations from every time you have participated in that type of event through your whole life.

Repetition can be exploratory. Joan Didion uses repetition this way (Rygiel, this volume), as did some of the proposals for this conference: A writer repeats, then goes a little further, then repeats again. One example is this: "[It is] in the act of didactically retelling a text to a listener, of teaching through repetition . . . [in] this act of reconstituting a story—of retelling it in a new language . . . reframing, that a story can bring a speaker to 're–vision,' to seeing a tale anew" (Macovski, conference proposal). This style produces a sense of spontaneity.

In religious rituals, exact repetition of certain parts of the ritual keeps involvement going and coordinates everybody around the ritual. It reinforces community values. Ritual has its very basis in repetition. There's a kind of security associated with repetition; it's not the meaning that even counts. When there are large groups of people, or when people are spread out, it is necessary to achieve shared attentiveness in order to engage in joint activity, so there are formal rituals. The Islamic call to prayer does this; so does the Pledge of Allegiance, though less effectively. Ritual that is too automatic may cease to draw people's involvement.

Linguistically, parallelism is extremely common in liturgical discourse all over the world. It may be that repetition in language does something to the way language and other kinds of behaviors are cognized. When you talk certain formulas over and over again, you're reframing them, unconsciously factoring out what they have in common, and constructing a more abstract representation. Obviously, though, not everything in the performance is going to be identical; certain things are going to be marked as having to be identical, and other parts may be variant.

At the same time as it reinforces a sense of community, repetition reinforces a sense of individuality. When you repeat you reinterpret the self. If every Sunday you say, "I believe in God," and follow with a prayer, you are a different *I* each week.

Repetition is the resource out of which aesthetics are created. In Hamlet's lines "To die, to sleep; to sleep: perchance to dream" (*Hamlet* III.i.64—65), the parallelism creates an association among the meanings, showing that the three verbs are close, but it builds a cumulative effect, too. And you know when Shakespeare's going to end a scene: All of a sudden people start to rhyme. The second occurrence of an element in a sonnet can give a resonance, a pleasure tingle. Many genres measure out repetition, how and where you repeat and where you change; certain literary periods, too, valued repetition (whereas appearing spontaneous is more important in other eras). In Thai poetry (Hudak, this volume), repetition is clearly defined as aesthetic; and this has to do with pleasing sound. Contemporary Thai poets have experimented with blank verse and free verse, leaving out the rhyme, but that is not regarded as poetry.

In postmodern novels, repetition postpones what would become an element in the plot, and so postpones making a plot—the plot virtually disappears for a while (D. Sherzer, this volume). When that happens, there is a focus on the language, a display of the language. It's not that the authors expect the readers to know the plot, as in traditional verbal art; they want to avoid the plot, to make sure readers don't get it. These authors are marking themselves as very different from the typical; they are drawing attention to the fact that they are setting themselves apart, and that intentionality is part of what we have to pay attention to when we read their texts. Other artists have different purposes for repeating: Andy Warhol makes a statement about the commercialization of art; Pinter and Stoppard point up the absurd quality of repetition in everyday interaction (Schnebly, Kelly, this volume); Philip Glass explores the possibilities of repetition in music, by imitating Balinese music; Picasso uses African sculptures for the plastic possibilities. Perhaps in the case of these artists, repetition signals something that is very foreign, whereas repetition in traditional texts signals traditional culture and ritual.

Another function of repetition is to inform, to be referential. Repetition is required for redundancy when there is noise, and for emphasis and highlighting, especially when people have to communicate through very controlled language. In aviation talk (Cushing, Volume

II), repetition appears to have this function: It ensures the safety of an aircraft by making sure that each speaker has feedback that the other actually heard what was said, and has it right. Or the address-ee says it again when he's not sure what was said. Repetition en-sures clarity in these "full readbacks."

One of the things that repetition might in general be doing is fore-stalling events or situations that people are afraid of, like silence or ambiguity or chaos or sense of formlessness. Repetition can be a very basic ordering principle that is reassuring. If you don't repeat, you forget, as Kundera points out in *The Book of Laughter and Forgetting*. Obsessive-compulsive behavior is repetitive. Many neu-rological disorders involve repetition, such as Tourette's Syndrome, a disease which causes people to get speeded up and start repeating out of control (Tannen, 1989, pp. 93–95). Perhaps scientists' drive to replicate experiments also arises out of fear, or at least from the satisfaction of following all the steps that you know you're supposed to follow in a prescribed way—though certainly not consciously.

In the movie "Being There," based on a novel by Jerzy Kosinski, Peter Sellers plays a man who is really sort of an imbecile, an idiot. But the one thing he knows how to do is repeat back what anybody says to him: They say, "I think it's a nice day today," and he says, "Nice day today." And each person who talks to him thinks he's absolutely brilliant. They think, "This person is really interested in me." And they just keep elevating him to higher and higher positions.

If you really want to tell somebody something you've already said, you recast; you don't repeat. If you've said something and somehow it wasn't communicated, you try something completely different, take another tack, such as perhaps a paraphrase. But if you want to do something new, then you're more likely to repeat.

Some would say that the way repetition is interpreted by the next speaker, and responded to, is what determines its function. There's an emerging quality to many repetition phenomena: As an utterance is being spoken, its functionality is up for grabs in the subsequent discourse. Function is in principle indeterminate at the moment of occurrence. So we might take objection to the presupposition that we can identify and taxonomize functions. We're in danger of objec-tification; function is always a hypothesis. What's really interesting about repetition is that the function is always open. We can identify a range of functions, but it's the context, after the fact, which really determines what's happening. The functions of repetition probably will be almost infinite; and any function that we can identify can be turned on its head.

Does Repetition Serve the Same Function On Different Levels?

Many languages employ reduplication in their morphologies, one kind of grammaticalized repetition. Reduplication tends to indicate some kind of plurality in nouns and some kind of distribution in space or iterative action in verbs. In sentences, it's common for repetition of a linguistic feature to establish thematic relations; subjects and verbs often have to agree, and many languages require negative concord. In order to produce a grammatical sentence, then, one has to repeat, and the texture of a language comes in many ways from these grammatically required phenomena. What is the relationship between this and repetition that is clearly intentional, when a speaker thinks, "What am I going to do now? OK, I'll say that again." Does repetition work the same way on all levels, on the level of sound, meaning, grammar, literary themes?

The kinds of repetitions that one finds in everyday language, and in the grammars of languages, are potentials for artistry in the poetries of languages. A little alliteration, on the phonological level, can be funny, just as are the multiple repetitions that create a joke (Norrick, Volume II), and the repetitions in playful talk. Repetition in Antiguan Creole appears as reduplication (which is in the grammar of the language), in narrative, in children's language; it can be seen as a unitary phenomenon, though the functions of grammaticalized repetition seem to be explicit, concrete, maybe iconic, in a way the discourse functions of repetition are not (Shepherd, this volume).

Repetition is grammaticalized in more different ways in Arabic than it is in English—there's more about the grammar that's repetitious, more juxtaposition. For example, adjectives agree completely with nouns, and in fact are for the most part identical to nouns, so all the marking is repeated when you modify a noun with an adjective. When writers are trying to persuade, they use the same strategy of juxtaposition, stringing ideas together in discourse, using coordinate clauses instead of subordination. Repetition is thus a basic structural principle on all levels (Johnstone, 1987b). Repetition is more available, so it's more likely to be used—and it is used much more often by Arabic speakers than it is by English speakers, and viewed more positively.

ARE THERE THINGS REPETITION ALWAYS DOES?

Does Repetition Always Change Meaning?

It makes sense to suppose that when you say the same thing again, the referential meaning stays the same. But something other than the referential meaning has changed. As an element is repeated, a history for it is created; as the context within which elements are used changes, their meaning changes. In Harold Pinter's *The Birthday Party*, for example, one phrase is repeated throughout: "Nice, very nice." At the beginning of the play, a wife serves her husband corn flakes and asks, "Is it nice? Are they very nice?" And he says, automatically, "Yes, they're very nice." And the next person comes down to eat: "Are they nice?" "They're very nice." Before the end of the play, the two men who have come in to take another man away and torture him are also using the phrase, "It's nice. It's very nice," but the phrase now sounds very black and scary (Schnebly, this volume).

When learners use repetition to capture an interlocutor's attention, to get across a message that they are unable to encode linguistically (Knox, this volume), there's no change in the referential meaning. But there's certainly a dimension added to the interaction. Nothing happens to the meaning of the utterance, the propositional content, but repetition certainly creates a cognitive effect.

If we're going to say that the meaning of a repeated expression is always different a second time, though, we need to think about meaning to whom. It is quite possible for Alzheimer's patients to repeat a text over and over until eventually they break out of that cycle, or to engage in a whole small conversation repeatedly (Brewer, this volume). It's like a mental stutter; from the speaker's perspective, the repetition is not used to change meaning, and there's no attitude change on the speaker's part. But to the hearer, the repetition does say something about the repeater.

Mayans often have the same conversation over and over, with the same people (Brody, Volume II). It's satisfying; everybody's happy with the conversation and will have it again later. Phatic contact is being forged between co-conversationalists. It is in fact a theoretical principle that, when something is repeated, its meaning changes. It's got a new box around it, because it happened a second time; we're committed to its having a different meaning. It's our job to say what the different meaning is.

But is it in fact the case that it's only nonreferential aspects of the meaning that change when an item is repeated? Smaller scale, more immediate repetitions, such as reduplications, get close, at least, to creating axiomatic or propositional meaning (plurality, for example). The more displaced the repetition gets, the more the meaning is discursive.

Does Repetition Serve Universal Cognitive or Interactional Functions?

The function of repetition in general is to point, to direct a hearer back to something and say, "Pay attention to this again. This is still salient; this still has potential meaning; let's make use of it in some way." This accounts, for example, for the cognitive utility of repetition to learners, getting the learner's attention on a token of input for a second round in order to have something to work with (Tomlin, this volume). We can also call attention to the fact that we're getting one's attention, and we can take that one step further, when awareness of the ability to manipulate allows us to play with attention. Immediacy may be poetic. We're always trying to gain the attention of the audience, and we only have a certain number of resources for doing that. Repetition is a resource, a cognitive pattern at our disposal, one of the ways our minds assimilate information. Repetition is a mode of focusing attention.

Is all repetition metalinguistic? It seems as if the kinds that count as intertextuality are: translation, plagiarism, allusion, parody, private or shared jokes, instructions, summation, quoting, anaphora, reporting. Repetition focuses attention on the makeup of both the repeated discourse and the earlier discourse. Repetition puts the utterance in brackets, making it impossible to treat the language as if it were transparent, by forcing hearers to focus on the language itself. In that sense repetition is metalinguistic, even though it's not conscious talk about talk.

Is there any discourse function that repetition couldn't serve? The functions of repetition may be the same as the functions of discourse. We can't say as a general principle that repetition is always going to be funny or it's always going to be aesthetic, but we know that it's always a resource ready to be used these ways, and others.

WHAT DISTINCTIONS IS IT USEFUL TO MAKE?

Formal/Semantic

What is the relationship among the experience of saying different sentences in the same intonational pattern, versus saying totally different words with the same intonational pattern, versus saying the same idea with totally different words, versus similar sentences bearing the words?

Immediate/Displaced

One distinction we found useful is the distinction between *immediate repetition* and *displaced repetition*. Immediate repetition would be when a unit is uttered and then immediately uttered again; it could be of any size from a syllable up to a whole conversation or written text. Immediate repetition and displaced repetition seem to be rather different kinds of things. Immediate repetition has to do again with whatever it was doing before: plurality, intensification, and so on; and displaced repetition seems often to have much more to do with textual cohesion. The function of immediate repetition wouldn't work if the items were displaced. Immediate reduplications and so on are localized and manageable, and as they get more and more displaced, they get harder and harder to manage. A displaced repetition might signal anaphora, or conversely it might signal topic change; in Burmese, the whole verb phrase is repeated at the beginning of the next sentence, as a way of indicating topicality. Rhyming is also a kind of displaced repetition, as is translation.

Exact/Non-exact

Reformulation, rather than exact repetition, is very often the real trigger for moving into another phase or level. When young children, in nursery school through first grade, want the teacher's attention, they say something like, "Can I go play with blocks now?" If the teacher is engaged with somebody else, they say, "I want to go play with blocks now." And then, "Can I go play with blocks now?" They may say the same thing five times. But as soon as the child says something a little bit different—"Ms. B., can I go play with blocks?" or "I'm going to go play with blocks" or "I'm going to do it"—the teacher's attention is on the child in a minute.

One sort of non-exact repetition involves changing only deictic terms, *I*s to *you*s or *he*s, *this*es to *that*s and *here*s to *there*s, with near verbatim repetition otherwise. In conversation, one can point out another speaker's error with exact repetition, which has the effect of saying "I'm repeating you verbatim because you made a mistake." Deictic-shifted repetition, on the other hand, may quote the original speaker in an encouraging way (Ferrara, Volume II). Variation can be deictic, in this way, or it can be lexical—you say *make* and I say *do*, but I'm still repeating you—or it can involve the intonation pattern (Simpson, Volume II), or the kind of reversal called *chiasmus* . . .

But what would we mean, precisely, by saying that some repetitions are more exact than others? How would we measure exactness? We might suppose that "To die, to sleep; to sleep: perchance to dream" is repetitive, but not to the extent that "He could hear the cry of bats. He could hear the cry of bats" is. There are a lot of words in the second example, and all of them are repeated. To put it more technically, we could count linguistically or otherwise analytically segmentable forms, and see how many of them are repeated from model to copy. But a paraphrase would be an example of a repetition in which no segmentable forms are repeated; the repetition is on the semantic level. Are we perhaps victims of folk ideologies about language here, saying that because something happens to be grammatically segmentable that therefore it's somehow more real? (See J. Sherzer, this volume.)

Degrees of Freedom

Some repetition is codified in ritual, which has to be said the same way every time. Other repetition is a matter of habit rather than being prescribed, a tendency that is a result of wanting to identify with the community. Still more free are repetitions that are part of an established game, patterns that are available but not habitual. Finally, there are spontaneous repetitions, more individual and exploratory, looking back, commenting or redefining.

Self-repetition/Other-repetition

Whether speakers are repeating themselves or others makes a difference in conversation. You can't disagree with yourself by just repeating yourself! Speakers say things like, "I went over there yesterday. No, I went on Tuesday," but that has a different effect than would another speaker's saying, "You went over there yesterday?" Self-repetition is self-repair, and it's in the middle of a turn. It doesn't change the flow of the conversation; nothing happens; nobody else is involved. On the other hand, though, a self-repetition like this could be seen as a three-turn corrective exchange . . .

What would the self/other distinction correspond to in written discourse? It might correspond to the difference between "monologic" versus "dialogic" text. For example, a Shakespearean sonnet in which it was clear that a lot was taken from an Elizabethan commonplace book would count as other-repetition; whereas if Shakespeare were paraphrasing something else he'd written, it would count as self-repetition. The distinction is more vague for written texts, though.

Culture

There is a range of tolerance for repetition in every culture, and the upper limits differ. Pedagogical handbooks for writing Modern English energetically proscribe redundancy and repetition, and Roget's Thesaurus is a resource for avoiding repetition. Academic culture values originality, though originality may be a recent goal. In the 14th and 15th centuries, repetition was more highly valued; the creation of fiction would have been odd, for example. Tolerance for repetition also depends on the stability of the social context. A situation of change makes it difficult to share large amounts of information, so repetitions go in other directions.

In cultural situations involving a group ethic for conformity, repetition is valued and necessary. Mayans repeat in their textiles, conversational topics, ritual, music, dance, and so on. Arabic uses repetition for persuasion in writing and speech, and it is always viewed positively. The Koran, a major source for Arabic writers and linguists, is highly repetitive, and it is taught through repetition: It was revealed orally to the Prophet, who was illiterate. Conversely, cultural groups in which verbal space is supposed to be less occupied, such as some Native American groups, or working class Americans, might be less receptive to phatic repetition.

Things often need to be said some specific number of times. In the Judao-Christian tradition, three is an important number; in some Native American traditions, four is the magic number. Stanzas are repeated four times; lines are repeated four times; ceremonies are done four times. Three is too little, five is too much. In traditional Islam and Judaism, a man says, "I divorce thee" three times, and he is divorced. In American jokes, three seems to be the number; on the third repetition the punchline occurs.

Language

Repetition is a more available resource in some languages than in others. Does it do the same work in different languages? Repetition is not very salient in English, for example, and perhaps not as often used as a resource; the intolerance of the language for repetition can be seen in pronominalization (unless pronouns are seen as repetitions), indefinite agent deletion. Most of the reduplication in English is lexical (*choo-choo, willy-nilly, shilly-shally*), though earlier in the verb system in Germanic there was some reduplication. One grammatical instance of repetition in many varieties of English is multiple negation.

Malayo-Polynesian languages utilize morphological reduplication. It's an open process; the clowns in traditional shadow theater play with it all the time. So even morphological repetitions can be open-ended in function. Reduplication can be used for intensification, which makes iconic sense, but it can also be used for *dis*intensification. An example translated from Malay would be *to walk* and *to walk walk. Walk walk* doesn't mean going with greater purpose, it means going with no purpose at all, just wandering around, strolling. This phenomenon occurs often in grammar: A grammatical strategy can do one thing or the exact opposite.

Genre

In situations that heighten replication, repetition, and parallelism, such as ritual, a different kind of meaning is operative, a kind of meaning that isn't accessible to segmentation (Urban, Volume II). Nonparallel discourse, such as that of mathematics, perhaps, is more propositional, involving the kind of meaning that is explicitly encodable in the surface forms. Not all discourse is poetic; some instances of discourse are designed around relatively linear propositional axiomatics (and it's when these sorts of discourse are privileged that proscriptions about repetition are generated). The ideology of the artistic/aesthetic side is the ideology of parallelism, repetition, and so forth; the ideology of the logical/deductive side, even though its discourse may include repetition (see Porter & Sullivan, Volume II), is the ideology of linearity and transparent reading. You would expect repetition to be more celebrated in the language-equals-play school of thought than in the flattened-discourse-propositional school of thought.

Does repetition function differently in literary texts than in non-literary texts? When readers approach a work of art, it's marked as a work of art, and they may not expect natural language. They may expect artificial language. Some authors attempt to model natural language more closely than others do—Donald Barthelme, Ann Beatty, people classified as minimalists—and for those who try to create the illusion of everyday language, there will be a high correlation between how we interpret their repetition and how we interpret repetition in everyday language. But in the work of authors who heighten their language or stylize it in a way that removes it from everyday talk, readers may attend to other kinds of rhetorical devices (see Ehrlich, this volume). One of the effects of repetition in literature can be defamiliarization, making strange. Even hyperrealism, for that matter, can have this effect. It can be a joke on the notion of imitation. There's a focusing of attention in art, even if it's a focusing of attention on the everyday.

Informative discourse includes a lot of repetition, but it takes a different form than the repetition in conversation. It takes the form of lexical repetition or pronominalization, whereas conversational discourse has larger elements repeated. There's just as much repetition, it's just that certain kinds get backgrounded and other kinds get foregrounded. And the primary function of the repetition may be different; repetition may have a more narrowly cohesive function in informative discourse, as opposed to a more interactional, collaborative function in conversation.

Modality

One of the effects of the repetition of "very nice" in *The Birthday Party* is that the increasingly sinister uses of the phrase retroactively make even the first uses seem sinister. The repetition forces the reader to go back to the beginning again, to reread the lines about the "very nice" corn flakes. If somebody has said something in the past, and you hear it repeated or manipulated in some way, you may go back and reinterpret whatever meaning it had the first time (see Gault, this volume). But it's easier to do that with a written text; our memories of conversation aren't very long. Pinter expects us to reinterpret; Ionesco starts plays over again so that you will go back.

Lectures in American Sign Language often include *sandwiching*: The verb is given at the beginning of an utterance, and then there is a little offshoot, and then the verb is repeated. Short sentences are often repeated two and three times. And the verb inflections are all reduplications of some sort or another. The high incidence of repetition may have to do with the fact that the audience has to be looking directly at the person signing, and people look away so often that the signer often has to repeat. (See Winston, Volume II, on another reason for repetition in ASL.) When you speak you don't have to repeat as much, because listeners don't have to be paying attention the same way.

Power

Even in a society in which repetition is devalued, there are certain uses by powerful people that are encouraged and accepted (see Rockwell, Volume II). Propaganda is one example of a use of repetition by someone in a powerful position. The functions of repetitions by relatively powerless individuals seem to be somewhat different. Powerless individuals use repetition to find acceptable ways to express unacceptable meanings. Powerless people also use repetitions as assertions of power—as when people chant at baseball games. In teacher–student interactions, there are real power differentials, so that there is a different pattern of repetition than there is in a more symmetrical situation. Teachers get very hesitant student requests for clarification, and teachers use repetition when control has been lost; it's a way to regain control, just as children use repetition to get attention and in that sense gain control.

Repetition is a multifaceted phenomenon. Repetition can mean agreement or disagreement, joking or hostility, work or play. It can be both cohesive and disjunctive. The more something is repeated, the more people come to expect it to be repeated; repetition eventually becomes the *less* foregrounded option, and suddenly *not* repeating is foregrounded. Whenever we talk about repetition, we have to talk about its opposite number. You can do something new by repeating yourself, and you show that you are not doing anything new by repeating yourself. Are there in fact only two things we can do in discourse, either repeat or do something different?

REFERENCES

Briggs, C. L. (1984). Learning how to ask: Native metacommunicative competence and the incompetence of fieldworkers. *Language in Society*, *14*, 1–28.

Demuth, K. (1986). Prompting routines in the language socialization of Basotho children. In B. B. Schieffelin & E. Ochs (Eds.), *Language socialization across cultures* (pp. 51–99). Cambridge, UK: Cambridge University Press.

Ferguson, C. (1979). Baby talk as simplified register. In C. Snow & C. Ferguson (Eds.), *Talking to children: Language input and acquisition* (pp. 209–235). Cambridge, UK: Cambridge University Press.

Johnstone, B., Ed. (1987a). *Perspectives on repetition.* Special issue of *Text, 7*(3).

Johnstone, B. (1987b). Parataxis in Arabic: Modification as a model for persuasion. *Studies in Language, 11*, 85–98.

Merritt, M. (1977). The playback: An instance of variation in discourse. In R. W. Fasold & R. W. Shuy (Eds.), *Studies in language variation: Semantics, syntax, phonology, pragmatics, social situations, ethnographic approaches* (pp. 198–208). (Colloquium on New Ways of Analyzing Variation, 3rd.) Washington, DC: Georgetown University Press.

Schieffelin, B. B. (1979). Getting it together: An ethnographic approach to the study of the development of communicative competence. In E. Ochs & B. B. Schieffelin (Eds.), *Developmental pragmatics* (pp. 73–108). New York: Academic Press.

Tannen, D. (1989). *Talking voices: Repetition, dialogue, and imagery in conversational discourse.* Cambridge, UK: Cambridge University Press.

Watson-Gegeo, K. A., & D. W. Gegeo. (1986). Calling-out and repeating routines in Kwara'ae children's language socialization. In B. B. Schieffelin & E. Ochs (Eds.), *Language socialization across cultures* (pp. 17–50). Cambridge, UK: Cambridge University Press.

Part I
Methodological Issues

Chapter 2
Repetition in Situated Discourse—
Exploring Its Forms and Functions

Marilyn Merritt

Center for Applied Linguistics
Washington, DC

SITUATED DISCOURSE

I am interested in locating indices of creativity in the human mind, and in the human capacity to share that individual newness with others. Understanding these will in turn help in understanding the nature of collective behavior and achievement. To that end, my work in discourse analysis has focused on spoken interchanges in naturally occurring social situations, where the eventful particularity of that situation has been the trigger for spontaneous creativity. The spoken interchanges I have selected are not casual interchanges between socially well-acquainted peers (the interpretation of which often requires mutual biographical information) but rather are drawn from the arena of public encounters, involving sometimes strangers: those interchanges surrounding the transaction of service, "service encounters" (reported in Merritt, 1976a,b, 1977, 1979a,b, 1984), and those interchanges that take place in primary classrooms (based on two research projects, reported in Merritt, 1979a,b, 1982a,b; Merritt & Humphrey, 1979, 1980; Merritt, Cleghorn, & Abagi, 1988; Merritt, Cleghorn, Abagi, & Bunyi, 1992; Cleghorn, Merritt, & Abagi, 1989).

An important aspect of all these interchanges is that the situation (including those role relationships of participants that derive from the situation) is the primary determinant of the pragmatic interpretation of the discourse (the social meaning assigned to items of language in their context of use). This is in large part a by-product of the fact that these situations are *externally structured* by the social institutions and places in which they occur (e.g., service encounters in stores, teacher–student interchanges in primary classrooms). A second important aspect of all these interchanges is that the main activity (transacting a service, conducting a lesson) is constituted of both talk and human actions other than talk.

In every chunk of natural language discourse the "situation" (see Goffman, 1964) directly affects the interpretation of discourse (and the interaction of which it is a part). In the case of externally structured situations like those I have analyzed, we can ask in a fairly straightforward way, "What are the situational demands on the discourse?" (what is it that the situation wants the discourse to get done—transact a service, teach and learn lessons, etc.), and "What are the situational resources available to meet those demands?" Thus, my data are situated in such a way as to lend itself easily to functional analysis.

Communicative demands differ from situation to situation, although there are also general demands that hold for almost all situations (such as making the communication perceivable to the intended interlocutor). Communicative resources also vary somewhat from situation to situation, but most are similar from one situation to the next. The function served by any resource can vary from one interchange or discourse to another, but there is usually a potential range of functions for any resource. Because of this we are able to speak of general functions served by language and at the same time find specific functions in particular situations, functions that are responsive to the particular communicative demands of that situation. This is how we are able to work toward discovering the basic mechanisms of pragmatics, by drawing generalizations from many types of situations.

The use of situated discourse as data thus provides a methodological advantage for analysis. Because different situations do share demands and resources—thereby making it possible to learn and generalize from almost any set of "real" natural language—we often forget that a deeper understanding of the power of general resources and their functions only comes with a deeper understanding of situated demands. It is in highly particularized situations that we can document the functionality of specific linguistic forms and thereby foreground the new and creative ways language is continually used.

RESOURCES FOR ANALYSIS,
INCLUDING REPETITION

Since the study of language has primarily focused on discovering units that are no larger than a single sentence, the study of natural language behavior (including written texts), in which language occurs in much larger chunks, is immediately confronted with basic problems as to how to proceed with any degree of formal rigor. With discourse data collected from appropriately similar sets of known situations, I believe that methodologically sound analyses can be achieved through a careful weaving back and forth between formal and functional categories. Briefly, I have developed the following steps as a way to begin: (a) select a locus of observation; (b) locate something "formally identifiable" within that locus; (c) try to analyze the function(s) of the form within that setting (e.g., look for co-occurrences and sequential regularities); (d) having identified the function(s), look for other forms that satisfy the same function(s); (e) look for patterns in the functions; and (f) speculate on larger generalizations and test these against other data.

The occurrence of repetition in the data provides a fundamental resource for analysis: It gives us a place to begin, a kind of anchor, that "formally identifiable" something. Crucial to qualitative analysis, and basic also to measurement theory, is the notion of identity, of being able to define and/or identify two or more objects as being "the same," of being able to categorize occurrence A as an instance of X. Later, we may want to extend the notion of identity to the identification of a set of objects, or (sets of) objects that share only some trait(s).

If we can identify or formally specify a "piece" of language (or some other analogous behavior or behavioral trace), then we have, if not a unit of analysis, something that occurs more than once and can be related to other parameters in the natural language setting. If we have a chronologically or sequentially arranged body of data, then we might speak of the first occurrence of a designated piece of communication behavior, and subsequent *recurrences*; or we might say that there was an occurrence and that it was repeated, or that there were *repetitions* of the piece in what follows.

That we are able to identify and mentally set apart these recurrences gives us a kind of methodological handle on the structure of the entire body of data. We can analyze and compare each occurrence with respect to how it is placed and patterned. How does it function in the situation at hand?

The easiest kinds of pieces to identify are exact recurrences of (sequences of) words. These are formally (as distinct from functionally) identifiable recurrences. For example, in studying service encounters, I found many occurrences of the word *O.K.* By looking at each instance in its discourse context and noting how it seemed to work in the situation, it was possible to see a general pattern in the way that *O.K.* worked (as an approbative response) and to suggest a local discourse function for *O.K.* (as a verbal place-holder while shifting the action to the nonverbal channel).

Once a particular function was specified for *O.K.*, it was possible to look for other forms that serve the same discourse function in that situation (such as *All right*), and then to notice that other semantically similar forms (such as *yes*) may not serve the same pragmatic function. Thus, by using the phenomenon of repetition as a formal anchor, I was able to interrogate my data for function, and then find the same function in different forms, and then analyze how the various forms work. It was possible to achieve a better understanding of the demands of the situation (here the communicative event "service encounter"), as well as a better understanding of the particular function of *O.K.* By looking at many instances of *O.K.*, and observing the range of situational functions, it was possible to postulate a general (as an extension of the local or particular) function or "meaning" of the form *O.K.* In a somewhat analogous way, I have analyzed the recurrence of formal categories like question and functional categories like request for attention.

THE NATURE OF REPETITION IN DISCOURSE AND INTERACTION

Within this framework I have encountered the phenomenon of repetition in many guises, over the years exploring its forms and functions within situated data (drawn primarily from three research projects cited above, dating from the mid-1960s to the present). In the remaining space I summarize in 10 points what I think I have learned so far about repetition. Each theme is designated with capital letters, with analytical terminology italicized. I use the term *repetition* as a general inclusive term for all kinds of "happening again," and introduce more specific terms as needed (e.g., *repeat, reformulation, replay, playback*).

Repetition is a Universal Phenomenon. It occurs in all languages, in all societies, and in almost all situations.

Repetition is a Major Resource in Communication. In natural language data, repetition can always be seen as a response to a situational demand, thereby assuming a situational function. Forms may often have multiple functions, of course.

Repetition is Associated with Canonical Form. Within a particular situation (especially an externally structured situation), there is often a *canonical form* for a structured sequence of discourse, one that is "typical," or even "basic," to the situation. For example, service encounters typically begin with a tacit offer of service, followed by a tacit request for service, followed by a formal offer of service, followed by a formal request for service.

One major type of repetition occurs when the whole sequence is repeated from one event to another; that is, participants and onlookers recognize that "the same thing is happening." (This is, of course, what makes it possible to abstract from pieces of discourse to a notion such as canonical form.)

Another type of repetition occurs within one event sequence. This is probably the type we most commonly think of as repetition. Sometimes these repetitions are planned as part of a canonical form. For example, in Kenyan classrooms, teachers often instructed students to repeat after them, as in the following: T: "Say 'those are books.' " Ss: "Those are books." T (again): "Say 'those are books.' " Ss (again): "Those are books." T: "That's a very nice sentence."

Once canonical forms are established, deviations from the norm can be recognized, such that unexpected or spontaneously repeated forms are highlighted for attention and interpretation. For example, when a customer queries, "Do you have key chains?" and the server responds, "What?" and the customer responds, "Do you have key chains?", the repetition of form in the customer's second turn is highlighted, in part because it is a deviation from the canonical sequence (as is the server's response). When we see these occurrences in our data, we can ask ourselves, What discourse-marking or interactional work is being done by the repeated form?

Repetition is Associated with Ritual. The fact that there is a canonical form(s) for a particular situation, of course, indicates that there is a routine way of doing things. Routine ways of doing things frequently become so normative that they can be considered rituals (routines that carry socially symbolic significance). This is, in general, true for repetitions that occur across events (the first type discussed above).

Repetition is at the core of the process through which an element acquires meaning and becomes symbolic. The author Carlos Fuentes (1988), for example, speaks of the way in which individuals need to name and rename the salient aspects of their culture, and that the name and the naming—the recurrence or repetition of the name or the specific words used—become thereby intensely symbolic and meaningful for the participants. Many formalized rituals involve planned repetition in canonical form (as shown, for example, in J. Sherzer, this volume).

In a related way we have all noted that repetition, and perhaps most notably partial repetition, can have tremendous *echoic carrying capacity*—a capacity to invoke a sense of the whole or the original contextual occurrence. For example, Walker and Adelman (1976) describe a stunning example from a primary classroom in England: Early in the year someone had brought to the class some strawberries to share, and the whole day was then surrounded with an ambience of cooperation and group involvement. Later in the school year, whenever anyone said, "Remember the strawberries?" the class would immediately respond positively, in a kind of echo of the day with strawberries.

Repetition Facilitates Rhythm and Group Synchrony. A salient property of linguistic repetition is that it occupies verbal space and therefore can be used as a kind of "filler." This is particularly useful when there is an ongoing rhythm in the discourse that is an integral part of sustained group participation and involvement. In whole group lessons in primary classrooms, for example, there is usually an orientation to the main *line of action* in the verbal/oral-aural channel where the teacher is presenting new information. The continuous production of verbal behavior needed to sustain group involvement and the primacy of the verbal/oral-aural channel is often achieved through the use of repetition and the establishment of *participatory rhythm*. Besides self-repeating, teachers often employ a number of discourse patterns (canonical forms) with choral responses by students.

There are two by-products of this: (a) The repetition of the same form, with no new information, automatically creates a longer time period in which the information being conveyed can be processed. So if the teacher says, "Air is everywhere" and then repeats "Air is everywhere," the time required to say the phrase twice provides twice as much cognitive processing time to process the same information (minus a small amount of time for recognizing the repetition). (b) The repetition also provides "catch-up" time for anyone whose attention may have lapsed or who did not hear the first time. As a result, the rhythm-sustaining properties of repetition also provide a means for establishing group synchrony (for example, in choral responses). This may involve repetition of an item, repetition of a format (canonical form), or repetition of both item and format.

In many whole group primary lessons in Kenya, teachers used combinations or *layers of repetition* to build and bind group participation. For example, after teachers self-repeated an item, teachers frequently used a call and refrain form of repetition, when the teacher would say something and expect students to repeat what had been said: T: "When air is strong," Ss: "When air is strong," T: "it is called wind," Ss: "it is called wind." This format would then sometimes be combined with overall repetition, such that the entire teacher–student interchange was repeated before moving on to the next informational point. Some teachers made use of bilingualism to effect repetition or content across linguistic codes. An example from one third-grade classroom: T: "We say air has got strength. Air has got?" Ss: "Strength." T:"Hewa ina nini? Ina? (Swahili: Air has what? It has?)" Ss:"Nguva (strength)." T: "Hewa ina nguva (Air has strength)."

The Rhythmic Property of Repetition Provides a Resource for the Management of Ongoing Nonverbal Activity. For example, in service encounters there is frequently a need to transact an exchange of money and goods. When this happens, the line of action may shift from the verbal channel to the nonverbal channel. Repetition often provides a resource for marking the verbal channel and maintaining verbal rhythm, although the main action has shifted to the nonverbal channel.

In one service area that I observed at length, customers often came to the cashier to buy cigarettes which were stored in display shelves behind the counter. The server's response to a request for cigarettes thus always involved a body orientation shift away from the customer in order to get the cigarettes. Often in these transactions the server would repeat the customer's order—sometimes with rising question intonation and sometimes with falling declarative intonation—as he was turning to the cigarette display. For example, C: "A carton of Winston, please." S: A carton of Winston. O.K.," and C: "C'n I have a pack of Doral, please?" S: "Doral menthol?" C: "Regular." The server would repeat, or *play back* the customer's request, as though to keep the rhythm in the verbal channel at the same time as the line of action in the encounter had shifted from the verbal/aural to the non-verbal channel (getting the cigarettes).

Such a playback repetition, of course, satisfies other functions in the encounter. It displays *engagement* in the encounter even though the server has turned away. Secondly, it provides an opportunity for customer confirmation or error correction. In the case of the questioning playback, the customer would routinely make a verbal response either confirming (e.g., "Right") or providing correction or further clarification (e.g., "Regular"). In the case of the declarative or assertive playback a verbal response by the customer was optional unless there was a need to correct or clarify the order.

In classrooms teachers also often use linguistic repetition to mark verbal cadence when primary information and/or action is being conveyed nonverbally—for example, when writing on the blackboard, or while demonstrating equipment. When nonverbal action is required by the students—for example, getting out books, putting away exercise materials—the teachers often use repetition to maintain ongoing rhythm and focus on the teacher.

Teachers are aware of the dominance of the verbal/aural channel as the most official channel for action in the classroom and often design exercises that engineer use of the verbal channel even when the main activity is nonverbal. For example, in one Kenyan classroom, when students were asked to copy the letter *p* in their exercise books, writing a whole page of *p*s, they were also instructed to recite aloud "I am writing sound p for pencil" over and over as they wrote in their books.

Repetition of Function May Involve Reformulation of Form. In an earlier example from the service encounter setting, I analyze the second occurrence of "Do you have key chains?" not only as a repetition, but also as a *replay* of an interactional *move* (a piece of behavior that comprises a single social act) in the discourse. The customer is making her move again, so to speak (in this case because the server indicated that he had not heard). In terms of the situation, the replay is designed to carry the same function as the original move.

In general, once we have recognized the repetition of function, it is usually easy to find examples in which the replay is not an exact *repeat*, but rather a (usually slight) variation in form or a *reformulation*. A replay may thus take the form of an exact repeat, a partial repeat, or a reformulation. For example, the customer's second turn might be "Key chains?" (partial repeat) or "Have you got any key chains?" (reformulation).

In one classroom, I observed teachers query, "Are they all gonna be there? Are all your fingers gonna be there?", "How many did you get? How many peanuts are on your paper?", and "How come? What happened?" In bilingual classrooms the availability of a second (or even third) language can provide an additional resource for reformulation. I observed one teacher saying, "Close the books you have.

Shut your books. Funga vitabu kila mtu (Swahili: close books every-one). Grace, hinga ibuka (Gikuyu: close (your) book)."

Repetition is Associated with Attention. All of us engaged in social interaction want to control the attention of our interlocu-tors. We want to get attention, direct it, and be able to (re)focus it. The control of attention is a major part of every teacher's work. In order for any information to be learned, it must be conveyed to students who are paying attention, whose attention is engaged in the interaction with the teacher, whose attention is engaged in that aspect of what is going on in the classroom—the particular *vector of activity*—that the teacher is developing through his or her lesson (or other participation structure).

Because the human sensory apparatus is neurologically pro-grammed to pick up instances of repetition in our environment, any form of repetition can serve as a way of drawing attention to what is being repeated. But the human mind not only picks up instances of repetition, it also learns to tune out repetition, or to lower attentive-ness, when too much repetition, especially "exact" repetition (a *repeat*), occurs. We can thus think of reformulation as one kind of generic repetition, and we can think of this form of repetition as an added resource to exact repetition, one that may encourage atten-tiveness on the part of the interlocutor because of the variation. In the case of classrooms, where teachers must work constantly to keep students involved in the appropriate vector of activity, repetition is a valuable resource for classroom management. The teacher can use repeats and reformulations to take up verbal/aural space (thereby maintaining a constant verbal/aural focus, which is always the offi-cial action channel in classrooms), maintain the rhythm of the en-counter (so that all participants can easily align and/or or realign themselves to what is going on), give students more cognitive pro-cessing time to understand new information and/or time to under-take some nonverbal action, as well as gain and maintain attentive-ness on the part of students.

Reformulation of Form may do Special Discourse Work. There is a counterpoint between repetition and variation or variety in terms of enhancing attentiveness in general, and, in the case of the classroom, in terms of enhancing learning. On one hand, rep-etition is positive because of all the ways in which it functions as a resource: to provide more processing time, facilitate ongoing rhythm in the encounter, provide another opportunity to perceive the information accurately, gain the interlocutor's attention, focus that attention, or even display attentiveness to what the interlocutor has contributed.

But too much repetition can have negative effects. That is, if repetition continues beyond the time needed for full processing time of new information, or for behavioral alignment, repetition becomes boring, and students (or other interlocutors) lose attentiveness because they anticipate that there will be no new information. In one Standard One classroom in Kenya, we noted a teacher having her students repeat, "It's a pen" 60 times! In this case students were practicing English pronunciation, associating the words with the teacher's demonstration of the object, and aligning themselves to a coordinated choral response in which more than 50 students were behaving in synchrony. Still, an observer may wonder if 60 times might not be a case of overkill.

Variety is positive because it keeps the flow of information exchange (or new action) moving along in the interaction. There is economy in the use of time to convey new information. There may also be increased attentiveness on the part of the interlocutors because of the need to perceive and process the communication accurately. At the same time, however, variety can be negative. There may not be enough processing time for the interlocutor to assimilate new information (this may be especially true when using a second language), such that variation may lead to confusion. There may be too much noise in the channel for accurate perception with only one play of the message, again resulting in confusion. There may be a need for group synchrony, which may be difficult to achieve without repetition.

Reformulation can be thought of as a kind of middle ground between exact repetition and something that is entirely new. Reformulation seems often to serve the function of reestablishing or maintaining attentiveness through providing some variety in the form, while at the same time increasing processing time by introducing minimal new information. Many teachers use a series of repeats and reformulations when introducing important new information, in responding to students, while waiting for students to formulate a response, or when making a behavioral transition in the classroom activity. For example, "How does evaporation take place? What makes evaporation to take place?" and, in response to a student's answer of "It heats," "It heats. It is able to make this water hot. The heat from the sun is able to make this water become warm. . . ." Students also use reformulation to get attention. In one classroom, a student playing a game called out "My turn" five times with no response from the teacher. When, on the sixth replay, he reformulated to "I said my turn," the teacher immediately responded.

I have often noted that a shift from exact repeat to reformulation signals a change in the speaker's sense of urgency and an increased effort to engage the interlocutor's attention more fully. In bilingual classrooms this reformulation may take the form of code switching. Individuals often also introduce reformulations as a way of remediating or repairing a previous move/message (see Jefferson, 1972; Schegloff, Jefferson, & Sacks, 1977). For example, one student, tracing her body on a piece of paper said, "Now I won't have to cut a hand off. Now there won't be a cutted hand off."

Repetition is Associated with Learning and Cognition. In learning situations such as the classroom, we can note additional ways in which repetition serves as a special resource. The recurrence or repetition of an item gives it a sense of familiarity to the perceiver. The recurrence or repetition of an item in a particular context imbues it with meaning or symbolic value. (In fact, this is true for virtually all forms of elaboration of items; items acquire meaning and symbolic value through *elaboration*, one type of which is repetition.)

Familiar items require less processing time as part of more complex messages. Hence familiar items can function much like concrete items in building the foundation for comprehending abstract messages. Cognitive accessibility (ease of learning) of an item, can, in fact, perhaps be conceptualized in terms of something like degree of *experiential reachability*—with concrete items as 100% experientally reachable. This may be why abstract messages are so often repeated, since through repetition they become more familiar, and through familiarity they become more experientially reachable. In Kenyan classrooms teachers often repeated concept phrases like "Air is a gas" many times. They also drew upon concrete items from students' home background to use as analogies for abstract subject matter. Another teacher strategy is to use culturally familiar formats, such as call and refrain, to make the "doing" of lessons familiar even though the topics may be abstract. Through association with classroom experiences, abstract concepts become elaborated and familiar, and ultimately more meaningful.

An important manifestation of repetition in learning is imitation. Many societies practice a form of learning in which novices first observe an expert for some time and then only later, after feeling that they have visually learned the skill (when it has become familiar and fully experientially reachable), do they begin to try to perform the task of the expert. We say that the novice learns by imitation, by internalizing the neurosensory record of repetition (usually through sight) and then allowing that neurosensory record to be played back through his or her neuromotor system (as behavior). With this type of learning, long periods of observation are usually required to learn complex behaviors/activities.

A related form of imitation, synchronous imitation, is one most of us are familiar with in learning a new dance step. In this approach the expert demonstrates the behavior—often in short segments—and then repeats the behavior several times, asking the novices to join him or her in synchronous movement (i.e., moving at the same time as the expert, in rhythm with the expert). The repetition of the behavior renders it familiar and identifiable; the continuous presence of the expert performing (leading the novices) makes it possible for novices to begin to perform before their neurosensory systems may have been completely familiarized. The continuous presence of the expert's example makes it possible for the novice to keep performing, even though the novice may experience short lapses of neuromotor memory.

Where material objects or equipment are involved as part of the desired behavior, we may see yet another pattern: the expert may first demonstrate to the novice and then monitor the novice imitative performance, sometimes physically guiding him or her through the use of the materials. The early instruction of handwriting in primary classrooms is a good example.

In all these ways repetition develops familiarity, even for unusual or abstract items. Familiarity provides a base for experiential reachability. That which can be concretely experienced (or reached experientially through familiarity) can be learned, and imbued with contextual or symbolic meaning.

REPETITION AND NEW MEANING

Repetition as part of an interest in creativity may seem like a contradiction in terms. I have tried to show, first, how instances of repetition present themselves as special opportunities for analyses and interpretations that are grounded in the particulars of a situation. Secondly, I have tried to illustrate the range of forms and functions that can be identified with repetition in the situated discourse of service encounters and learning situations. Repetition directs our attention. Repetition is also a resource for "doing" that is almost always available to participants.

Because the enactment of every communicative event carries the potential for becoming a new situation, participants must be prepared to adapt their communicative resources to meet the new demands. On-the-spot marshalling of resources to meet the demands of the new situation is creative behavior, the resolution of problem, the establishment of new function or meaning. We establish meaning through doing and through making connections between familiar and new. The interface between exact repetition and reformulation may give us insight as to how such increments of familiarization take place in our minds. Familiar behavioral routines may be as important as familiar ideas in successful learning environments. In actual social situations there is a "competence of doing" that is associated with understanding. The study of repetition may bring us closer to comprehending this phenomenon.

REFERENCES

Cleghorn, A., Merritt, M., & Abagi, J.O. (1989). Language policy and science instruction in Kenyan primary schools. *Comparative Education Review, 33*, 21–39.

Fuentes, C. (1988). Forum lecture at George Mason University, Fairfax, VA.

Goffman, E. (1964). The neglected situation. *American Anthropologist, 66* (6), 133–136.

Jefferson, G. (1972). Side sequences. In D. Sudnow (Ed.), *Studies in social interaction*. Glencoe, IL: The Free Press.

Merritt, M. (1976a). *Resources for saying in service encounters*. Unpublished doctoral dissertation, University of Pennsylvania.

Merritt, M. (1976b). On questions following questions—in service encounters. *Language in Society, 5*, 315–357.

Merritt, M. (1977). The playback: An instance of variation in discourse. In R. W. Fasold & R. W. Shuy (Eds.), *Studies in language variation*. Washington, DC: Georgetown University Press.

Merritt, M. (1979a). Building higher units and levels: The case for the strategic "locus of observation". In P. R. Clyne, W. F. Hanks, & C. L. Hofbauer (Eds.), *The elements: A parasession on linguistic units and levels*. Chicago: Chicago Linguistic Society, University of Chicago.

Merritt, M. (1979b). "Communicative loading" and intertwining of verbal and non-verbal modalities in service events. *Papers in Linguistics, 12*, 365–392.

Merritt, M. (1982a). Repeats and reformulations as windows on the nature of talk engagement in primary classrooms. *Discourse Processes, 5*, 127–145.

Merritt, M. (1982b). Distributing and directing attention in primary classrooms. In L. C. Wilkinson (Ed.), *Communicating in the classroom*. New York: Academic.

Merritt, M. (1984). On the use of "O.K." in service encounters. In J. Baugh & J. Sherzer (Eds.), *Language in use*. Englewood Cliffs, NJ: Prentice-Hall.

Merritt, M., & Humphrey, F.M. (1979). Teacher, talk, and task. *Theory into Practice, XVIII* (4), 298–303.

Merritt, M. & Humphrey, F. M. (1980). *Service-like events during individual work time and their contribution to the nature of communication in primary classrooms.* Final report to the National Institute of Education. Washington, DC: Center for Applied Linguistics. (ERIC ED 196277 FLO 12029)

Merritt, M., Cleghorn, A., & Abagi, J. O. (1988). Dual translation and cultural congruence: Exemplary teaching practices in using English, Swahili, and mother-tongue in three Kenyan primary schools. In K. Ferrara, B. Brown, K. Walters, & J. Baugh, (Eds.), *Linguistic change & contact.* Austin, TX: Department of Linguistics, University of Texas. (Vol. 30 (special issue) of *Texas Linguistics Forum*)

Merritt, M., Cleghorn, A., Abagi, J. O., & Bunyi, G. (1992). Socialising multilingualism: Determinants of codeswitching in Kenyan primary classrooms. *Journal of Multilingual and Multicultural Development 13,* 103–121.

Schegloff, E., Jefferson, G., & Sacks, H. (1977). The preference for self-correction in the organization of repair in conversation. *Language, 53,* 361–382.

Walker, R., & Adelman, C. (1976). Strawberries. In M. Stubbs & S. Delamont (Eds.), *Explorations in classroom observation* (pp. 133–150). London: John Wiley.

Chapter 3
Transcription, Representation, and Translation: Repetition and Performance in Kuna Discourse

Joel Sherzer

Department of Anthropology
University of Texas at Austin

The Kuna Indians are probably best known for their molas, colorful appliqué and reverse-appliqué blouses made and worn by Kuna women and sold all over the world. They are one of the largest indigenous groups in the South American tropics, numbering more than 30,000 individuals, the majority of whom inhabit San Blas, a string of island villages stretching from near the Canal Zone to the Panama-Colombia border, quite close to the jungle mainland, where they farm. Living on the edge of modern, urban civilization, the Kuna have managed to maintain their cultural uniqueness through a creative integration of old and new, constantly adapting and manipulating traditional patterns to make them fit new situations.

The Kuna have a rich and dynamic verbal life. Like most tropical forest and lowland South American Indian societies, the Kuna's world is permeated by and in fact organized by means of their discourse—the mythical chants of chiefs; the histories, legends, and stories of traditional leaders; the magical chants and secret charms of curing specialists; the speeches and reports of personal experience of all men and women; and the greetings, leave-takings, conversations, and joking of everyday life. All of this is oral—spoken, chanted, sung, shouted, and listened to.

Kuna verbal art, because of its ongoing diversity and vitality, provides a laboratory for the study of Native American verbal art in particular and for an exploration of the complex nature of oral discourse more generally. The structuring principles and processes involved in the performance of Kuna verbal art are complex; they constitute the poetics of performance. Attention to details of transcription and representation enable us to appreciate this poetics in action. Presenting an oral performance in written form reveals the native conception and perception of the performance, as well as performance strategies. Providing different transcriptions and representations of the same performance brings out the very different aspects of its structuring and poetics.

My focus here is on repetition and parallelism, a central feature of the poetics of Kuna performance. While repetition and parallelism are present in all Kuna speaking and chanting, they are most strikingly apparent, indeed omnipresent, in the most ritual and formal Kuna verbal genres. In this sense, the Kuna provide a representative instance of Native American oral poetry, in which repetition and parallelism of various kinds play an important role. Many forms of verbal art in Native America, especially those used in ritual and ceremonial contexts, are structured through the repetition of sounds, words, phrases, lines, and verses. This structure moves the texts along, provides an incantatory tone, and aids in the memorization of fixed verbal forms as well as the creative performance of flexible or adaptable verbal forms. In parallelism, the repetition is of a frame, within which there is variation. Here is a small portion of the Navajo *Blessing Way*, which ensures health and well-being.

> Earth's feet have become my feet
>   by means of these I shall live on.
> Earth's legs have become my legs
>   by means of these I shall live on.
> Earth's body has become my body
>   by means of these I shall live on.
> Earth's mind has become my mind
>   by means of these I shall live on.
> Earth's voice has become my voice
>   by means of these I shall live on.
> Earth's headplume has become my headplume
>   by means of these I shall live on. (Witherspoon, 1977, p. 26)

The esthetic coherence and unity of these lines is created by the exact repetition of the line: "by means of these I shall live on," alternating with the parallel lines generated by the frame: "Earth's [body part] has become my [body part]."

More specifically, the role of repetition and parallelism in Kuna verbal art should be seen in the context of both Mesoamerica and lowland, tropical South America, in which parallel couplets, extensive lists, and stacking of poetic lines are quite common, indeed characteristic of the public oral performance of verbally artistic discourse. In Mesoamerica, the metaphorical couplet, which was a major organizing principle of the verbal art of the classic Aztec and Mayan civilizations, is a linguistic reflection of the dualistic mode of thinking which has been noted for these civilizations. In the words of Miguel León-Portilla, the foremost scholar of Aztec and Mayan literature:

> Anyone who reads indigenous poetry cannot fail to notice the repetition of ideas and the expression of sentiment in parallel form. Sometimes a thought will be complemented or emphasized through the use of different metaphors which arouse the same intuitive feeling, or two phrases will present the same idea in opposite form. A few examples will make this clear. In an Aztec poem which exalts the Sun, Huitzilopochtli, who is invoked by priests and people alike, the same thought is expressed twice:
>
> > From where the eagles are resting,
> > from where the tigers are exalted . . .
>
> And the parallelism reappears in the same poem singing the greatness of Mexico-Tenochtitlan:
>
> > Who could conquer Tenochtitlan?
> > Who could shake the foundation of heaven? (León-Portilla, 1969,
> pp. 76–77)

Couplets, as well as triplets, are characteristic of the poetic structure of the classic Mayan epic, the *Popol Vuh*. Here is an example from a speech in which the gods who are the makers and modelers of humankind call upon older gods who are diviners and artisans to help them:

So be it, fulfill your names:

Hunahpu Possum, Hunahpu Coyote,
Bearer twice over, Begetter twice over,
Great Peccary, Great Tapir,
lapidary, jeweler,
sawyer, carpenter,
Maker of the Blue-Green Plate,
Maker of the Blue-Green Bowl,

incense maker, master craftsman,
Grandmother of Day, Grandmother of Light. (Tedlock, 1985,
     pp. 80–81)

In lowland, tropical forest South America, extreme parallelism is
characteristic of curing chants which communicate with represen-
tatives of the spirit world. Here is an example from the Suyá Indians
of Mato Grosso, Brazil, of a curing song for a child with fever:

1. Blowing [physical blowing]
2. Master of the still waters
3. Master of the still waters
4. Master of the still waters
5. Master of the still waters
6. Master of the still waters
7. Rough-skinned white cayman his hand is spread out. How
   come?
8. Animal, Animal, that lies there still.
9. Master of the still waters
10. Master of the still waters, white cayman
11. Master of the still waters
12. Master of the still waters
13. Master of the still waters
14. Master of the still waters
15. Master of the still waters
16. Master of the still waters
17. White cayman, master of the still waters
18. His hand is spread out, his neck skin is spread out, his hand is
    spread out, he trembles not. How come?
19. Animal, animal, lying there
20. Master of the still waters
21. Master of the still waters
22. Master of the still waters (Seeger, 1986, pp. 74–75)

Seeger (along with Greg Urban) analyzes the parallel structure of
this chant as follows:

There is a structure to the curing song, involving a parallelism between certain parts. This curing song can be divided into six parts as
follows:
     A: lines 1, 2, 3, 4, 5, 6,
     B: lines 7, 8, 9,
     C: lines 10, 11
     D: lines 12, 13, 14, 15, 16
     E: lines 17, 18, 19
     F: lines 20, 21, 22

There is a structural parallel between A, C, and F (repeating the phrase "master of still waters"), and also between B and E. This leaves lines 10 and 11 as a kind of pivot. The lines are part of the central core of the song, and they combine both the name of the animal and the mastery of the still waters. The lines thus represent a synthesis of AB/DEF. (Seeger, 1986, p. 75)

While it is not my purpose here to provide an extended discussion of repetition and parallelism in general, it seems appropriate, as part of my exploration of Kuna repetition and parallelism, to offer some remarks on the relationship between repetition and parallelism. Repetition, in its most general sense, is the basis of structural pattern, in that elements which are in some sense the "same" are established and defined and thus distinguished from elements which are "different." With regard to language structure, the elements involved can be smaller or larger, from sound patterns to grammatical units such as words, phrases, and sentences, to discourse units such as lines, verses, and episodes. According to this way of looking at things, parallelism, the poetic process which has been defined and exemplified by Roman Jakobson and others, is a type of repetition, in that "sames" of some kind or at some level or to some degree are repeated in order to create a parallel pattern. At the same time, since one kind of parallelism is exact or total repetition, repetition is a type of parallelism. In this sense, we have two types or concepts of repetition, which we can call repetition (1) and repetition (2). Repetition (1) is the most general and abstract, which provides the possibility of pattern and structure. Poetic parallelism is an instance of or a type of repetition (1). Repetition (2) is a particular type of pattern, in which a form is repeated totally, exactly. It is this repetition (2) which is a type of parallelism.

TYPES OF PARALLELISM IN KUNA

There are many types of parallelism in Kuna verbal art, involving phonology, morphology, syntax, and semantics. Parallelism is closely tied to line organization and structure in that it sets up correspondences based on, and cutting across lines and units composed of, lines, such as verses. Sometimes adjacent lines are identical, with the exception of the deletion of a single word. Sometimes adjacent lines differ only in nonreferential morphemes, such as stem formatives. Sometimes a series of lines differs only in that a single word is replaced by others with slightly different meaning within a same semantic field. Sometimes the pattern underlying the parallel structure is not a single line, but rather an entire set of lines, a verse, or a stanza, a frame which is repeated over and over with changes in one or more words. The result of all of these types of parallelism is a slow-moving narration, advancing by slight changes in referential content, added to repeated information. Extreme attention is paid to minute and precise detail.

The parallelistic structure of curing and magical chants in particular involves all levels, from the most macro—repetition of whole verse and stanza patterns—to the most micro—repetition of words and morphemes. The result is an overlapping and integration of various parallelistic patterns, a verbal polyphony composed of a tenacious array of cohesive and contrapuntal forms and meanings.

As an example of the pervasive role of parallelism, as well as the different types, in curing and magical chants, consider *The way of the snake*, a magical chant used to raise a dangerous snake in the air. (The full text is presented in Sherzer, 1990.) In *The way of the snake*, certain crucial lines are repeated identically or almost identically throughout the text, punctuating it by marking the boundaries of sections within it. Examples are:

> *Maci oloaktikunappi nele* is present (5 times).
> The specialist/he counsels/is counseling *Maci oloaktikunappi* (12 times).

Two lines differ in nonreferential morphemes (and the possible deletion of a word):

> The specialist is sharpening *(nuptulu-makke-kwiciye)* his little knife.
> He is sharpening *(nuptulu-sae-kwiciye)* his little knife.

in which the verb stem formative *-makke* of the first line is replaced by the verb stem formative *-sae* of the next line.

Two lines are identical except for the replacement of a single word, the two words being slightly different in meaning and within the same semantic field:

> He is cutting small bushes.
> He is clearing small bushes.

> The specialist moves.
> The specialist advances.

A stanza-like frame is repeated, each time with a change in the word used to fill a particular slot. In a long section of the chant in which the specialist demonstrates his intimate knowledge of the parts of the snake's body, the following frame is repeated nine times:

"How your [body part] was formed, put in place.
The specialist knows well."
The specialist is saying.

In this way, all of the body parts of the snake are listed. It seems worth noting here, since Goody (1977) and others have pointed to the list as a characteristic of written discourse, that this example of the use of parallelism to perform orally a list of items is but one of the many such cases in Kuna and other nonliterate societies. In fact, one of the functions of this kind of frame-parallelism in oral discourse seems to be precisely the memorization and performance of lists.

Parallelism thus serves a set of intersecting and overlapping functions in *The way of the snake*. It often involves the syntagmatic projection of a paradigm or taxonomy (of body parts, medicines, or movements). In addition to its poetic function (in the sense of Jakobson), this process of projecting taxonomies onto a fixed line, verse, or stanza enables the generation of a long text or portion of text. Length is an important aspect of the power of magical chants. The more recalcitrant the snake, the longer the specialist will make the text, precisely by generating more lines by means of parallelistic structures. At the same time, the performer's intimate knowledge of the nature of the spirit world, especially its parts and taxonomic classification, is also displayed by parallelistic structures and processes. And since specialists must memorize these texts, parallelistic line, verse, and stanza frames seem to provide mnemonic aids to memorization. Finally, this extensive parallelism aids in actual performance, providing both time and procedures for moving from line to line, narrative description to narrative description. It is no wonder, given these various functions, that parallelism is so pervasive in *The way of the snake*.

TRANSCRIPTION, REPRESENTATION, AND TRANSLATION

A most useful and interesting way to approach the role of repetition and parallelism in the structuring of Kuna discourse, and in fact in the structuring of any oral discourse, is by paying serious and careful attention to issues of transcription, representation, and translation. For it is in our experimentation with ways of representing the oral discourse of a particular group of people that we can best appreciate the group's own experimentation, in actual performance, with the structuring and indeed representation of discourse.

Breaking with an earlier generation, recent researchers, myself included, believe that Native American oral discourse and especially verbal art is best analyzed and represented as linear poetry rather than block prose. In particular, we pay considerable attention to such features of poetic organization as grammatical and semantic parallelism, intonation, pause patterning, and other oral features of the dramatization of the voice so characteristic of, and so essential to, verbal performances. The determination of line and verse structure is central to the enterprise. Line and verse structure is intimately related to repetition and parallelism.

My investigation of Kuna discourse has revealed that each of the line- and verse-marking devices, grammatical, intonational, musical (in the chase of chanting), and social interactional, is highly elaborated and developed in and of itself, and enters into different types of relationships with the others, sometimes congruent, synchronic, and isomorphic, sometimes creating contrasts, tensions, and counterpoint. Given this situation, it might then seem appropriate to provide several written representations of the same performance, according to each of the different organizational criteria. In my work to this date, I have not done this but rather have opted for a single transcription and representation of each performance which aims at capturing as much as possible of what members of a Kuna audience actually feel in listening to a performance. Here, however, I propose a different approach, namely to experiment with different modes of representation of a single performance, precisely to unpack the different structuring principles involved in performance and to highlight each of them, hopefully at the same time demonstrating that the Kuna performers themselves are manipulating, playing with, and creatively experimenting with modes of representing their own discourse. Each representation I present here highlights different aspects of the repetition and parallelism which pervade Kuna discourse.

My example is *pisep ikar (The way of the basil plant)*, performed by Pranki Pilos from the San Blas island of Mulatuppu. It is a verbal mosaic of intersecting and overlapping repetitions and parallelistic patterns of all kinds. This magical chant, addressed to the spirit of the basil plant (named *inapiseptili* in Kuna magical, ritual language), is used to insure success in the hunting of wild animals in the jungle. The hunter bathes in a potion made from the fragrant basil plant and has this chant performed for him by a specialist. The opening portion of the chant, which is my focus here, deals with the birth (symbolically described) of the basil plant.

In my first representation of the performance, lines are determined by a parallelism of melodic shape, as well as grammatical and semantic parallelism. Pairs of lines constitute verses. There is a short pause after the first line of a verse, and a laryngeal tightening followed by a long pause after the second line of a verse. Here is a transcription and representation which highlights the extreme repetition and parallelism of words and grammatical affixes, by lining them up, stacking them under one another.

inapiseptili olouluti tulalemaiye
         olouluti tulallemaiye

inapiseptili olouluti sikkirmakkemaiye
         olouluti sikkirmakmamaiye

inapiseptili olouluti wawanmakkemaiye
         olouluti wawanmakmainaye

inapiseptili olouluti aktutumakkemaiye
         olouluti aktutulemainaye

inapiseptili olouluti kollomakkemaiye
         olouluti kollomakmainaye

inapiseptili olouluti mummurmakkemaiye
         olouluti mummurmakmainaye

Notice a crucial feature of this representation, namely that, in order to highlight the parallelism so strikingly characteristic of this text, I have left blank spaces at the beginning of the second line of each verse, even though there is no long pause in the oral performance, which is what blank spaces conventionally represent. In the translation of this passage, I propose another representation, namely one in which the short pauses are not represented by blank spaces:

Inapiseptili in the golden box is moving
In the golden box is moving

Inapiseptili in the garden box is swinging from side to side
In the golden box is swinging from side to side

Inapiseptili in the golden box is trembling
In the golden box is trembling

Inapiseptili in the golden box is palpitating
In the golden box is palpitating

Inapiseptili in the golden box is making a noise
in the golden box is making a noise

Inapiseptili in the golden box is shooting out
In the golden box is shooting out

Notice that this representation captures the flow of the voice, of the melodic pattern, but no longer highlights the striking grammatical and semantic parallelism, which was so well demonstrated in my first representation.

Another representation was made on Sound Edit, a computer program which displays a sound in terms of amplitude and pause pattern. Figure 3.1 shows the first two verses, labelled as follows: 1a is the first line of the first verse, 1b is the second line of first verse, 2a is the first line of the second verse, and 2b is the second line of the second verse.

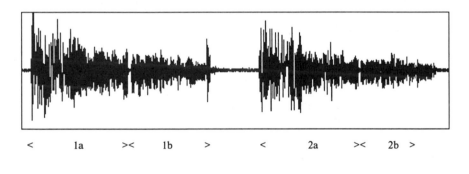

<   1a   ><   1b   >   <   2a   ><   2b   >

1a inapiseptili olouluti tulalemaiye   2a inapiseptili olouluti sikkirmakkemaiye

1b olouluti tulallemaiye   2b olouluti sikkirmakmamaiye

Figure 3.1 Sound Edit display of first 2 verses of *The way of the basil plant.*

This representation/display shows the parallelism of the two verses with regard to the flow of the voice, by displaying amplitude, from high to low. The sharp burst of amplitude at the end of the first verse is a loud laryngeal tightening which sounds very much like a cough. Notice the long pause between verses, the very short pause between lines within a verse.

Still another transcription is a more conventional linguistic representation and specifies the grammatical divisions of the text as well as its most literal meaning. Words are divided into morphemes (minimal meaningful and grammatical units) by means of dashes. This representation is multilinear.

1	inapiseptili	olouluti	tulalemaiye
2	ina-pisep-tili	olo-ulu-ti	tula-le(k(e))-ma(i)-ye
3	RP-NOUN-RS	RP-NOUN-RS	ADJ-PAS-POS-OPT
4	medicinal-basil-nominal	golden-box-nominal	alive-is-horiz-hopefully
5	Inapiseptili	in the golden box	is moving

1		olouluti	tula(l)emaiye
2		olo-ulu-ti	tula-le(k(e)-ma(i)-ye
3		RP-NOUN-RS	ADJ-PAS-POS-OPT
4		golden-box-nominal	alive-is-horiz-hopefully
5		In the golden box	is moving

1	inapiseptili	olouluti	sikkirmakkemaiye
2	ina-pisep-tili	olo-ulu-ti	sikkir-makk(e)-ma(i)-ye
3	RP-NOUN-RS	RP-NOUN-RS	VERB-V FORM-POS-OPT
4	medicinal-basil-nominal	golden-box-nominal	swing-verbal-horiz-hopefully
5	Inapiseptili	in the golden box	is swinging from side to side

1		olouluti	sikkirmakmamaiye
2		olo-ulu-ti	sikkir-makk(e)-ma(i)-ma(i)-ye
3		RP-NOUN-RS	VERB-V FORM-POS-POS-OPT
4		golden-box-nominal	swing-verbal-horiz-horiz-hopefully
5		In the golden box	is swinging from side to side

1	inapiseptili	olouluti	wawanmakkemaiye
2	ina-pisep-tili	olo-ulu-ti	wawan-makk(e)-ma(i)-ye
3	RP-NOUN-RS	RP-NOUN-RS	VERB-V FORM-POS-OPT
4	medicinal-basil-nominal	golden-box-nominal	tremble-verbal-horiz-hopefully
5	Inapiseptili	in the golden box	is trembling

1		olouluti	wawanmakmainaye
2		olo-ulu-ti	wawan-makk(e)-ma(i)-na(e)-ye
3		RP-NOUN-RS	VERB-V FORM-POS-DIR-OPT
4		golden-box-nominal	tremble-verbal-horiz-go-hopefully
5		In the golden box	is trembling

1	inapiseptili	olouluti	aktutumakkemaiye
2	ina-pisep-tili	olo-ulu-ti	aktutu-makk(e)-ma(i)-ye
3	RP-NOUN-RS	RP-NOUN-RS	VERB-V FORM-POS-OPT
4	medicinal-basil-nominal	golden-box-nominal	palpitate-verbal-horiz-hopefully
5	Inapiseptili	in the golden box	is palpitating

1		olouluti	aktutulemainaye
2		olo-ulu-ti	aktutu-le(k(e))-ma(i)-na(e)-ye
3		RP-NOUN-RS	VERB-PAS-POS-DIR-OPT
4		golden-box-nominal	palpitate-verbal-horiz-go-hopefully
5		In the golden box	is palpitating
1	inapiseptili	olouluti	kollomakkemaiye
2	ina-pisep-tili	olo-ulu-ti	kollo-makk(e)-ma(i)-ye
3	RP-NOUN-RS	RP-NOUN-RS	VERB-V FORM-POS-OPT
4	medicinal-basil-nominal	golden-box-nominal	make noise-verbal-horiz-hopefully
5	Inapiseptili	in the golden box	is making a noise
1		olouluti	kollomakmainaye
2		olo-ulu-ti	kollo-makk(e)-ma(i)-na(e)-ye
3		RP-NOUN-RS	VERB-V FORM-POS-DIR-OPT
4		golden-box-nominal	make noise-verbal-horiz-go-hopefully
5		In the golden box	is making a noise
1	inapiseptili	olouluti	mummurmakkemaiye
2	ina-pisep-tili	olo-ulu-ti	mummur-makk(e)-ma(i)-ye
3	RP-NOUN-RS	RP-NOUN-RS	VERB-V FORM-POS-OPT
4	medicinal-basil-nominal	golden-box-nominal	shoot out-verbal-horiz-hopefully
5	Inapiseptili	in the golden box	is shooting out
1		olouluti	mummurmakmainaye
2		olo-ulu-ti	mummur-makk(e)-ma(i)-na(e)-ye
3		RP-NOUN-RS	VERB-V FORM-POS-DIR-OPT
4		golden-box-nominal	shoot out-verbal-horiz-go-hopefully
5		In the golden box	is shooting out

Line 1 of each row in the representation is a phonemic transcription of the tape recording of the performance. In line 2, morpheme boundaries are indicated by dashes. The morphemes are presented in their fullest, deepest, most abstract form. Parentheses surround vowels which are potentially deletable according to Kuna rules of phonology and morphology. In line 3, the grammatical categories of morphemes are labeled. RP stands for *ritual prefix*, a nominal prefix used in magical chants. NOUN stands for noun stem. RS stands for *ritual suffix*, a nominal suffix used in magical chants. ADJ stands for *adjectival stem*. PAS stands for *passive suffix*. POS stands for one of four *verbal suffixes* which indicate the *position of the subject of a sentence* in ongoing movement. OPT stands for *optative mood*. VERB stands for *verb stem*. V FORM stands for *verb formative suffix*. DIR stands for one of *verbal suffixes* which indicate the *direction of the subject of a sentence*. Line 4 provides a literal translation of morphemes. Line 5 is a freer translation.

A close examination of the multilinear representation demonstrates considerable repetition and parallelism at many levels. It also reveals a certain degree of play, manipulation, and, apparently, experimentation with the basic structure of this memorized chant on the part of the performer, Pranki Pilos. One of the invariables of the text is the syntactic structure of the lines and verses: The first line of each verse consists of two nominals followed by the verb, and the second line of each verse parallels the first without the initial nominal. Another invariable is the inclusion of the positional verbal suffix and the final verbal suffix, the modal *ye*.

The variable aspects of the text draw on the potential provided by the polysynthetic structure of this language, in which many suffixes are potentially strung along, especially after verb stems. Here are some examples. The most abstract, underlying form of the verb formative suffix is *makke*, represented as *makk(e)* on line 2 of the multilinear representation. This is also the usual ritual form this morpheme takes, its more everyday variant being *mak*. Interestingly, Pranki Pilos alternates *makke* and *mak*, the ritual and everyday forms, in lines 1 and 2 of verses 2, 3, 5, and 6 of this performance. A related manipulation involves an alternation between the verb formative suffix and the passive suffix. The passive suffix is used in both lines of verse 1, and in this sense this verse contrasts with all other verses. The two lines of verse 4 exploit this contrast as well. Line 1 of this verse has the verb formative suffix; line 2 has the passive suffix. Both of these examples involve breaking with an overall pattern of repetition and parallelism and creating another within it. The *makke/mak* alternation is particularly striking, in that it inserts an everyday, colloquial form into a ritual performance, a possibly dangerous move, but one which provides one more level of poetic tension and which in itself provides still another pattern of repetition and parallelism.

Another performance manipulation is the reduplication of the positional suffix *mai*, which occurs only in line 2 of verse 2. In lines 2 of verses 3 through 6 *mai* is followed by the directional suffix *nae*, which creates another pattern of parallelism. From the point of view of ordinary Kuna grammar, this sequence is ungrammatical and illogical. Since *nae* appears in its short, everyday form *na*, it may be ambiguous with *nai*, a positional suffix meaning "hanging" or "perched." This provides even more tension in the text.

What this at first glance purely linguistic representation captures is individual creativity, play, and manipulation against the backdrop of a highly ritual, repetitive, parallelistic, memorized chant. In all of this, grammatical, semantic, sociolinguistic, and logical rules and structures are played down and poeticized, in the service of

Pranki Pilos's performance in which formal patterning competes with referential meaning.

This leads to still another representation of this performance, a most abstract one, which highlights the formal patterning of repetition and parallelism, of variants and invariants. In this representation, a and b stand for the nominals *inapiseptili* (the name of the basil plant) and golden box; c, d, e, f, g, and h stand for the various verb stems; p stands for the passive suffix; W and w stand for the verb formative suffix, W in its ritual form and w in its everyday form; x stands for the positional suffix; y stands for the directional suffix; and z stands for the optative suffix.

a	b	c	p	x		z
	b	c	p	x		z
a	b	d	W	x		z
	b	d	w	x	x	z
a	b	e	W	x		z
	b	e	w	x	y	z
a	b	f	W	x		z
	b	f	p	x	y	z
a	b	g	W	x		z
	b	g	w	x	y	z
a	b	h	W	x		z
	b	h	w	x	y	z

Each of the representations of Pranki Pilos's performance of *The way of the basil plant* presented here reveals different aspects of the poetic structuring of the actual performance. A comparison of all of them brings out the dynamic intersection of all of the resources that Kuna performers draw on—grammatical, lexical, intonational, paralinguistic, and musical—and demonstrates quite clearly the interplay of congruences, isomorphisms, repetitions, and parallelisms, as well as tensions, contrasts, and counterpoints, so characteristic of the dynamics of Kuna verbal art. In this particular performance we have an excellent illustration as well of the interplay of memorization and creative improvisation, both involving an intersection and overlapping of repetition and parallelism. This also becomes evident in a comparison of the different representations.

This chapter has a double focus, on the one hand the central role of repetition and parallelism in the structuring of Kuna discourse and on the other the transcription, representation, and translation of this discourse. These two foci are intimately related.

The pervasive patterns of repetition and parallelism, which are characteristic of the structuring of, especially, ritual forms of Kuna discourse, result in an interesting tension between form and content. While patterns of parallelism can frame and highlight, thus enhance and foreground referential content, overlapping and intersecting patterns of repetition and parallelism can overwhelm and thus almost obfuscate referential content. (Note the interesting parallel here between Kuna oral discourse and the mola or woman's blouse, the principal form of Kuna visual art; see Sherzer & Sherzer, 1976.)

In my presentation, discussion, and analysis of Kuna patterns of repetition and parallelism, I do not consider transcription, representation, and translation to be in any way incidental, secondary, or marginal. Quite the contrary. It is precisely through careful attention to issues of transcription, representation, and translation that the structuring principles involved in Kuna performance practices become apparent. That is, the complex networks of overlapping and intersecting repetition and parallelism which underlie the structuring of Kuna discourse, as in the example I present here, are brought out by experimentation with different models of transcription, representation, and translation. Furthermore, the different models of transcription, representation, and translation enable us to focus on and understand the distinct though related esthetic principles that different performers and members of audiences attend to during performances.

Roman Jakobson taught us that parallelism is a guide to the intuitively covert structure of the grammar of a language and that simultaneously attention to the grammar of a language is crucial to our understanding of such poetic processes as parallelism. Jakobson's insights are also at the core of an approach to discourse which has come to be called ethnopoetics. Through experimentation with multiple modes of representation of a single Kuna performance, I hope to have contributed to a key concern of ethnopoetics, namely, the complex structure, often emergent, of how people talk, perform, hear, and interpret.[1]

REFERENCES

Goody, J. (1977). *The domestication of the savage mind.* Cambridge, UK: Cambridge University Press.

Léon-Portilla, M. (1969). *Literatures of Mexico.* Norman, OK: University of Oklahoma Press.

---

[1] More complete reports of my research on the Kuna are presented by Sherzer (1983, 1990).

Seeger, A. (1986). Oratory is spoken, myth is told, and song is sung, but they are all music to my ears. In J. Sherzer & G. Urban (Eds.), *Native South American discourse* (pp. 59–82). Berlin: Mouton de Gruyter.

Sherzer, D., & Sherzer, J. (1976). *Mormaknamaloe: The Cuna mola.* In P. Young & J. Howe (Eds.), *Ritual and symbol in Native Central America* (University of Oregon Anthropological Papers 9, pp. 21–42). Eugene, OR: University of Oregon.

Sherzer, J. (1983). *Kuna ways of speaking: An ethnographic perspective.* Austin, TX: University of Texas Press.

Sherzer, J. (1990). *Verbal art in San Blas: Kuna culture through its discourse.* Cambridge, UK: Cambridge University Press.

Tedlock, D. (Trans.). (1985). *Popol Vuh: The definitive edition of the Mayan book of the dawn of life and the glories of Gods and kings.* New York: Simon and Schuster.

Witherspoon, G. (1977). *Language and art in the Navajo universe.* Ann Arbor, MI: University of Michigan Press.

Part II
Repetition in Literary Discourse: Echoes Across Texts and Within

Chapter 4
Staging Repetition: Parody in Postmodern British and American Theater

Katherine E. Kelly

Department of English
Texas A&M University

REPETITION WITH DIFFERENCE:
TWO MODELS OF ARTISTIC PARODY

Literary and cultural theorists have attempted to account for a surge in interartistic quotation, mimicry, and appropriation of various kinds in the Western arts of the past several decades. One type of recent artistic borrowing calls attention to itself by repeating (with difference) the languages, images, motifs, and/or genre markers of particular (and usually well-known) prior works. In 18th and 19th century British and American drama, prior works or conventions in an "other" artistic context were often (but not always) performed as mocking burlesques. For this and other reasons, *parody* was, until recently, defined as a subset of satire. However, more recent examples of parodic recycling not only fail to mock the sources they repeat but actually pay them homage. Consequently, Linda Hutcheon (1985, p. 6) has broadened the definition of parody to include a wide range of "imitation characterized by ironic inversion." The various kinds of artistic borrowing elsewhere called by other names—*satire, trans-contextualization, literary recycling, hypertextuality* and *in-tertextuality*—can, she insists, be contained by her definition, which she delimits by subject and treatment. To begin with, the source text of a parody must always be either another work of art or another form of coded discourse (p. 16). Second, the parodist's implied intention must not be to conceal a source but to mark a difference from it through irony. The effect of the irony may be but need not be comic (pp. 37, 39).

Gary Morson's theory of parody (1989), an extension of Mikhail Bakhtin's work on dialogism, is similar to Hutcheon's but significantly different from it in one respect. Morson uses three qualifying criteria for admitting a work into the class of parodies: (a) It must evoke or indicate another text, (b) it must be antithetical to that other text, and (c) it must clearly be intended to have "higher semantic authority than the original" text (p. 67). Morson's model insists more vehemently than does Hutcheon's that the texts implicated in parody should be in oppositional relation. He implies this requirement in his third criterion, which addresses cases in which the reader/spectator does not know which of the two texts in dialogue is being granted greater authority (i.e., which is the "winner" and which the "loser"). When this third criterion goes unsatisfied, Morson declares the dialogical relation to be, not that of parody, but of what he calls *metaparody*—a genre of parodies that mock not only a "target" text but also their own superior reworking of that prior text. Here Morson is attempting to acknowledge those cases where the readers/spectators of a parody are cut off from a single or a final interpretive resolution of the dialogical play between texts. Hutcheon does not need to create such a category, as she refrains from insisting that parodic intertextuality must imply a hierarchy of the texts in dialogue. In the place of such a hierarchy, Hutcheon posits a deliberately broad and inclusive range of intentionalities and responses. In Hutcheon's terms, we can, for example, legitimately class works as parodies that explicitly defer to their sources (e.g., cinematic *homages*). Not only can we call such works parodies but also we must recognize that all parodies—even those that mock— also reinforce their targets: "parody's transgressions ultimately remain authorized . . . by the very norm it seeks to subvert" (p. 75). Parody is never a mere subjugation of one text or convention by a posterior imitation, but a complex and varying transaction between texts that can be experienced as mockingly comic or movingly elegiac.

Hutcheon's model of parody has the virtue of pragmatism. Both flexible and inclusive, it allows her to classify and account for recent aesthetic recycling strategies in an historical context. Morson's more polemical extension of Bakhtin's remarks on parody assumes the centrality of conflict (or dialectical clash and synthesis) as a principle of cultural change and is therefore less able than Hutcheon's model to account for recycling practices that do not in any obvious way reflect the dialectical process. However, the vigor of Morson's assertions carries persuasive weight. His remarks on parody's role in literary and cultural history are especially intriguing: "Parody works by etiology. . . . A text or genre will be vulnerable to parody . . . to the extent that it ignores or claims to transcend its own originating context. . . . Parody historicizes, and in so doing, it exposes the conditions that engendered claims of unconditionality" (1989, p. 78). The historicizing function of parody will prove central to the works of both of the theater artists discussed here.

PARODY IN THE THEATER

Both Hutcheon and Morson apply their models of parody to actual works of art, but favor prose fiction when selecting their examples. My own interest in extending the applications of these two models of artistic parody to dramatic texts may, therefore, clarify their central assumptions in new ways. The double function of a dramatic text distinguishes it from other literary texts intended to be received through reading alone. To ask what is unique about literary parody in the theater is also to ask what is unique about spoken language in the theater. If, as Richard Bauman (1977, p. 16) has suggested, repetition can be a sign that speakers are performing, then might not the inverse also be true: When speakers (i.e., actors) are performing on stage, they are always repeating something—most obviously, words written for them by a playwright, less obviously, "natural" occurrences of speech and action adapted from an extraartistic context. As Michael Issacharoff (1989, pp. 4–5) has suggested, "theatrical utterance, if it may even be called utterance, is linked to the issue of repetition and quotation"; "theatre dialogue is no more than display discourse" (p. 9).

But why have a number of influential postmodern playwrights chosen to heighten this display by composing their discourse from the already-written texts of earlier authors? Literary parody has emerged in the modern European theater under pressure of a debate concerning the supremacy of spoken language on the stage. The key assertions in this debate could be said to define some of the essential conflicts in the theater of the past few decades. Over and against the British and American literary theater of the canonical past perpetuated by the academy—Shakespeare, Jonson, Sheridan, Shaw, O'Neill, and so on—a significant group of 20th-century theater artists has attempted to assert the primacy of nonliterary theatrical signs. E. Gordon Craig's assertion that "the eye is more swiftly and powerfully appealed to than any other sense" (1968, p. 115) was only one of his arguments for an environmental theater that would minimize dialogue in favor of raising setting and scenery to a new level of dominance in the theatrical event. Antonin Artaud (1968, p. 59) called for a nondiscursive, oneiric language that would circumvent logic: "It is not a question of suppressing the spoken language, but of giving words . . . the importance they have in dreams." More recently, Roland Barthes (1982, p. 75) has written, "What is theatricality? It is theatre-minus-text, it is a density of signs and sensations built up on stage starting from the written argument. . . . (In) great theatre . . . the written text is from the first carried along by the externality of bodies, of objects, of situations; the utterance immediately explodes into substances." Commenting upon Artaud's "theatre of cruelty," Jacques Derrida (1978) associates a text-centered drama with a logocentric ("theological") stage space: "The theatrical practice of cruelty, in its action and structure, inhabits or rather *produces* a nontheological space. The stage is theological for as long as it is dominated by speech, by a will to speech, by the layout of a primary logos which does not belong to the theatrical site and governs it from a distance. . . . an author-creator who, absent and from afar, is armed with a text and keeps watch over . . . the meaning of representation" (p. 235).

These objections to text-centered theater are distinctly motivated and theoretically grounded, but they all share an interest in dispersing the locus of theatrical power heretofore heavily invested in the playwright. As it has been used by Tom Stoppard (1975) and Robert Wilson (1977), parody can either erode or reinforce this power, sometimes doing both at once.

TOM STOPPARD'S *TRAVESTIES*: AUTHORIAL POWER AND PARODY

Stoppard's *Travesties* offers an example of parody used to flatter the audience's knowledge of texts central to literary history, thereby promoting a self-congratulatory pleasure in the spectators as well as a cohesion between author and spectator as members of a *cogno-*

scenti. Travesties also uses parody to display and celebrate author Stoppard's linguistic virtuosity. Clearly, this play values the power of the author. But in its parodic doubleness, it also mocks that power and the privilege accorded the canonical texts it displays. As a parody, *Travesties* poses the question: How seriously should we take the power of the author/artist, and what does the artist owe society in exchange for being taken seriously as an artist? In its range of parody, from the mocking to the barely ironical, *Travesties* can best be described using Hutcheon's pragmatic model, although Morson's description of the historical function of parody can help to account for Stoppard's choice of texts and for the moral impulse behind the playwright's recycling strategies.

Travesties opens with a scene set in the Zurich Public Library during the First World War in which actors portraying James Joyce, Lenin and his wife, and the Dadaist Tristan Tzara are displaying the writing of *Ulysses*, Lenin's *Imperialism, the Highest Stage of Capitalism*, and a (pseudo)-Dadaist poem. Parodic repetition takes several forms in this scene, such as the actors' exaggerated resemblances to the historical figures they represent (in the London production, "Joyce" wore a jacket covered with oversized shamrocks; in an allusion to Dadaist literary technique, Tzara is provided with an actual hat from which he draws slips of paper) and the actors' literal embodiment of details reported about the historical person. (Joyce's biographer, Richard Ellmann [1959, p. 409], wrote that Joyce "never wore a complete suit, always the jacket of one and trousers of another." Stoppard's Joyce accordingly wears the opposite halves of two suits in the play's two acts.)

In addition, parody in the prologue takes the form of textual repetition with difference—the actors repeat (or, in the case of Tzara and the Lenins, seem to repeat) fragments of actual literary and nonfictional published works. The textual parodies themselves are also quite distinct. Joyce repeats lines from *Ulysses*, while Tzara pulls pieces of paper out of a hat that compose "for him" an extended cross-lingual punning poem describing the Dadaist and his doctrine. Finally, Lenin and his wife do not parody literary discourse at all but "natural conversation" reconstructed (and delivered in Russian) by author Stoppard from Lenin's collected writings and Lenin's wife's *Memories of Lenin*. Stoppard's "parody" of the Lenins' conversation, while based on a nonfiction source, is nevertheless, by Hutcheon's definition, authentic parody, as Stoppard repeats this (admittedly constructed or adapted) discourse within the limits of another fictional text. Morson's criterion of conflict, on the other hand, does not seem to apply to the Lenins' statements: the prior "text" evoked by their lines is not clearly antithetical to the parody of that text being spoken on stage, nor can the spectator determine which of the two is being preferred.

There is, however, a heightened irony (in Hutcheon's phrase) in this opening scene. It arises not so much from the difference between the original texts and their (mis)representations—although such differences exist—but from the difference between all of the characters' speech and so-called ordinary English. They all sound different from how we expect them to sound, in that they all speak in a foreign language, a "code" of sorts: Tzara speaks Dada pseudononsense; Joyce speaks primarily in *Ulysses* dialect; and the Lenins speak in Russian. That they are all repeating texts as well as writing them may not be, at this point in the play, apparent to all readers/ spectators, but it will become apparent in the course of the first act.

The opening scene parodies the reader/spectator's expectation that the characters will address one another in some form of represented "natural" speech. Instead, we hear writers "writing" their speeches. This "writtenness" is, like the parodic procedure itself, foregrounded by repetition, a formal feature of both Joyce's and Tzara's modernist texts that Stoppard transcontextualizes by showing the authors dictating a representative series of repetitions or variations aloud.

JOYCE: (dictating to GWEN): Deshill holles eamus . . .
GWEN: (writing): Deshill holles eamus . . .
JOYCE: Thrice.
GWEN: Uh-hum.
JOYCE: Send us bright one, light one, Horhorn, quickening and womb-fruit.
GWEN: Send us bright one, light one, Horhorn, quickening and womb-fruit.
JOYCE: Thrice.
GWEN: Uh-hum.
JOYCE: Hoopsa, boyaboy, hoopsa!
GWEN: Hoopsa, boyaboy, hoopsa!
JOYCE: Hoopsa, boyaboy, hoopsa!
GWEN: Likewise thrice?
JOYCE: Uh-hum. (1975, p. 18)

The humor of this particular occurrence of "display discourse" turns not only on the oddity of Joyce's diction but also on the oddity of his structured repetitions and on our position as spectator or reader overhearing in the public space of a library the dictation of a literary text. In choosing to open his play with these various parodic displays of writing, Stoppard signals his subject to be that of writing or literary art itself.

As we move into act I, narrator Henry Carr becomes a kind of metawriter, staging for us in his unreliable memory/imagination his recollection of his days in the British Consulate in Zurich during the First World War. Carr's long narrative introduction to himself and his occasion for speaking to us informs us of the central texts which we have heard and can expect to hear again—Joyce's *Ulysses*, Lenin's writings, Tzara's poems, and Oscar Wilde's *The Importance of Being Earnest*. The latter plays an especially large role in Carr's recollection, as he had played the role of Algernon in James Joyce's Zurich production of the play, during which he became embroiled in a dispute with Joyce over reimbursement for the cost of his costume.

While Carr claims in the first act to be presenting his memoirs, Stoppard gives him a textual frame—dialogue, characters, situations—borrowed closely from Wilde's play. Thus, when Henry Carr begins his memoirs, he writes them as an unwitting parody of Wilde's *Earnest*, in relation to which his own text of "senile reminiscence" is, by all traditional literary standards, vastly inferior.

Carr begins his narrative of his experiences in Zurich with Joyce, Lenin, and Tzara during the Great War only to become distracted from his narrative goal by his own authorial excesses—strings of cliches, bouts of temper, irrelevant details. In his repeated attempts to restart and complete his memoirs, Carr parodies not only the memoir genre but also the convention of narrator reliability and the figure of the playwright himself, playing fast and loose with history in his desire to tell a good story. The key scenes in the first act of the play—marked by the repeating restarts of Carr's narrative—feature an ideological argument between Young Carr and Carr's multiple caricatures of Tristan Tzara. In this argument scene, which repeats with variation, Carr and Tzara debate the relation between art and politics, with Carr insisting that an artist is under no obligation to serve a particular ideology, and Tzara insisting that art is directly implicated in politics and commerce, which, in their degenerate state, have given rise to antiart. Each of the disputants parodies his position in the mocking sense, by pushing it to a point of absurdity. Philistine Carr drops all pretense of reason and civility in attacking Tzara:

> I went to war because I believed that those boring little Belgians and
> incompetent Frogs had the right to be defended from German militar-

ism, that's *love of freedom* . . . and I won't be told by some yellow-bellied Bolshevik that I ended up in the trenches because there's a profit in ball-bearings! (p. 40)

Tzara responds by interpreting the outbreak of the War as the chance coincidence of the Austrian heir's wedding anniversary and his decision to inspect the army in Bosnia:

> *Quite right!* You ended up in the trenches, because on the 28th of June 1900 the heir to the throne of Austro-Hungary married beneath him and found that the wife he loved was never allowed to sit next to him on royal occasions, except! when he was acting . . . as Inspector General of the Austro-Hungarian army—(p. 40)

As readers of Stoppard know, virtually all of his works question the artist's responsibility to the extraartistic world, although his position on the question has not always been either clearly understood or fairly stated. Both Tzara and Carr, as diminutive spokespersons for Lenin and Joyce, respectively, mock their own positions. But neither Joyce nor Lenin—the play's two "giants"—mock themselves, although both are parodied in the sense that they and their texts are represented within an *other* work of art. To locate Stoppard's own implied position on the art–politics debate, we must recognize that he repeats texts for reasons other than mockery and that even mockery can function as back-handed praise. The first act of the play, devoted largely to presenting in various parodic forms Joyce's neutralist position during the War (and, by extension, his position on art's disinterestedness) concludes with Henry's Carr's recollection of a dream he had of cross-examining Joyce: "I had him in the witness box, a masterly cross-examination, case practically won . . . and I *flung* at him—'And what did you do in the Great War?' 'I wrote *Ulysses*,' he said. 'What did you do?' Bloody nerve" (p. 65). The power of the author/artist, in this case James Joyce, is both eroded by mockery and parodic quotation of various kinds in the first act, and validated by serving as the central model of artistic accomplishment during the Great War. In answer to the question, "How seriously should we take the power of the artist and what obligation do artists have to the societies in which they live," act I implies that Western democracies take art and artists more seriously than they should, and that artists have only the obligation to be grateful to the society in which they practice their art. Henry Carr, sometimes privileged with speaking lines echoing other Stoppard characters and even Stoppard-the-author, puts it as follows: "The idea of the artist as a special kind of human being is art's greatest achievement, and it's a fake!" (p. 47).

But the first act answers the question once only. In order to "count" in this play, an event, a question, a character, or an action must be marked by repetition. *Travesties'* problematic act II presents "Lenin" and his "wife," through whom Stoppard asks the question again, this time from the point of view of a political rather than an artistic authority. Lenin's protegee Cecily opens the act with a long lecture on the history of Marxism at the time of the Russian translation of *Das Kapital*. In its London premiere, this opening nearly capsized the play, as spectators were bewildered (not to mention disappointed) by the abrupt style shift from Wildean comedy of manners to Brechtian epic narrative. Stoppard had to decide whether entertaining the spectators or using parody to present the problem of art versus politics was more important. He kept the lecture, but made it shorter.

The key scenes in act II are also staged in a documentary style. In these scenes, "Lenin" quotes from a variety of his writings on the role of art in the Revolution. The parodic effect of these speeches is dependent not upon a distortion of Lenin's original texts (presumably familiar only to a handful of spectators) but upon their having been recontextualized in the milieu of Stoppard's parody of Wilde's *Earnest*. The intertextual relation of the *Earnest* frame plot and the Lenin documentary scenes is frankly antithetical in both content and style. When "Lenin" poses the question of how seriously we should take art and what does the artist owe to society, he arrives at answers diametrically opposed to those suggested in act I:

> Today, literature must become party literature. . . . Literature must become a part of the common cause of the proletariat, a cog in the Social Democratic mechanism (p. 85). I don't know of anything greater than the Appassionata. Amazing, superhuman music. . . . But I can't listen to music often. It . . . makes me want to pat the heads of those people who while living in this vile hell can create such beauty. (p. 89)

From Lenin's point of view, the artist must serve the Revolution or be expelled from the Party. Art must not be taken too seriously as it can soften the hearts of revolutionaries who "can't pat heads or we'll get our hands bitten off" (p. 89). Following closely after "Lenin's" last soliloquy, Stoppard's stage directions suggest that *Earnest* retakes the stage, as "The 'Appassionata'. . . . degenerates absurdly into *Mr. Gallagher and Mr. Shean*" (p. 89). Stoppard reintroduces the *Earnest* frame at the play's close, underscoring its privileged status as a normative (albeit parodied) text by means of which not only stylistic but also ideological coherence can survive the play's radical shifts in idiom.

The second act of *Travesties* devoted to Lenin is flawed, not because it opens on a surprising note but because it fails to parody Lenin's position with the variety, ingenuity, and playfulness characteristic of the parodies of Joyce and Henry Carr. So that while Stoppard was compelled by the conventions of intellectual fair play to devote one of the play's two acts to "Lenin's" view of the role of the artist, he fails to convince readers and spectators that he takes "Lenin's" view as seriously as he takes "Joyce's." It is finally the playfulness of parody itself that emerges the victor in the art–politics debate.

ROBERT WILSON'S CELEBRATION OF THE IMAGE

Just as Stoppard's parodies attempt to diffuse the power of the author by locating the center of the action in the spectator's recognition of (mis)quoted texts, genres, and conventions, so Robert Wilson's theater pieces attempt to empower the spectators by granting them a vast space and time within which to receive and respond to a series of images and verbal texts offered for their viewing. Robert Wilson is one of the most striking and successful proponents of a non-text-centered theater to practice in the United States in recent years. Notorious for their length (several have run for as long as 12 hours, some have run for days), for their dreamlike stretching of time and space, and for their visual sumptuousness, Wilson's events relegate "dialogue" to secondary status. While not all of them feature literary parody, they are all parodic in the broad sense of the term— they quote and transcontextualize written and visual texts, transforming them most typically through spatial extension and repetition over time.

Wilson's 1974 piece, *A Letter for Queen Victoria*, foregrounds stage utterance as "display discourse" by treating it as an element in the mise-en-scene and by offering an alternative to conventional stage language in the writings of Wilson's colleague Christopher Knowles. Entitled for an actual letter written to the queen and then rewritten (i.e., parodied) for Wilson by Stefan Brecht, *Victoria* opens with a simultaneous recitation of two versions of this letter, one read by Christopher Knowles, the other read by three cast members. As with the Lenin's statements in *Travesties*, we cannot know which of these parodic versions of the original text to prefer, as we haven't heard the original text. Over the course of the play, Wilson will make clear his preference for Knowles's parodies of "ordinary" or even of stage discourse.

Despite the piece's title and its opening verbal barrage, its coherence is primarily visual, keyed by four basic stage pictures, framed by the same scene at the beginning and end. A string quartet plays continuously, while two dancers spin on downstage ramp areas. Each act begins with a tableau into which people move; brightly lit stage objects appear in a downstage "dead" zone. Images and themes repeat sporadically over the course of the piece: the American Civil War, an Edenic garden, murder scenes, suggestions of imperial domination, cliche language, natural sounds, bomb blasts, and so on. But no narrative emerges. Instead, carefully placed repetition marks borders, like the opening and closing scenes marking each act.

Wilson's critique of the destructive hegemony of verbal language as a communicating medium in modern culture emerges through verbal parody. Bonnie Marranca (1977, p. 40), the editor of the published version of the play, has suggested that Wilson poses the critique and implies a solution in Edenic, Utopian terms. Christopher Knowles's language performances (and, by implication, his heretofore disempowered mode of "autistic" cognition) are offered as alternative and superior models—perhaps even as therapeutic correctives—to a culture dominated by verbal language as a rational medium. In this piece, Wilson parodies display discourse by treating words as a scenic element. Not only does he arrange symmetrical blocks of words as backdrops, as in the projection of a Knowles piece of writing during the entr'acte, but also he comments upon language in another piece of scenery, the "dam drop," a backdrop on which words are drawn as if falling down and breaking up like water over a dam. Part of his inspiration for this critique came from his acquaintance with Christopher Knowles, a so-called autistic child brought to Wilson's attention by a mutual friend after Christopher had begun making tapes about his sister watching television. Wilson, who overcame his own youthful struggle with a severe speech impediment after working with a dance instructor, became fascinated with these tapes, some of whose word arrangements he reproduced during the staging of *Victoria*. He met Christopher and began to invite him to perform his repetitive language pieces at selected moments during Wilson's own events. Christopher's alternative way of organizing information offered Wilson a model of a privileged cognition uncorrupted by a logocentric bias. As an innocent and self-contained child, Chris was both the Edenic past and the promise of better future. Unlike the figure of Queen Victoria, implicated in torrents of language and in violence by the screams she and others occasionally perform in the piece, Chris appears on stage to play language games. This excerpt from Bonnie Marranca's script suggests how the Knowles–Wilson entr'acte dialogue sounded:

> (Chris on stage right and Bob on stage left, each clapping two wooden blocks in their hands. Show curtain is behind them.)
> 1   what
> 2   we're doing the four acts act one act two act three and act four
> 1   what
> 2   we're doing "a letter for queen victoria"
> 1   what
> 2   we're doing the speaking
> 1   what are we doing
> 2   we're doing the blocks. (Marranca, 1977, p. 71)

In Wilson's terms, real communication between the two of them is being displayed, even though spectators may dismiss this dialogue as illogical, redundant, and pointless. At other places in the piece, Wilson reproduces traditional stage discourse in fragments, clearly marked by mocking parody. Act 3 opens with a large backdrop stretching across the stage, painted with a symmetrical design of the words "CHITTER" "CHATTER" in four columns across, 10 lines deep. With this commentary as backdrop, the scene's dialogue begins:

> 1A   I cannot tolerate living in the city all year
> 2A   If it weren't for our country home I don't know what I'd do
> 1A   It's such a charming place
> 2A   So quaint you know. (p. 89)

Wilson's distinctly slow tempo and use of minimal, repetitive musical scores has struck many as merely a faddish appropriation of 1960s and 1970s Soho minimalism. And while Wilson was, during these years, influenced by the New York culture he worked in, his preoccupation with removing himself from the theater event predated his move to New York, beginning with his work with disturbed children and senior citizens living in institutions. Slow motion, repetition, and large scale were and still are essential strategies in his attempt to decenter the theater event—to give the spectator control over how and at what pace they will select from what he is offering them to view: "I use the kind of natural time . . . it takes the sun to set, a cloud to change, a day to dawn. I give you time to reflect" (quoted in Shyer, 1989, p. xvi). Parody is an additional device for involving the spectator in a game with texts and their deformed repetitions.

While simpler than Stoppard's multiple parodic strategies, Robert Wilson's mockery of verbal culture in *A Letter to Queen Victoria* may well be aimed at a similar target: the spectators' beliefs that the wise and powerful author has something to "tell" them. Both Stoppard and Wilson use parody to interrupt the author myth: a special knowledge of the personal and the historical moment. Both use parody to empower the spectators, granting them the means, the space, and the time through which to construct their participation in the staged event.

REFERENCES

Artaud, A. (1968). *The theatre of cruelty* [First and Second manifestoes]. In E. Bentley (Ed.), *Theory of the modern stage* (pp. 55–75). Harmondsworth, UK: England: Penguin Books Ltd. (Original work published 1938.)

Bauman, R. (1977). *Verbal art as performance.* Rowley, MA: Newbury House.

Barthes, Roland. (1982). Beaudelaire's theatre. In S. Sontag (Ed.), *A Barthes reader* (pp. 74–81). New York: Hill and Wang.

Craig, E. Gordon. (1968). The art of the theatre: First dialogue. In E. Bentley (Ed.), *Theory of the modern stage* (pp. 113–37). Harmondsworth, UK: Penguin Books Ltd. (Original work published 1911.)

Derrida, J. (1978). *Writing and difference.* (Alan Bass, Trans.) Chicago: University of Chicago Press.

Ellmann, R. (1959). *James Joyce.* New York: Oxford University Press.

Hutcheon, L. (1985). *A theory of parody.* New York: Methuen.

Issacharoff, M. (1989). *Discourse as performance.* Palo Alto, CA: Stanford University Press.

Marranca, B. (Ed.). (1977). *The theatre of images.* New York: Drama Book Specialists.

Morson, G. S. (1989). Theory of parody. In G. S. Morson & C. Emerson (Eds.), *Rethinking Bakhtin* (pp. 63–86). Evanston, IL: Northwestern University Press.

Shyer, L. (1989). *Robert Wilson and his collaborators.* New York: Theatre Communications Group.

Stoppard, T. (1975). *Travesties.* New York: Grove Press.

Wilson, R. (1977). *A letter for Queen Victoria.* In B. Marranca (Ed.), *The theatre of images* (pp. 37–109). New York: Drama Book Specialists.

Chapter 5
Effects of Repetition in the French New Novel

Dina Sherzer

Department of French and Italian
University of Texas at Austin

The French New Novel, which began appearing in the late 1950s, developed into the New New French Novel in the late 1970s. Its influence is felt in feminist writings, as well as in the present Newer New Novel (Porter, 1988). Its impact has been a systematic deconstruction of the conventions of the novel with innovative techniques. While there is a wide variety of new novels, they share basic features resulting from similar strategies. By manipulating discourse possibilities, they make language mean differently, and they represent experience differently (Sherzer, 1986).

Repetition is a discursive and referential technique that is widely used in the New Novel, and it takes many forms. It can be a montage of discourses borrowed from other texts and presented as such, as in *Mobile* by Michel Butor (1962), which is a patchwork of American items of culture including geography, names of different ethnic groups, names of cars and ice creams, and translations of portions of treaties and documents. It can be an intertextual construct in which two texts are made to mean together, one underlying the other, as in the case of *Les Géorgiques* by Claude Simon (1981), a rewriting of Virgil's work against war and in favor of nature and agriculture (Sherzer, 1986). Or it can be a parody, a desacralisation of a traditional item of culture with a feminist bent, as in the case of Monique Wittig's (1976) *Brouillon pour un dictionnaire des amantes* ('Rough copy for a lover's dictionary'), a dictionary which has no entry in the masculine. Every item is feminine or feminized. In these texts, which are considered postmodern, there are prior texts, that is discursive forms and referential elements from previous texts, which are repeated, transformed, and manipulated to create something new and old.

During the period of the New New Novel, one mode of representation stands out as particularly interesting because of its formal and stylized features. It is commonly associated with Alain Robbe-Grillet, who began his career with disconcerting works such as *Dans le labyrinthe* and *La jalousie*, which rendered the obsessions of his main characters by means of repetition of a certain number of elements. He is also the author of the scenario of Alain Resnais's *L'année dernière a Marienbad*, an enigmatic film also constructed by means of repetition. But two other new novelists as well, Jean Ricardou and Claude Simon, found it challenging to experiment with repetition. In what follows I will analyze Jean Ricardou's (1965) *L'Observatoire de Cannes*, Alain Robbe-Grillet's (1965) *La Maison de rendez-vous*, and Claude Simon's (1973) *Triptyque*, which I will refer to as *O de C*, *M de R*, and *T*. They are three verbal configurations constructed by repetition, three variations on repetition.

O de C, *M de R*, and *T* share a certain number of characteristics. They are constructed by the juxtaposition of strips of representation in which places, characters, and actions can be visualized. Chronology and plot, that is temporality, causality, and logical links, are absent. In these strips various elements are repeated as they are, or slightly modified. There is no sense of an ending, since no referential or formal component brings about completion of an activity or of a state of affairs. Other variations and repetitions could be added to the existing ones, lengthening the text but not changing it otherwise. The narrators in these texts, while behaving as neutral and uninvolved characters, are in fact very subjective in their objectivity. They sustain the same flow of words and elaborate a detached and precise prose. Standard syntax and formal, standard vocabulary, precise yet not overly technical, are defining features of their style. Embellishments, improprieties, and slang are avoided, as are self-conscious interventions showing approbation or disapprobation, reinforcing or undermining what is written. In addition, the present tense is usually used to the exclusion of all others, and what happens takes place in an atemporal world which is always here and now. Ricardou, Robbe-Grillet, and Simon create texts in which the

enunciation and the enunciated yield a strangely uncanny representation.

L'OBSERVATOIRE DE CANNES

What can one do in Cannes on the French Riviera? One can go to the
beach, sit or lie on the sand to get tanned, swim, snorkel, and catch
an octopus, make sand castles, and play ball. On the beach there
might be a sudden storm. One can take a train up a hill to look at the
panorama of the port, the coast, and the islands in the sea off the
coast. One can look at the Cannes hills, landscape, and cityscape
from the beach. One can take pictures and buy postcards, and go
to a night club. This is precisely what is going on in *O de C*. The
characters involved are a newlywed couple, a middle-aged bald man,
a grandmother and her granddaughter, and a young blonde woman.
With this semantic set and minimum narrative material a complex,
continuous game of repetition is elaborated across the 31 sections of
the novel.

The actions of looking, of observing, and of using various optical
apparatuses are constantly repeated. In the train, the tourists look
at each other and watch the landscape through the windows. At the
observatory, they look at the landscape with binoculars, they look at
the landscape drawn on a ceramic table, and they look at postcards
displayed on a rack. On the beach, they look at other people and at
an octopus which has just been caught; they watch a ball game and
a cover girl being photographed for a magazine; the man with the
camera takes pictures, the blonde woman looks at photographs in
an album; someone watches a striptease show, and someone else
looks under water with a snorkeling mask.

The same strip of representation is repeated with slight variations in a least two different anchorings. For instance, the fat woman with a red swimsuit seen on a postcard reappears with the
same characteristics. In another strip she is the fat grandmother
wearing a red swimsuit on the beach, where she watches her granddaughter. One strip recurs insistently, that of the blonde girl wearing a two-piece swimsuit, but elements change slightly from strip to
strip because the situation or the anchoring has changed. On page
30, the blonde girl is lying on the reclining wall bordering the beach.[1]
The two-piece swimsuit is described again on page 31, but now it is
part of a listing of items which protect her. On page 46, a sudden
storm causes people to go away, but the blonde girl remains, protected by a little wall. She is photographed by a man, and the three

---

[1] I refer to the pages in the French text.

triangles of the swimsuit stand out on her tanned body. On page 57, the girl is swimming, and her body wearing the swimsuit and moving in the water is described. On page 83, on the postcard rack, in the picture of a young girl on her knees and bending backwards, the girl wears the same two-piece swimsuit with green and white squares. On page 96, the blonde girl looks at photographs of herself in an album. She is seen in a two-piece swimsuit, but this time the squares are black and white. On page 133, a cover girl is being photographed on the beach. She wears a two-piece swimsuit with green and white squares. On page 144 the blonde girl finds a clearing in the woods around the observatory and goes there to tan herself. She undresses, and as she is removing her blouse and her pants, the two-piece swimsuit appears. On page 174, we are in the middle of a striptease show, and, as the girl removes her clothes, the triangles of her panties and bra, made of green strass, suddenly emerge, shining under the projectors.

Syntactically the swimsuit is permuted in different positions. It can be one element in an enumeration, then the object or the subject in a clause. Different verbs are used. Some underscore the swimsuit's function of hiding, of covering (*enfouir*, to tuck; *cacher*, to hide), therefore pointing insistently at what is covered and hidden. Other verbs, on the contrary, suggest a bursting out of forms and sharp delineation of them (*se détacher*, to stand out; *jaillir*, to jut out; *saillir*, to shoot out).

Characters reappear, always associated with a set of elements such as an item of clothing, a physical detail, or an object they carry. The blonde girl is tanned and wears a white blouse, pants with green and white stripes, and sandals called *spartiates*, a sole tied with yellow laces. She also wears a two-piece swimsuit made from white and green checkered material, hemmed with a scalloped edge of white lace. She carries a circular beach bag with a yellow cord. The middle-aged man is bald, wears a rain coat, and carries a camera dangling on his belly. He wipes his forehead with a white handkerchief with green stripes. The young woman of the couple wears a pink dress and has her hair tied up in a chignon. Her husband wears a white shirt. The grandmother is frequently described as being fat, and on the beach she wears a red swimsuit. The conductor of the train has a cap with gold letters. These elements are fully or partially repeated every time the character appears, and the same lexical items are used to characterize them.

Objects also always reappear with the same characteristics. Thus there is a red ball dotted with white sail boats. A beach bag has yellow cords. On the beach there are festoons of seaweed, little pieces of wood. Sometimes the same object reappears but different synonyms are used to refer to it, as in the case of the octopus, which is called *une pieuvre, un poulpe, un céphalopode.*

The same shape reappears in heterogeneous entities. An octagon recurs, actualized in objects that have this shape, or in groupings of people or objects that form it. A table where the landscape is painted on ceramic tile in the observatory is octagonal; the young husband reproduces this octagon on a postcard when he explains the landscape to his wife. Graffiti on a wall form an octagon. Young people form an octagon when they play ball on the beach. The little girl makes an octagon with her sand cakes on the beach. The triangle is singled out in many items. It is mentioned in the description of the V-neck opening of the young girl's blouse. Her swimsuit is referred to as three triangles. Graffiti form V-shapes or triangles. Legs, branches, sails of a boat, and clothes drying in the sun form triangles. Other forms keep recurring, such as the ellipse made by the head of the blonde girl swimming, by the tuft of hair under her arms, by the tuft of pubic hair of the stripteaser, by the snorkel in the water, and by the moss and seaweed pushed by the sea onto the beach. The scalloped edge of the young girl's swimsuit has the same configuration as the foam on the wave, the festoon of debris in the sand, and the contour of a cloud. Rectangles, squares, circles, straight lines, parallel lines, oblongs, spirals, and cylindrical and conical volumes are isolated everywhere in objects, the landscape, and characters as well as colors and numbers.

Far from being static repetitions and variations, these strips of representation in *O de C* are the focus of intense activities and of *"minuscules révolutions,"* to borrow a title from another work, by Ricardou (1970). Any lexical or syntactic element or component or frame of any kind is available for repetition and permutation. This creates modifications in the representation and even reaches a certain climax, since what might be called the adventure of the triangle ends with the removing of the triangles during the striptease, revealing what was hidden up to that point. With the repetitions Ricardou constructs a text which is carefully and minutely contrived, and which proposes adventures of shapes, colors, movements, syntax, and lexicon in different settings, creating minute revolutions with words.

LA MAISON DE RENDEZ-VOUS

Violence, sadism, drugs, prostitution, assassination, suicide, sexy Eurasian girls with tight-fitting dresses, rich Europeans involved in illicit deals, Hong Kong with its European and Chinese neighborhoods, Kowloon and Aberdeen, its ferries and its streets teeming with life: such is the semantic material with which Robbe-Grillet plays in order to set up repetitions in *M de R*. This semantic material constitutes in itself a repetition, as it calls on familiar detective story imagery. Robbe-Grillet draws on a genre of popular culture, which he rewrites into an experimental text. However, instead of constructing a linear novel where events unfold successively with more or less temporal manipulations, Robbe-Grillet invents strips of representation in which the same elements keep recurring. Whereas in the *O de C* the anonymous narrator is an uncertain, unmarked originator who does not take part in the actions, the narrator of the *M de R* participates in some of the events of the novel, speaks in the first person, and even at times interacts with some of the characters. The characters of the novel are Lady Ava, seen as a hostess receiving her guests in her elegant residence and brothel called the Villa Bleue, in which there is a theater; the narrator, one of these guests; Ralph Johnston, called the American, who deals in drugs and women and wants one of Lady Ava's protégées, Lauren, to belong to him exclusively; Edouard Manneret, drug dealer, money lender, and drug experimenter; Kim and Lucky, two Eurasian girls who work as servants for Lady Ava, Kim being her lover at times; and John Marchand, who commits suicide in his car.

M de R deploys different types of repetitions. Readers repeatedly come across a type of scene in which the same semantic material is expressed with different components. One type involves a scene in which one character dominates another. For example, Lady Ava gives orders to Lauren, who listens with submission. Kim is in the same submissive relationship with regard to Lady Ava. Ralph Johnson looks at Lauren as if she were his object/subject, ready for any of his whims. A young Japanese girl is the object of Kim's domination. And toward the end of the novel Lauren treats Ralph Johnson as an object/subject she can control. Another group of scenes also shares the same underlying semantic content. In them a young girl or a young woman is threatened, tortured, or abused physically by an animal or a man. The first occurrence opens the novel. The narrator explains how he is obsessed with the flesh of women, especially when they are tied or beaten (1965, pp. 11–12).[2] On page 27, the narrator specifies that he participates at an evening reception at the Villa Bleue. At one point he says that he steps out in the garden, where he comes across a sculpture which represents a young girl whose clothes are being torn by a tiger. Back in the house (p. 31) he watches a theatrical representation. On the stage a young Eurasian

---

[2] I refer to the pages in the French text.

is being attacked by a black dog, just as in the garden sculpture. In another stage representation a dog must now tear the clothes off the body of a young frightened Japanese girl. During this play, a man describes to his neighbor a statue from the Tiger Balm garden in Hong Kong which depicts an orangutan carrying away a frightened girl on his shoulders (p. 55). One of the guests at the reception wears a ring which represents a sculpted woman lying on a bed, "wriggling with pleasure or pain" (p. 75). On page 76, Manneret looks at the Eurasian girl lying motionless in bed, in disorder. Then Kim is seen crouching in the corner of a room, a man bent over her trying to overcome her. Stepping out in the garden again the narrator gets lost in a small alley leading to a secret room, where he comes across a statue of a naked girl fighting a man bent over her (p. 134). On page 167, the narrator explains that Manneret has performed experiments with drugs on a Japanese girl.

There is another type of repetition of strips of representation. This one does not repeat the same activity or situation with different components; rather, the narrator tells several times what happened one time. The narrator describes what he sees at the reception at Lady Ava's house and on the stage of the theater. Later, with the pretext of wanting to understand what has happened, he imagines again the scenes, describing the same setting, the same activities, the same groups of individuals, and the arrival of the police. He also describes repeatedly the crowded streets and a scene involving a street sweeper looking at propaganda against drug use on a piece of illustrated newspaper. Toward the end of the novel, often instead of retelling a whole scene he recalls and even lists what he has described by means of short sentences. The assassination of Manneret is repeated several times. Early on it is mentioned as having happened, then Manneret is described as being shot by Johnson, and another time Manneret is bitten to death in the neck by Lady Ava's dog.

As in *O de C*, in *M de R* there is the repetition of a specific feature associated with a character or an object. I have already mentioned the tight-fitting dresses worn by the Eurasian girls. Kim often carries a fat brown envelope which seems full of sand. Lauren is repeatedly described as wearing a low-necked, wide-skirted white dress. Several times she appears in a reclining position on furs or black silk, her body offered to Sir Ralph. The street sweeper wears blue clothes and a conical hat. The English policemen always appear wearing khaki shirts and shorts and white socks. The fat man, who is always telling stories, is always mentioned as having a red or congested face. The Chinese characters are described as being mysterious and impassive, and one utterance is always associated with Lady Ava: "Won't you have a glass of Champagne?"

Repetition of the same lexical set in different frames or anchorings is also used in this novel. A Eurasian girl wearing a tight-fitting dress is walking a dog. She looks at the window of a shop, where she sees a model wearing the same type of dress and holding a dog on a leash. Kim is seen quite often wearing a tight-fitting dress and walking Lady Ava's dog. Then a girl walking in the street, another one working in a restaurant, or a girl sculpted on a ring also wears a tight-fitting dress. Often the dress is said to make creases at the waist and on the stomach as it closely molds the supple and flexible young bodies.

Robbe-Grillet is obviously playing with and manipulating language and narrative in the *M de R*. With discontinuities, interruptions, unresolved situations, and repetitions he encodes the elements of a detective novel set in the Orient with all of the eurocentric stereotypes that might be found in them. But rather than developing these elements or linking them into a plot, he indexes them with a few semantically charged components, which he keeps repeating.

TRIPTYQUE

On the cover of *T* we find the following statement, presumably written by Simon himself: "In painting, a triptych is a work consisting of three panels. If the actions or the characters depicted can be connected more or less closely (for example, several episodes of a legend) at other times the subjects of each panel are different. But in one way or another the entire work constitutes an indissociable whole, as much by the unity of construction as by the calculated way in which the different forms and colors match and balance each other." *T* is a verbal configuration organized precisely according to this description. Simon repeats, or, more precisely, he transcreates the fragmentation and unity of a visual experience into a verbal one.

In the three different sections or panels that form *T*, Simon invents three different settings, three different sets of characters, and three different mininarratives, which can be reconstructed by readers only at the end of the book. The first mininarrative takes place in a typical ordinary French village. Men have just come back from hunting. The hunters and others, including a young woman accompanied by a little girl, surround a wild boar which has been killed. Later, leaving the little girl to play with two little boys, the woman joins the hunter in a barn, where they usually meet to make love.

Instead of staying with the little girl, the boys go the barn and watch the couple having intercourse. Meanwhile, the little girl drowns in a river. The actions of the second narrative take place in an elegant seaside resort, in an upper-class hotel. A woman has just made love with an influential man in exchange for the help he might give her son, who has been caught with drugs. And for the third narrative we are in a dirty, noisy, industrial city. In an alley a barmaid is making love with a young man wearing a tuxedo. The young man, who has just been married, has gone drinking with his friends in a bar where the barmaid is his former lover, and the two of them have slipped out in the night, while the bride is waiting alone in a room.

Instead of presenting each narrative in one of the panels, the material of the three narratives is distributed across the panels, so that it is possible to read a strip of representation referring to the village scene, then, without transition, typographical, syntactic, or referential, to find oneself in a strip describing something having to do with the city narrative or the seaside resort narrative. Fragmentation is also caused by an exuberance of details and by the extreme diversity of juxtaposed entities. Indiscriminately, algae and a trout undulating in a river, the meandering of this river, striations on cow excrement or on wood, the rising of the tail of a cow, ripples of water, waves of the sea, a penis entering a woman's body, people drinking in a bar, buildings and palm trees, and a rabbit lying dead on a table are described, making of the text a dense inventory of disparate elements.

Simultaneous with this fragmentation deployed so carefully by means of several discourse strategies, a whole array of unifying devices is deployed equally carefully, and by means of various types of repetition. An anonymous, extradiegetic narrator presents the content using the same precise, elegant, and objective style in the three panels. Vocabulary, syntax, and tone remain the same whether the narrator describes a rabbit, a butterfly, or male or female anatomy. In the content, repetition is present at many levels of the text. The referential content of the three narratives is about the same topic: illicit love making. In the city, in the village, and at the seaside resort, a couple who are not supposed to meet make love on the run, hiding. In addition to these actual happenings, the text describes an engraving, the poster of a film in the village, and a film being shot at the seaside, all also about illicit lovers meeting clandestinely. Thus the same narrative matrix underlies the referential content disseminated in the three panels.

Reduplication is also a device used in *T*, as in *O de C* and in *M de R*. The actions or features of living characters are filmed or reproduced in paintings, filmstrips, or posters. The scene of the woman and the hunter making love in the barn is repeated on an engraving representing a maid and a valet making love on bales of hay. The black curly hair and sheep-like face of the man making love in the alley with the barmaid are also the characteristics of a man on a movie poster placed in the village. The scene of a woman lying in bed while she talks to a man standing up on a balcony overlooking the sea is also a sequence in a film being shot.

The recurrence of one item in different contexts constitutes a type of repetition that unifies elements. For instance, the verb *luire* (to gleam) in its present participial form qualifies a man's penis in *son membre luisant* (his gleaming member); the effect of a white shirt in the night is described with the same verb in *le plastron blanc de sa chemise qui luit dans l'ombre* (his white shirtfront gleaming in the shadow); the make-up of a clown gleams because of its greasiness in *la sueur délaye le blanc gras du maquillage qui luit sur ses tempes et ses joues* (sweat thins out the white greasepaint that gleams on his temples and cheeks); the shininess of the blade of a knife, and of railroad tracks under the rain, is described with the same verb. Colors—brown, black, red, and green—are used in the same fashion, reappearing in different entities. One shape keeps recurring, singled out in many parts of the body, objects, and items of topography. Here are some examples:

- A long cliff of blinding white façades, with rococo decorations, *follows the curve* of the bay in a gently *sweeping arc* (Simon, 1976, p. 1).[3]
- The orchard extends as far as the river, just before the *bend* it makes as it heads past the village. Just past the *bend* the current is partially diverted into the millrace, which flows underneath the first *arch* of a stone bridge, the second arch . . . spans the sparkling free water flowing rapidly between little islands with *clumps* of water willows and enormous pale bluish green leaves shaped like flaring *funnels* (p. 2).
- Underneath the paper is a photograph . . . of a naked girl with big *breasts*, kneeling down . . .
- Her *round* pendulous breasts narrow to pointed tips . . . Foamy *whirls* circle her thighs and form *bracelets* around her wrists (p. 54).
- The *bent* silhouette is leaning with both hands on the handlebar

---

[3] I refer to the pages in the English translation.

of a baby buggy . . . From time to time one can see the gleam of the *curved* blade of the *scythe* lying diagonally across the buggy (p. 84).

Thus the same shape, that of a curve, is made to appear in the shape of a scythe, in cheeks, breasts, curly hair, a bay, plants grouped into a clump, a river making a bend, a person bending, and bridges arching over a river.

Movements are inscribed massively in a wide variety of phenomena. Thus one reads about water falling over a wall, cracks forming on cow excrement which has just fallen, jerks agitating the body of a rabbit that has just been killed, tops of trees waving in the wind, shivers of poplars agitated by a breeze, masts of yachts swaying in the wind, concentric ripples formed around a stone or an object in the river, the back of a man shaken by spasms as he vomits, movements of lovemaking, and strings of mist undulating in the air. All these repetitions are actualized by an exuberant display of lexical items belonging to the semantic fields of undulating movements and curves. Some examples of the verbs are *to oscillate, to undulate, to wiggle, to meander, to bounce, to spring up, to stoop, to swing, to twist in an arc,* and *to swell.* Nouns such as *cracks, swellings, windings, undulations, jolts, jerks, shakes, curvatures,* and *wrinkles* are constantly used.

In the preface to *Orion aveugle,* in which he explains how he writes and what writing means to him, Simon (1970, p. 9) speaks of the prodigious power of words that enables them to bring together and to compare what without them would remain scattered. In *T he* demonstrates that repetitions have the singular power of bringing together unrelated but familiar items, animate and inanimate, and thus of conferring an uncanny quality to the representation.

EFFECTS OF REPETITION

I have explained how repetitions are deployed in the texts and what functions they serve in them. But repetitions also mean and do something in themselves. They represent an idiosyncratic use of language. They encode a specific type of representation. They affect the reading process. They are specific cultural markers, and they open up toward other forms of experience and culture.

In the three novels, in using a common device in discourse, repetition, and in expanding its use, the writers have made it work differently. In doing so, they have experimented with new possibilities in the structuring of discourse. In the 31 sections of *O de C*, in the continuous text of *M de R*, and in the three panels of *T*, repetitions are on the one hand disruptive forces: They bring about too much redundancy, hence unbalance in the discourse texture. Yet, on the other hand, they are a cohesive force. They take the place of plot and of causal and logical links, which normally have that function. They introduce changes in discourse as well. They affect its composition, as well as its structuring and the ordering of elements. Because of the massive presence of repetitions, sameness and similarity are deployed syntagmatically, in contrast to the usual syntagmatic deployment of difference and contiguity.[4] The other change affects which function of language is foregrounded in novelistic discourse. Typically the referential function plays the dominant role. But in the novels I consider here repetitions draw attention to the phonic aspect of language, and consequently the referential function is played down. Readers focus on the meaning of discourse, but its aurality also comes forward. Repetitions draw out and foreground the phonic resources of discourse and display them in new ways.

O de C, *M de R*, and *T* constitute explorations in the possibilities of repetition. The notion of *isotopy* used in French semiotics (Greimas et al., 1972) is useful in order to construct a typology of the repetitions found in the three novels. An isotopy is the iteration of a unit of language, and in discourse there can be referential, semantic, lexical, and phonic isotopies. One sort of referential isotopy is a repetition of a prior text, as in the case of *M de R*, which is a rewriting of a detective story. A referential isotopy can be elaborated by a semantic deep structure underlying various strips of representation, such as the action of looking in *O de C*, the sadomasochistic relationship in *M de R*, and illicit love making in *T*. An isotopy can be created when the same semantic material appears in different frames or anchorings with the same lexical and syntactic organization, as in the case of the Eurasian girl wearing a tight-fitting dress and walking a black dog that looks at a shop window. Another isotopy used in these novels is formed by the fact that the same semantic material is always associated with the same person and expressed with the same lexical and syntactic units. Examples include the bald man carrying his camera hanging down from his neck on his stomach, and the checkered swimsuit of the blonde

---

[4] Genette (1966), using Jakobson's notions of the paradigmatic and syntagmatic axes structuring discourse, has pointed out that already in his first novels Robbe-Grillet manipulates the components of these axes by introducing repetitions syntagmatically.

girl. These isotopies form semantic axes which traverse the novels syntagmatically. Furthermore, smaller local semantic isotopies are formed by means of the use of synonyms, as in the case of *O de C*, where the octopus that has been caught keeps being referred to but with different terms *(poulpe, pieuvre, cephalopode)*.

In addition to these semantic axes one finds semantic grids which model the representation by means of various isotopies. A shape, geometric figures, colors, or movements reappearing in many entities form such grids. The constant tone, the uniform and neutral style with no positively or negatively charged elements modifying the lexical items used in each of the three texts, is another isotopy deployed in the representation. Concomitant with semantic isotopies formed by the recurrence of the same lexical units, phonic isotopies are created by the repetitions of sounds, the order of words, and rhythms. The consequence of the presence of all these types of isotopies is that the discourse of the novels is sculptured, shaped by effects of alliterations, assonances, echoes, parallelisms, paronomasis, rhymes, and synonyms, not deployed in one or two sentences but generalized in the verbal texture. What these texts show is that repetition is both elementary and sophisticated.

The use of repetitions in the representation in French novels is not new. Proust, for instance, in *Remembrance of Time Past*, repeats the same type of scenes. The protagonist, Marcel, at various times in his life, participates in receptions, soirées, and concerts, with various members of the Parisian aristocracy and bourgeoisie. The repetition of such scenes constitutes a paradigm deployed over the several volumes of the work. Their function is to show the passing of time and the changes in society, in Marcel and in the others.[5] Balzac, in his *Human Comedy*, has several characters reappear with different identities and characteristics. These repetitions bring suspense, unity, and continuity to the multivolume work. Akutagawa's *Rashomon*, and Faulkner's *Sound and Fury*, are other texts which use repetitions in order to explore how a story can be told from different points of view. For Ricardou, Robbe-Grillet, and Simon, repetitions are not narrative strategies in the service of the plot. Nor are they means to show the relativity of experience or the arbitrariness of the telling. Rather they are formal elements to be played with in order to elaborate another kind of representation. In their texts everything can be repeated, not only an item of referential content, a particular occurrence or character, but colors, forms, textures, frames, actions, lexicon, and syntax as

---

[5] For a study of various forms of repetition in narrative see Genette (1980).

well. In these novels, narrative with beginning, middle, end, and progression is replaced by isomorphisms, that is, the recurrence of shapes and movements in different entities.

The other striking innovation brought about by repetitions as they are used in these novels is that the novels' narrators are presented as *seeing* rather than as telling or retelling. Instead of telling a story they stage simulations resulting from the experience of seeing. A simulation is the result of the application of formal rules or models in order to explore the possibility of generating new expressions and formulations of experience. The writers in the works I discuss construct formal representations with repetitions. In this regard, the neutral tone of the text provides a perfect background against which to foreground formal elements. Ricardou privileges geometry. For instance, the body, clothes, and objects of the blonde girl are simulated in terms of triangles, cylinders, ellipses, stripes, and oblong shapes. Robbe-Grillet privileges the erotico-sadistic with his insistence on the tight-fitting dress on the bodies of young Eurasians, and with the scenes of violence perpetrated on the body of young girls. Simon constructs his simulation with curves and movements that are made to appear in many components of reality and experience.[6]

These novelistic discourses in which form tends to dominate over sequence and plot raise interesting questions about language and experience and language and culture. Do we perceive reality through the semantic entities given by our language, or is it reality which makes us use language in specific ways? Recent studies have demonstrated that discourse mediates between language and culture and language and experience; that is, in a certain sense our perception of reality is constructed by discourse (see J. Sherzer, 1987). The texts I study here are a case in point. With their repetitions they foreground forms, textures, and movements, and by so doing they defamiliarize the familiar, and familiarize the unfamiliar, creating discourses which express an idiosyncratic reality and experience.

Are there purely formal relationships in the representations of these three novels? As I mentioned earlier, these texts are objective and at the same time very subjective, and this is precisely because of the repetitions. Although there is no overt indication of state of

---

[6] See Quéau (1986), who discusses various types of simulations. He provides illustrations of simulations by visual artists (p. 92), some of them recalling Ricardou's geometrical orientation. Simon (1972) explains how, in *La route des Flandres*, he uses the principle of set theory to inscribe chromatic and formal isomorphisms in his text. He uses this simulation again in *T*.

mind, the repetitions create a redundancy suggestive of the narrators' subjectivity. In *O de C* the repetitions focusing obsessively on the triangle of the swimsuit of the young blonde girl, and the geometrical way of apprehending the world, reveal the obsession of a narrator whose point of view is at the intersection of reality and phantasm. The choice of the semantic material in *M de R* certainly is that of an individual in the grip of erotic and sadistic impulses. And the detailed descriptions of things, individuals, settings, and activities reflect a solipsistic and narcissistic desire to observe oneself mastering the diversity and the complexity of experience through writing, in *T*.

By virtue of their repetitions, these texts belong to a specific Western cultural moment while at the same time opening up to other cultures as well. In the first place, they are very much French creations. They are New Novels, that is, the products of an intellectual effervescence and linguistic fetishism or fascination with language that permeated Parisian life in the 1960s and 1970s. They are the creation of novelists who are consciously, deliberately, playing with and experimenting with language, who are of the opinion that novels should not so much be the writing of adventures as the adventures of writing, and who write novels that are implicit deconstructions of the conventions of the novel by proposing new modes of representation and new signifying practices. Exploring the possibilities of repetition in language in order to structure discourse differently, as I have described here, constitutes one of these deconstructive practices.

Besides being French New Novels, the texts I consider are also postmodern texts, again because of the repetitions with which they are constructed. They are discontinuous texts, the result of linguistic and referential manipulations. In them, the repetitions form networks of elements amounting to a rhizomatic structuring by means of elements that are the same and different.[7] The fact that they repeat the content of popular fiction is also a postmodern feature. Repetition is a salient feature that has been exploited in other postmodern creations, for example by visual artists such as Andy Warhol and Titus-Carmel, who, preceded by Escher, expanded the possibilities of repetition that already existed in painting with

---

[7] Deleuze (1976) uses the notion of rhizome to describe structures patterned by a mesh where any item can be connected to any other, thus replacing narrative in novels and preventing any hierarchies or closure from being established.

the form of the diptych, or the triptych, and with the device of *mise en abyme*.[8]

In the representation they invent through and with their repetitions, Ricardou and Robbe-Grillet do one more thing. They repeat phallocentric clichés and, in the case of Robbe-Grillet, eurocentric ones as well. By repeatedly representing half-naked or naked bodies of women, they reify that patriarchal gesture so endemic to Western culture and to its modes of representation of woman. In *Ways of Seeing*, John Berger (1979) examines how woman is represented in art and offers a series of repetitions on the same motif which begins with Titian's *The Venus of Urbino*, repeated by Goya's *Maia* and by Manet's *Olympia*. These women are naked or half-naked, reclining on a bed and offered to the gaze of men. In *O de C*, the blonde girl on the beach, the one doing the strip tease, and the one whose picture is being taken for a magazine cover are part of such a series. In *M de R* the Eurasians with their tight dresses are such objects, but in addition Robbe-Grillet overtly and consciously repeats the stereotypes of the woman offered to the gaze of the man when he describes a painting in which Lauren is reclining on a bed with a hibiscus flower in her left ear. He calls this painting *La Maia* and identifies it as a work by Edouard Manneret, playing with the name of the painter Manet who painted *Olympia*, a painting with similar characteristics.[9] The question is: Are these writers unconsciously repeating phallocentric clichés, or are they playing with them precisely in order to denounce them? Robbe-Grillet, who has been attacked for being phallocentric, replies that Freud had already pointed out all our pathological obsessions, and that he, Robbe-Grillet, repeats them and recycles them, as ludic material in his works (*Nouveau Roman*, 1972, p. 141). Simon does not single out women in a voyeuristic fashion. His characters are couples in the act of making love. Here is what he says about his strategy in an interview (Du Verlie, 1974, pp. 17–18): "Challenge, fragmentation, repetition, for these are the characteristics of my texts, whether it be a question of leaves, clouds, battles, or sexual matters. As you can see I treat sexual objects exactly the same way I treat all the rest." One might ask whether Simon succeeds in this: Topics in discourse do not all

---

[8] Jan Van Eck's *The Bethrothal of the Arnolfini* (1434) is a frequently cited example of *mise en abyme*.

[9] Quoting and repeating works by painters is one of Robbe-Grillet's favorite techniques. See *La belle captive* (1980), a montage of a text by Robbe-Grillet accompanying paintings by Magritte.

have the same semantic and cultural connotations and charges, and chances are that readers do not react neutrally to the repetitions involving sexual matters.

I mentioned earlier that the repetitions in these texts are not only of a referential nature, but also, since sounds are repeated as well, readers not only visualize the strip of representation, but also have an aural experience. They are made to hear the text mentally by the continuous presence of the same phonic elements, by the order of recurring words, and by the rhythm of specific units. This aurality is one striking feature of these postmodern texts. Because of these phonic features they have many of the characteristics of ritual oral performances in traditional societies. For instance, the recurring description of the swimsuit in *O de C*, and of the tight-fitting dress of the Eurasian girl in *M de R*, are akin to the formulas or refrains that reappear in *The Odyssey* or in old French epics. Thus the most postmodern meets the most traditional in these texts, where language and discourse are made to work and mean in many ways. Other oral experiences come to mind as one reads these texts, experiences of non-Western artistic creations that resonate with the European texts. One of the features of these experimental texts is that they are not linear, causal progressions starting from a calm state of affairs and rising to a crisis which culminates in some kind of climax and ends up in a resolution. Rather they encode variations with strips of representations where various elements are repeated, but there is no rise and fall. Balinese gamelan music has the same characteristics.[10]

What do these texts that deploy massive amounts of repetitions do for readers who are used to, programmed by, difference? They provide a challenging reading experience. Typically the beginnings of novels propose a set of unmarked elements out of which certain ones become salient and a narrative mesh begins, out of which little by little one thread, then another, then several, are pulled forward and backward, advancing the story and thickening the plot. The same anaphoric and cataphoric system is at work in *O de C*, *M de R*, and *T*. But what recurs repeats what was already said, then repeats it again as is or with a slight variation, so that the narrative progression stalls and is ultimately suppressed. If readers anticipate a novel complete with action and resolution, they will be frustrated. But the

---

[10] For an analysis of the characteristics of Balinese gamelan music, see Bateson (1972, p. 113). This type of music is the point of departure and a source of inspiration for the minimalist works of Philip Glass, where repetitions aim at creating a non-Western aesthetics.

point of these novels is to make language work differently, to construct a different kind of representation, and consequently to make readers read differently. What happens after a few repetitions is that repetitions become foregrounded, so that readers anticipate them and wonder what will be repeated next and how what is repeated will be combined in a new context. The experience these texts offer is the discovery of the similar, the rediscovery of the known, the strangeness of repetition, and the interest or fascination of play.

REFERENCES

Bateson, G. (1972). *Steps to an ecology of mind.* New York: Ballantine.

Berger, J. (1979). *Ways of seeing.* New York: Penguin.

Deleuze, G. (1976). *Rhyzome.* Paris: Minuit.

Du Verlie, C. (1974). Interview with Claude Simon. *Sub-Stance, 8,* 3–20.

Genette, G. (1966). Vertige fixé. *Figure II.* Paris: Seuil.

Genette, G. (1980). *Narrative discourse.* Minneapolis: University of Minnesota Press.

Greimas, A. J. et al. (1972). *Essai de sémiotique poétique.* Paris: Larousse.

Nouveau roman: hier et aujourd'hui, 2 (1972). Paris: UGE.

Porter, C. A. (1988). After the age of suspicion: The French novel today. *Yale French Studies* [Special Issue].

Quéau, Ph. (1986). *Eloge de la simulation.* Paris: Presses Universitaires de France.

Ricardou, J. (1965). *L'observatoire de Cannes.* Paris: Minuit.

Ricardou, J. (1971). *Révolutions minuscules.* Paris: Gallimard.

Robbe-Grillet, A. (1965). *La maison de rendez-vous.* Paris: Minuit.

Robbe-Grillet, A. (1980). *La belle captive.* Lausanne-Paris: Bibliothèque des arts.

Sherzer, D. (1986). *Representation in contemporary French fiction.* Lincoln: University of Nebraska Press.

Sherzer, D. (1986). Ubiquité de la répétition. *Neophilologus, 70,* 372–380.

Sherzer, J. (1987). A discourse-centered approach to language and culture. *American Anthropologist, 89,* 295–309.

Simon, C. (1970). *Orion aveugle.* Paris: Skira.

Simon, C. (1972). La fiction mot à mot. *Nouveau roman: hier et aujourd'hui, 2,* 73–99.

Simon, C. (1973). *Triptyque.* Paris: Minuit.

Simon, C. (1976). *Triptych.* New York: Viking.

Chapter 6
Repetition and Point of View in Represented Speech and Thought*

Susan Ehrlich

Department of Languages, Literatures and Linguistics
York University
North York, Ontario, Canada

INTRODUCTION

Many linguistic studies of repetition have investigated its function in spoken language, specifically, in conversation (Tannen, 1987a, b, 1989; Norrick, 1987). And not surprisingly, many of the functions imputed to repetition in conversation are related to the physical and cognitive characteristics of language production in the spoken (as opposed to the written) mode. For example, Tannen (1987a, 1989) discusses the way in which repetition facilitates the production of spoken language in that it "enables a speaker to produce fluent speech while formulating what to say next" (Tannen, 1989, p. 48). Likewise, repetition is said to facilitate the comprehension of spoken language to the extent that it allows for the production of "semantically less dense discourse" (p. 49). In both cases, repetition

* I thank Barbara Johnstone for her comments on an earlier version of this chapter.

provides a relief from the demands of face-to-face interaction: the speaker is provided with an opportunity to plan what he or she will say next while the listener's processing demands are diminished with the redundancy that accompanies repetition. Clearly, then, some functions of repetition (though not all) are directly related to the language mode being investigated and, in particular, to the speed with which speaking and listening must take place.

In this chapter, I examine repetition in written, literary discourse. In line with the discussion above, I argue that the function of repetition in the texts under investigation here is directly related to their mode. More specifically, the fact that these texts are written and highly crafted determines, to a large extent, how the repetition is interpreted (i.e., how it functions). In the remainder of this section, I discuss characteristics of spoken vs. written discourse and planned vs. unplanned discourse (Ochs, 1979) that have implications for the function of repetition in these various discourse types.

Spoken vs. Written Discourse

Psycholinguistic studies investigating differences in the comprehension of spoken and written language (Olson, 1977; Hildyard & Olson, 1982) have suggested that reading a text may produce a bias towards what is actually *said* in the text, whereas listening to a text will produce a bias towards what is *meant* by the text. Hildyard and Olson (1982) comment on the differences between the way meaning is retained in spoken and written discourse:

> In oral language, the point, intention or significance of the language, the "speaker's meaning" is preserved in the mind of the listener; as the actual words, syntax and intonation are ephemeral, they are rapidly exchanged for those interpreted meanings which can be preserved. In written language, the words and syntax, the "sentence meaning," is preserved by the artifact of writing, and mental recall becomes the precise reproduction of that artifact. (p. 20)

Norrick (1987), writing on the function of repetition in conversation, distinguishes between "random repetition"—instances of repetition that "are explicable in terms of the speaker's task of production in face-to-face conversation," and "significant repeats"—instances of repetition that perform some identifiable operation on their previous occurrence (Norrick, 1987, p. 247). For Norrick, random repetitions "require no special attention by either the speaker or the hearer" (p. 246) and are "those repetitions that we produce unintentionally, and interpret sublimally" (p. 248). He provides the following example:

(1)   C: so this is why I'm floating round. I gave up my permanent (cough) my permanent job here. (p. 246)

Random repetitions, then, while easing the demands of face-to-face conversation, are not linguistic forms that are remembered or focused on to any great extent. In this sense, they are emblematic of spoken language as Hildyard and Olson characterize it; that is, speech is generally more "ephemeral" than writing, with the linguistic forms of speech being "rapidly exchanged for those interpreted meanings that can be preserved." I am not suggesting that Hildyard and Olson's dichotomy can be used to characterize all repetition in spoken discourse as ephemeral. Rather, I am suggesting that *some* instances of repetition in spoken language (i.e., Norrick's random repetition, and Tannen's instances of repetition that facilitate the production and comprehension of spoken language) are more closely tied to the demands of the oral medium than are others. And, while it may share some functions with oral repetition, repetition in most genres of written, planned discourse is not likely to be random repetition. Indeed, Norrick (1987) claims that random repetitions "are those which careful speakers and writers edit out when they have a chance to pre-plan their discourse" (p. 248).

Unplanned vs. Planned Discourse

Ochs (1979) defines *unplanned discourse* as "discourse that lacks forethought and organizational preparation" and *planned discourse* as "discourse that has been thought out and organized (designed) prior to its expression" (p. 55). There is, of course, no one-to-one correspondence between unplanned and spoken discourse, on the one hand, and between planned and written discourse, on the other. While speech is more likely than writing to be unplanned, there are genres of spoken language that are relatively planned (e.g., a formal speech) and genres of written language that are relatively unplanned (e.g., casual letter writing). Literary discourse constitutes an extreme point on the planned/unplanned discourse continuum, a point that Ochs characterizes in the following way: "verbal behavior in which every idea and every lexical item and every structure in which the idea is to be expressed is considered and designed in advance" (p. 55). It is precisely because literary texts are highly crafted and planned that readers of literature undoubtedly approach them with the expectation that their linguistic forms will be extremely significant. Thus, not only will there be no instances of random repetition in the texts under investigation here, from the reader's point of view there will be no instances of repetition without specifiable semantic effect, given the expectation that "every lexical item and every structure . . . is considered and designed in advance."

In what follows, I demonstrate that the repetition of predicates denoting narrative events has the effect of shifting the point of view from which the events in question are seen. I argue that repetition has this effect in literary texts as a result of the texts' written and highly planned nature. That is, the instances of repetition discussed below would not necessarily have the same function in spoken, unplanned language, where linguistic forms are more ephemeral and may be interpreted as less significant (in some sense) to the overall meaning of a discourse.

REPRESENTED SPEECH AND THOUGHT

The examples cited in this chapter come from two novels by Virginia Woolf, *To the Lighthouse* (1964b) and *Mrs. Dalloway* (1964a). These texts are characterized by what Auerbach (1968) has called a multipersonal representation of consciousness: "The essential characteristic of the technique represented by Virginia Woolf is that we are given not merely one person whose consciousness (that is, the impressions it receives) is rendered but many persons, with frequent shifts from one to another" (p. 536). The formal distinctiveness of this style lies in its blurring of the distinction between direct and indirect discourse. Following Genette (1980), I distinguish between the formal speaker of a text (i.e., the narrator) and the vantage point from which events and descriptions are conveyed in a text. In these texts by Woolf, the narrator remains constant throughout (in other words, the formal speaker does not change), but the person whose point of view orients the events shifts between the narrator and the characters. Characters within these texts are designated by third-person pronouns, and the time of the narrated events is represented by the past tense. Therefore, the act of telling the narrative is performed by someone distinct from the characters and occurs at a point in time after the narrated events. Within this context of indirect discourse, however, the subjective impression of characters become evident. (See Dry, 1975, Fillmore, 1981, Banfield, 1982, and Ehrlich, 1987, 1990a,b, for a more detailed linguistic description of this style.)

One of the linguistic means by which a character's (a third person's) point of view emerges is the interspersing of direct discourse constructions within the border context of indirect discourse. The passage below *(italics added throughout)* contains a number of exclamations that do not normally occur in indirect discourse.

(2)   He was really, Lily Briscoe thought, in spite of his eyes, *but then look at his nose, look at his hands,* the most uncharming human being she had ever met. *Then why did she mind what he said?* (Woolf, 1964a, p. 99)

The person whose perspective is apparent in exclamations like *but then look at his nose, look at his hands* and *Then why did she mind what he said?* in (2) is not the formal speaker or narrator of the text but the referent of *she,* Lily Briscoe. Despite the fact that this character does not speak 'directly,' these exclamations (direct discourse constructions) serve to invoke her point of view. On the one hand, features of indirect discourse create a formal speaker who is distinct from any of the characters within the text. On the other hand, features of direct discourse create a point of view that can only be attributed to one of the characters. This almost verbatim rendering of characters' speech and thought has been called *represented speech and thought* (RST) by Banfield (1982).

I have argued in previous work (Ehrlich, 1990b) that an adequate linguistic account of the interpretation of point of view in RST must go beyond a treatment of the internal properties of sentences to the larger context of the discourse. In other words, there are many sentences within these texts that contain none of the sentence-internal properties of RST (e.g., direct discourse constructions) yet are interpreted as reflecting a character's point of view. Included among the discourse devices that contribute to the emergence of characters' perspectives is repetition. In particular, the repetition of predicates denoting narrative events can often serve to invoke a different viewing position on the events in question.

TEMPORAL STRUCTURE OF NARRATIVES

It is a distinguishing characteristic of narratives that they create a timeline—a narrative present—in which the represented events occur. Readers or listeners are aware of a narrative past, present, and future, with events of the narrative present functioning to move time forward in the depicted world. Recent work in discourse semantics (Dry, 1983; Dowty, 1986) has attempted to isolate the linguistic properties of clauses responsible for the perception of time movement in narrative discourse. Dry (1983) points out that predicates that refer to the initial and/or final endpoints of situations create the impression of time movement. This is illustrated in example (3) below.

(3) Fred walked into the room. The janitor *sat down* on the couch.
(4) Fred walked into the room. The janitor *was sitting down* on the couch.

In (3), the event represented by the predicate *sit down* is interpreted as occurring later than the time of Fred's walking into the room. Because the simple past tense in English refers to the endpoints of the situation its predicate represents (Smith, 1983), the second sentence of (3) moves the reference time of the narrative forward. When the same predicate occurs in the past progressive (which refers to a point that is not a situation's endpoint), as in (4), its event is interpreted as contemporaneous or overlapping with the previous sentence's event. The second sentence of (4) does not have the effect of pushing the reference time of the narrative forward.

The aspectual alternation between the simple past and past progressive interacts with predicate-type to the extent that only events (as opposed to states) in the simple past tense will create the impression of time movement. Using Vendler's (1967) taxonomy of predicate-types, Dry categorizes both achievements and accomplishments as events and both activities and statives as states. Within this system, *achievements* are defined as situations with a punctual occurrence having a natural endpoint (i.e., reaching the top, blinking). *Accomplishments* also have natural endpoints but are situations of greater duration than achievements (i.e., building a house, typing a letter). *Activities* (i.e., running, swimming) and *statives* are classified as states rather than events, because neither have natural endpoints, only arbitrary ones. Statives are different from activities in that there is no energy required to maintain them (i.e., knowing someone, being short, owning a car). The effect of predicate-type on the movement of narrative time is illustrated below.

(5) Fred walked into the room. Susan *got up* from her chair.
(6) Fred walked into the room. Susan *sat* in her chair.

Because the second sentence of (5) contains the achievement predicate, *got up*, it refers to the endpoint of this situation and therefore is interpreted as denoting an event which occurs later than the previous sentence's event. In contrast, the second sentence of (6) contains an activity predicate, and thus the state denoted by this predicate is interpreted as overlapping with the previous sentence's event; the reference time of the narrative does not move forward.

Repetition of Narrative Events

Of specific concern to this chapter are instances of repetition where an achievement or accomplishment predicate in simple past tense is repeated. That is, I am concerned with the repetition of predicates that should have the effect of pushing time forward in the narrative world. Consider the following examples:

(7)   Judging the turn in her mood correctly—that she was friendly to him now—he was relieved of his egotism, and told her how he had been thrown out of a boat when he was a baby; how his father used to fish him out with a boat hook; that was how he had learnt to swim. One of his uncles kept the light on some rock or other off the Scottish coast, he *said*. He had been there with him in a storm. This *was said* loudly in a pause. They had to listen to him when he *said* that he had been with his uncle in a lighthouse in a storm. Ah, thought Lily Briscoe, as the conversation took this auspicious turn, and she felt Mrs. Ramsay's gratitute. (Woolf, 1964b, p. 106)

In (7), the first instance of Mr. Tansley's (the referent of *he*) speech act is represented by an accomplishment predicate in the simple past tense and serves to move the reference time of the narrative forward. Thus, the second and third mention of Mr. Tansley's speech act seems to refer to a point in time that has already passed within the depicted world. Likewise, the repetition of the predicate, *went off*, in (8) also seems to represent a point in the narrative past, as the first instance of the event functions to push time forward within the narrative world.

(8)   They wavered about, went different ways, Mr. Bankes took Charles Tansley by the arm and *went off* to finish on the terrace the discussion they had begun at dinner about politics, thus giving a turn to the whole poise of the evening making the weight fall in a different direction, as if, Lily thought, seeing them go and hearing a word or two about the policy of the Labour Party, they had gone up on to the bridge of the ship and were taking their bearings; the change from poetry to politics

struck her like that; so Mr. Bankes and Charles Tansley *went off*, while the others stood looking at Mrs. Ramsay going upstairs in the lamplight alone. Where, Lily wondered, was she going so quickly? (Woolf, 1964b, p. 129)

In (9) and (10) below, different lexical items represent the second occurrence of the events in question (i.e., this is not exact repetition). The repetition of the events, however, denotes a point in time that has already passed within the narrative world.

(9) Now it was time to move and as a woman gathers her things together, her cloak, her gloves, her opera-glasses and gets up to go out of the theatre into the street, she rose from the sofa and *went to* Peter.
      And it was awfully strange, he thought, how she still had the power as she came tinkling, rustling, still had the power as she *came across* the room, to make the moon which he detested, rise at Bourton on the terrace in the summer sky. (Woolf, 1964a, p. 55)
(10) 'No going to the Lighthouse, James,' he *said* as he stood by the window, speaking awkwardly but trying in deference to Mrs. Ramsay to soften his voice into some semblance of geniality at least. . . .
      This going to the Lighthouse was a passion of his, she saw, and then as if her husband had not said enough with his caustic saying that it would not be fine tomorrow, this odious little man *went and rubbed it in* all over again. (Woolf, 1964b, 18)

In (9), Mrs. Dalloway's traveling across the room is repeated by a different predicate; in (10), Mr. Tansley's speech act is repeated by a different predicate.

In passages (7)–(10), events initially represented by accomplishment predicates in the simple past tense are repeated. The repeated events, however, are not represented as anterior to the current reference time of the narrative. Rather, they are represented in the simple past tense (not the past perfect) and, thus, as occurring for the first time within the narrative world. I suggest that this type of repetition functions to introduce a new point of view into the discourse. The temporal incoherence resulting from the repetition of completed events can be resolved if the second mention of an event is viewed as conveying a different perspective on the event. Rather than interpreting the second instances of the accomplishment predicates as referring to points in the narrative past, I am claiming that readers interpret their events as occurring for the first time (i.e., in the narrative present) but from the point of view of a different source consciousness. In (7), the point of view shifts from the referent of *he* to Lily Briscoe; in (8), the point of view shifts from a relatively objective one to that of Lily Briscoe; in (9) the perspective shifts from an objective one to that of Peter; and in (10), from Mr. Tansley's point of view (the referent of *he*) to that of Mrs. Ramsay.[1]

Hrushovski (1982), in a general discussion of strategies or procedures for imposing coherence on superficially incoherent texts, cites 'imposing a shift of speaker' as one such strategy. He provides the following example:

(11)   He opened the door. A few pieces of clothing were strewn about. He caught the fish in his net. (p. 162)

While the first two sentences in (11) are not connected by any formal or logical means, they are readily interpreted as coherent if we assume that readers draw inferences about doors being entrances to rooms, and rooms often containing clothes. According to Hrushovski, it is more difficult to interpret the third sentence of (11) as coherent with previous discourse, because fish are not normally caught with nets in rooms. At least two strategies can be used to restore coherence to this passage. A metaphorical interpretation is possible whereby the third sentence could be understood non-literally, for example, as a man entering a room and catching a thief. Alternatively, Hrushovski claims, a shift of speaker can be imposed upon the passage such that the sentence is interpreted as the man's thoughts (i.e., as a shift in point of view) as he enters the room. In a similar way, I am claiming that the temporal incoherence evident in passages like (7)–(10) is resolved by interpreting the repeated events as conveying a shift in speaker or source consciousness. This shift in point of view relies crucially on the similarity involved in repetition. The introduction of a *new* narrative event into the discourse would not necessarily invoke a shift in perspective; it is the repeating of "old" or "given" events (i.e., events that are predictable from the preceding context) that creates a 'new' perspective on them.

DISCUSSION

At the outset of this chapter, I suggested that the particular function associated with the repetition of narrative events in RST is directly related to these texts' mode. Because these are highly crafted, written texts rather than unplanned, spoken texts, readers assume that their linguistic forms (e.g., repetition) have been carefully consid-

---

[1] Repetition of completed narrative events is just one linguistic device by which shifts in point of view are signaled. Therefore, in passages (7)–(10), there may be other linguistic indicators of the shifts in question. For example, in passage (9), the presence of the verb *come* in the repeated event, *came across*, helps to invoke the perspective of the individual located at the goal of the motion (Fillmore, 1983), that is, Peter.

ered and designed in advance, and are not affected by the demands of face-to-face interaction. In other words, the repetition in these texts is not functioning to provide a speaker with planning time or a listener with redundant information. If readers assume that repetition in these texts is not meant merely to provide redundancy, then they will search for other interpretations to explain its occurrence. For example, as demonstrated above, they may interpret the repetition of narrative events as indicating a new perspective on "old" or "given" narrative material.

Given the differences between highly crafted, written texts and unplanned, spoken texts, one would expect a difference in the way shifts in point of view are signalled in the two modes. The repetition of events within an oral, unplanned narrative will be less readily interpreted as signalling a shift in point of view, given the other functions of repetition in spoken language, that is, facilitating the production and comprehension of speech. As illustrated in the following example (borrowed from Polanyi, 1982, p. 161, citing Schiffrin, 1981), shifts in point of view in spoken, unplanned discourse tend to be more linguistically overt.

(12)   And my grandfather says now I'm going to stick the broom under the couch. I'm going to pull it out and you start hitting. He's telling my father youse start hitting the rat with the hammer. You squash him, right?

Polanyi claims that the repetition of what the grandfather says above gives us two views of the same event, "one distanced somewhat (in the narrator's diction) and one much more intimate (in the grandfather's voice and thus from within his world)" (p. 161). While repetition is involved in the signalling of this shift in point of view, the crucial element to my mind is the change in diction that accompanies the repetition. If this speech event were repeated without the word choice that approximates the grandfather's style of speech (i.e., if the shift in perspective were less linguistically overt), it would be less readily interpreted as reflecting the grandfather's point of view. By contrast, the repetition of a narrative event in RST can invoke a shift in perspective, due to the significance attached to each and every structure in highly crafted, literary texts.

REFERENCES

Auerbach, E. (1968). *Mimesis.* Princeton, NJ: Princeton University Press.
Banfield, A. (1982). *Unspeakable sentences: Narration and representation in the language of fiction.* Boston: Routledge and Kegan Paul.

Dowty, D. (1986). The effects of aspectual class on the temporal structure of discourse: Semantics or pragmatics? *Linguistics and Philosophy*, *9*, 37–61.

Dry, H. (1975). *Syntactic reflexes of point of view in Jane Austen's "Emma."* Unpublished doctoral dissertation, University of Texas at Austin.

Dry. H. (1983). The movement of narrative time. *Journal of Literary Semantics*, *12*, 19–53.

Ehrlich, S. (1987). Aspect, foregrounding and point of view. *Text*, *7*, 363–376.

Ehrlich, S. (1990a). Referential linking and the interpretation of tense. *Journal of Pragmatics*, *14*, 57–75.

Ehrlich, S. (1990b). *Point of view: A linguistic analysis of literary style.* London: Routledge.

Fillmore, C. (1981). Pragmatics and the description of discourse. In P. Cole (Ed.), *Radical pragmatics* (pp. 143–66). New York: Academic Press.

Fillmore, C. (1983). How to know whether you're coming or going. In G. Rauh (Ed.), *Essays on Deixis* (pp. 219–227). Tübingen: Gunter Narr Verlag.

Genette, G. (1980). *Narrative discourse.* Ithaca, NY: Cornell University Press.

Hildyard, A., & Olson, D. R. (1982). On the comprehension and memory of oral vs. written discourse. In D. Tannen (Ed.), *Spoken and written language* (pp. 19–33). Norwood, NJ: Ablex Publishing Corp.

Hrushovski, B. (1982). Integrational semantics: An understander's theory of meaning in context. In H. Byrnes (Ed.), *Contemporary perceptions of language: Interdisciplinary dimensions* (pp. 156–190). Washington, DC: Georgetown University Press.

Norrick, N. (1987). Functions of repetition in conversation. *Text*, *7*, 245–64.

Ochs, E. (1979). Planned and unplanned discourse. In T. Givon (Ed.), *Discourse and syntax* (pp. 51–80). New York: Academic Press.

Olson, D. R. (1977). From utterance to text: The bias of language in speech and writing. *Harvard Educational Review*, *47*, 257–81.

Polanyi, L. (1982). Literary complexity in everyday storytelling. In D. Tannen (Ed.), *Spoken and written language* (pp. 155–170). Norwood, NJ: Ablex Publishing Corp.

Schiffrin, D. (1981). Tense variation in narrative. *Language*, *57*, 45–62.

Smith, C. (1983). A theory of aspectual choice. *Language*, *59*, 479–501.

Tannen, D. (1987a). Repetition in conversation: Towards a poetics of talk. *Language*, *63*, 574–605.

Tannen, D. (1987b). Repetition in conversation as spontaneous formulacity. *Text*, *7*, 215–43.

Tannen, D. (1989). *Talking voices: Repetition, dialogue, and imagery in conversational discourse.* Cambridge, UK: Cambridge University Press.

Vendler, Z. (1967). *Linguistics in philosophy.* Ithaca, NY: Cornell University Press.

Woolf, V. (1964a). *Mrs. Dalloway.* Harmondsworth, UK: Penguin Books. (Original work published 1925)

Woolf, V. (1964b). *To the lighthouse.* Harmondsworth, UK: Penguin Books. (Original work published 1927)

Chapter 7
Repetition and Failed Conversation in the Theater of the Absurd

Cynthia Schnebly

Arts and Sciences Division
University of Houston at Victoria

Paul Friedrich (1986) has described "all natural language" as "poetic in part," and envisions "the relation between poetic and natural language" as "not cyclical but rather that of two imperfectly parallel streams, which sometimes are almost out of earshot of each other and sometimes can converge" (p. 27). The image of the "imperfectly parallel streams" can also be applied to the relationship between conversational discourse and dramatic discourse. In creating dialogue for plays, playwrights use everyday conversation as a resource. In Friedrich's terms, "language [provides] rough drafts for poetry" (p. 35). Dramatic dialogue may mimic conversations as closely as possible, in two closely parallel streams, or move the discourse to poetry, in more distant parallel streams.

Analysis of conversation in plays thus provides a way into their meaning. And, since dramatic discourse highlights and foregrounds features of ordinary conversation, plays can also be sources of insight about the workings of everyday talk. Goffman (1974) reminds us that playwrights preselect the material for their texts, including conversations, just as speakers in conversation choose relevant details for their stories. Turn-taking rules in drama, Goffman says, are different from those of ordinary conversation. First, in dramatic discourse one speaker is given primary attention while other participants' actions are deemphasized. Second, turns in dramatic conversation are rarely interrupted, and time for audience response may be included in the script. Third, conversation turns are frequently "much longer and more grandiloquent than in ordinary conversation," especially since playwrights "have more time to contrive apt, pithy, colorful, and rounded statements than do individuals engaged in natural unstaged talk" (p. 143). Burton (1980) points out that the features of dramatic discourse make it ripe for conversational analysis. For her, "drama scripts are markedly tidied-up versions of talk" (p. 115). Tannen (1989) also emphasizes the need to study conversation in drama and other literary genres, arguing that "literary (in the sense of artfully developed) genres elaborate and manipulate strategies that are spontaneous in conversation" (p. 80).

In this chapter I focus on the effects of repetition in two plays by Edward Albee, *The Zoo Story* (1960) and *The American Dream*[1] (1959), and two plays by Harold Pinter, *The Birthday Party* (1961) and *One for the Road* (1984).[2] I describe the forms and functions of repetition in the play texts, focusing especially on how repetition works as an involvement strategy (Tannen, 1989) in creating relationships between the characters in the plays and between the texts and their audiences. Although Tannen argues that repetition in everyday conversation creates "interpersonal involvement" (p. 9) and "[gives] the impression of a shared universe of discourse" (p. 52), she points out that in plays such as *The Birthday Party* the repetition strategies are manipulated for other effects. I argue that the cumulative effect of repetition in these plays of Albee and Pinter illustrates a negative side of repetition in everyday conversation: Repetition can create conversations that are dull, lifeless, mundane, jammed with routinized expressions that can have a jarring effect on the audience. The characters often seem only marginally aware of what is being said, and they repeat to clear away the obligation to reply or to evade substantive response.

FORMS OF REPETITION

One of the ways plays in the Theater of the Absurd function is by making the audience feel they are overhearing everyday conversation and then exaggerating ordinary features of conversation until

---

[1] All quotations by Edward Albee have been reprinted by permission of The William Morris Agency, Inc., and the Putnam Publishing Group, Inc., from *The American Dream* by Edward Albee and *The Zoo Story* by Edward Albee.

[2] All quotations by Harold Pinter have been reprinted by permission of Matthew Drama, a division of Methuen.

the audience is uncomfortable. This is the effect of the repetition in the texts of Albee and Pinter. Repetitions in these plays range along a scale from exact repetition, to repetition with slight variations, to paraphrase. Repetitions of words, phrases and sentences, as well as themes, is common in all the texts. And repetition is common both in exchanges where speaker change occurs frequently and also in longer passages by the same speaker.

In Albee's *The American Dream*, exact repetition of words and phrases is common in both same speaker repetition and second speaker repetition. The repeats in example (1) illustrate this form of repetition. (Repeated words and phrases have been underlined for emphasis throughout the examples.)

(1)   Grandma.   My, my, my. Are you the van man?
      Young man.   The what?
      Grandma.   The van man. The van man. Are you come to take me
                    away? (p. 105)

Characters in the play often repeat words in sets of twos or threes, such as Grandma's "my, my, my" or "The van man. The van man."

In *One for the Road*, Nicholas repeats the word *death* with the impact increasing incrementally each time. Not only does he appear to like the sound of the word and of his own voice, as in examples of children's experimentation with words and sounds (Ochs, 1979), but his repetition also emphasizes the probable outcome of his interrogation of Victor.

(2)   Nicholas.   Death. Death. Death. Death. As has been noted by the
                  most respected authorities, it is beautiful. The purest,
                  most harmonious thing there is. (p. 45)

Repetition with slight variation is, however, more common than exact repetition. The repeated sequences may be expanded, the form may be changed from a statement to a question or exclamation, or the emphasis may be altered. In example (3), from *The Birthday Party*, Pinter uses repetition patterns reported in the speech of young children (Keenan, 1977). Meg and Stanley play a childlike game in which Stanley is supposed to imitate Meg's directions but does not cooperate.

(3)   Meg.   Do you want some tea?
                  Say please.
      Stanley.   Please.

Meg.   Say <u>sorry first</u>.
Stanley. <u>Sorry first</u>.
Meg.   No. <u>Just sorry</u>.
Stanley. <u>Just sorry</u>! (pp. 17–18)

Repetition of set phrases occurs frequently in the play texts of Albee and Pinter. *The American Dream* repeats sequences of "Oh, my child; my child," "Oh, so firm; so firm," and "Oh, he is; he is." In *The Zoo Story* sequences of "Oh, yes; the zoo" are repeated, as in example (4). The dialogue keeps returning to the untold story Jerry has promised to tell Peter.

(4) Peter. <u>The zoo</u>; <u>the zoo</u>. Something about <u>the zoo</u>.
     Jerry. <u>The zoo</u>?
     Peter. You've mentioned it several times.
     Jerry. <u>The zoo</u>. Oh, yes; <u>the zoo</u>. . . . (p. 20)

In Jerry's monologues, he also emphasizes the same sequence in "And, oh yes; the poor monster," and "Oh, yes; there's a grey-yellow-white color, too when he bares his fangs," which both echo his phrasing "Oh, yes; the dog."

Same Speaker Repetition

As many conversation analysts have noted (Norrick, 1987; Tannen, 1987, 1989), speakers frequently repeat their own words and phrases not only inside a turn but in subsequent turns and as themes in longer units of discourse. Same speaker repetition in the play texts of Pinter and Albee is used in many of the same ways we find it used in ordinary conversation—after false starts, for expansions of original statements, for reintroductions of a topic, and as prepatterned phrasings speakers incorporate into their own speech. Speakers repeat after false starts, as does the Young Man in these lines from *The American Dream*.

(5) Young Man. Oh, <u>almost anything</u> . . . <u>almost anything that pays</u>. I'll do <u>almost anything for money</u>. (p. 109)

His repetition includes the correction of the false start and a paraphrase with more specific information than the first statement. Same speaker repetition also includes expansions of the original phrase, as in (6).

(6)   Nicholas.   I'm prepared to be frank, as a true friend should. <u>I love
death</u>. What about you?
(Pause)
What about you? <u>Do you love death</u>? Not necessarily your
own. Others. <u>The death of others</u>. <u>Do you love the death of
others, or at any rate, do you love the death of others as
much as I do</u>? (*One for the Road*, p. 45)

By structuring this sequence as a series of expanding questions,
Pinter is able to show clearly the verbal torture Nicholas is using on
Victor, as he does again in (7).

(7)   Nicholas.   <u>What's the matter?</u>
(Pause)
<u>What in heaven's name is the matter?</u> (p. 52)

Speakers also use repetition to bring a topic or comment back
to the front of the discussion after intervening lines. Jerry asks a
question in the lines below from *The Zoo Story* and then waits nine
lines before reintroducing it as a statement with revised emphasis.

(8)   Jerry.   But <u>that's the way the cookie crumbles</u>.
. . . .
Jerry.   <u>That is the way the cookie crumbles</u>. (p. 16)

Albee says in the stage directions that Jerry's first lines are said in a
mocking tone, and the second are said softly. In forcing himself on
Peter, Jerry has been forward enough to question why Peter has only
female children, insinuating that the subject has been a difficult one
for Peter to come to terms with. Although this completely irritates
Peter, Jerry can't resist bringing his original insinuation back to the
surface of the conversation.

Borrowing readymade phrases from other characters is a recurring technique in *The American Dream*. In (9), Mommy interrupts
Daddy's sentence to provide extra information; then Daddy uses the
information she has just provided to begin his turn. He also borrows
the pattern he began in his first turn and builds on it.

(9)   Daddy.   When we took this apartment, <u>they were quick enough to
have me sign the lease; they were quick enough to take my
check for two months' rent in advance</u>. . .
Mommy.   <u>And one month's security</u>. . .
Daddy.   . . . <u>and one month's security</u>. <u>They were quick enough to
check my references; they were quick enough about all
that</u>. But now! But now, <u>try to get the icebox fixed, try to
get the doorbell fixed, try to get the leak in that johnny
fixed</u>! Just <u>try it</u>. . . <u>They aren't so quick about that</u>. (pp.
57–58)

Daddy's repetition of "they were quick enough" and "try to get . . .
fixed" serves to create patterns and rhythm more easily processed by
the listener and more easily produced by the speaker, a technique
Tannen (1989, p. 48) refers to as the production function of repetition.

Much of the same speaker repetition in the plays appears in
longer turns and emphasizes parallel phrasings. For the speech
below by Grandma in *The American Dream*, I've arranged the sentences to reflect the patterns in her dialogue.

(10) Because I'm old!
      When you're old   you gotta do something.
      When you get old,   you can't talk to people
                                 because people snap at you.
      When you get so old,   people talk to you
                                                        that way.

      That's why   you become deaf, so
                             you won't be able to hear
                                 people talking to you
                                                        that way.

      And that's why   you go and hide under the covers
                                 in the big soft bed,
                             so you won't feel the house shaking
                                 from people talking to you
                                                        that way.

      That's why old people die, eventually.
                             People talk to them
                                                        that way.
      I've got to go and get the rest of the boxes. (p. 65)

These patterns reflect Albee's theory (see Zindel & Yerby, 1988)
that plays contain "a kind of internal music that also relates to
music as it goes along—rather the total form of a piece of music—in
the same way that plays have their own kind of poetry" (p. 13).
Readers or listeners are automatically drawn to these lines by their
musical quality and by the series of parallel ideas. The third line
from the end of the sequence—"That's why old people die, eventually"—brings together the three key ideas: "that's why," "old," and
"people die." Grandma begins the lines by talking about her personal plight as an old person, moves to discussing the larger group of
old people as *you*, and then finally distances herself by referring to
the old people as *them*. The repetition in these lines closely follows
many of the examples Tannen (1989) has recorded from everyday
conversation and from public oratory.

Second Speaker Repetition

Speakers repeating the words of previous speakers in dramatic discourse also follow the same rules as speakers in normal conversation. They repeat in conversational openings and closings, to correct or contradict another speaker, to inquire about a previous utterance, to turn a question into a statement, and to agree with a previous speaker (Norrick, 1987). When Stanley meets McCann in *The Birthday Party*, he greets him in the same manner we use in greetings each day.

(11) Stanley.   <u>Evening</u>.
      McCann.   <u>Evening</u>. (p. 37)

In these plays second speaker repetition often corrects or contradicts the previous speaker's information. Example (12) shows Jerry incensed at Peter's addressing him as "my dear fellow."

(12) Peter.   <u>My dear fellow</u>, I . . .
      Jerry.   Don't <u>my dear fellow me</u>. (*The Zoo Story*, p. 20)

In (13), Grandma contradicts Mrs. Barker's comment by mocking it.

(13) Mrs. Barker.   Oh . . . is it? Nonetheless, I really do feel that I can trust you. Please tell me why they called and asked us to come. I <u>implore you</u>!
      Grandma.   Oh my; that feels good. It's been so long since anybody <u>implored me</u>. Do it again. <u>Implore me some more</u>. (*The American Dream*, p. 95)

The next sequence shows McCann questioning Stanley's previous statement by turning Stanley's words around.

(14) Stanley.   <u>You'll find it very bracing</u>.
      McCann.   Do <u>you find it bracing</u>? (*The Birthday Party*, p. 39)

In Pinter's *One for the Road*, the most common tactic for Nicholas to use as an interrogator is to take Gila's statements and turn them into questions to confuse her.

(15) Gila.   He was in <u>the room</u>.
      Nicholas.   <u>Room</u>?
                  (Pause)
                  <u>Room</u>?

Gila.	The same room.
Nicholas.	As what?
Gila.	As I was.
Nicholas.	As I was?
Gila.	As I was!
	(screaming) (pp. 63–64)

Gila finally registers her utter frustration by taking his question and turning it into an exclamation.

Second speaker repetition is also used to show acceptance of the previous speaker's comments. In this passage from *The Birthday Party*, Meg signals her understanding that Petey is right when she repeats "in winter."

(16)   Meg.   But sometimes you go out in the morning and it's dark.
          Petey.   That's in the winter.
          Meg.   Oh, in winter. (p. 10)

Goldberg shows Meg that he accepts her statement about the time for the upcoming party by repeating.

(17)   Goldberg.   We're going to give him a party.
          McCann.   Oh, is that a fact?
          Meg.   Tonight.
          Goldberg.   Tonight. (p. 33)

In these plays, then, when speakers repeat the words of the previous speaker, they follow the rules of second speaker repetition in everyday conversation.

CONVERSATIONAL DETACHMENT IN DRAMATIC DISCOURSE

The above examples offer ample support for what literary critics have been saying about dialogue in these plays: The conversations closely parallel ordinary speech. Pinter's language has often been described as conversation-like. Martin Esslin (1987) comments that "Pinter's clinically accurate ear for the absurdity of ordinary speech enables him to transcribe everyday conversation in all its repetitiveness, incoherence, and lack of logic or grammar" (p. 234). For Dina Sherzer (1978), it is this parody of everyday talk that defines conversation in the Theater of the Absurd:

The characters exchange the most commonplace, the most ordinary type of utterances, the most mechanical speech acts. In so doing they simulate the rituals of everyday interactions, but these interactions are foregrounded on on the stage, because there is nothing else. In traditional theater these types of interactions are understood to exist, but they are played down to give prominence to the main problem, to the predicament of the characters. In the Theater of the Absurd these interactions have become the very stuff of the plays. Consequently, the banal, the mechanical, and the perfunctory stand out. (p. 282)

Both Pinter and Albee have discussed the importance of writing about the failure of conversation to connect people. Albee firmly believes that people decide not to reach out to each other because they do not want to take chances (Anderson & Ingersoll, 1988). For Pinter (1964), communication is evasion:

I think that we communicate only too well, in our silence, in what is unsaid, and that what takes place is a continual evasion, desperate rearguard attempts to keep ourselves to ourselves. Communication is too alarming. To enter someone's life is too frightening. (p. 83)

In these four plays, characters appear to be having conversations like ours in ordinary speech, but their attempts to communicate most often fail. *The Birthday Party, The Zoo Story, The American Dream,* and *One for the Road* are all models of evasion of communication. Characters are not working hard to participate in the conversations, to show their level of commitment or their deep involvement. Their replies indicate deliberate attempts to satisfy conversational requirements minimally and to evade giving substantive information. The characters cling to routinized expressions to clear away obligations to participate fully. The repetitions are often an indication of how little of themselves they want to give away in conversation and how much they want to delay the presentation of painful information.

The effects of this repetition are twofold. First, it makes readers or listeners pay attention to how little information appears to be communicated through the surface words of conversations and how much comes through the subtext. Second, the repetition of mundane, dull expressions that the audience is familiar with can jar, shocking us into the realization of how the incremental buildup of repetition in conversation works. Bruce Kawin (1972) says this level of repetition works like a mantra:

Up to a certain point, repetition emphasizes the sense of what is repeated—builds, as it does in *King Lear*. Beyond that point, the repeated word loses its original meaning: it becomes a routine or cliche, a blank wall, a falsified memory, or a drone. But repeated past this point, the word can become a force, the drone primary sound. By repetition, a proposition can become a secular *mantra*. (p. 170)

Repetition in the dialogue between these characters shows a more negative side of repetition in conversation. Sometimes the act of borrowing a preformulated word or phrase or sentence from a previous speech indicates a speaker's unwillingness to be involved actively in the conversation. Characters may use frequent "communication checks," as Keenan (1977) terms them, much as children use them with adults to make sure they are paying attention. Pinter uses the "very nice" response in *The Birthday Party* as an indication that characters are forced to reply to a conversational question but don't actually want to be engaged in conversation.

(18) Meg. I've got your cornflakes ready. Here's your cornflakes. <u>Are they nice?</u>
 Petey. <u>Very nice.</u>
 Meg. I thought <u>they'd be nice.</u> (p. 9)

(19) Meg. <u>Is it nice out?</u>
 Petey. <u>Very nice.</u> (p. 10)

(20) Stanley. What's it like out today?
 Petey. <u>Very nice.</u> (p. 14)

(21) Meg. Here you are Petey.
 <u>Is it nice?</u>
 Petey. I haven't tasted it yet.
 Meg. I bet you don't know what it is.
 Petey. Yes, I do.
 Meg. What is it, then?
 Petey. Fried bread.
 Meg. That's right.
 (He begins to eat. She watches him eat.)
 Petey. <u>Very nice.</u> (pp. 11, 12)

Each time Petey responds with "very nice," he is responding to Meg's communication check, but he shows little interest in continuing the dialogue. Examples (18)–(21) all show Petey's unwillingness to do more than barely acknowledge his part in the conversation. Each time Petey responds with "very nice," he is supplying Meg with the response that he thinks will get him off the conversational hook.

In (21) he answers all of her questions, but not until he gives her the expected response is she willing to change topics. During the play other characters begin using the phrase. In (22) and (23) it is obvious that neither Meg nor Goldberg is in a hurry to give up more details in the conversation.

(22)   Goldberg.   We're pleased to meet you, too.
        Meg.   <u>That's very nice.</u> (p. 30)

(23)   Meg.   He's a deck-chair attendant.
        Goldberg.   <u>Oh, very nice.</u> (p. 31)

While the phrase begins the play as Petey's reply to Meg about the quality of cornflakes, its meaning takes on a decidedly ominous tone as the play proceeds. What makes this unsettling for the audience is the slow realization during the play that a mundane expression such as "very nice" can come to describe the inattentiveness with which people react to the horrors going on around them, in this case, Stanley being forcibly taken away by Goldberg and McCann. In (24) Meg uses the phrase to describe Goldberg and McCann; by (25) McCann is using it to describe the party they are planning for Stanley.

(24)   Stanley.   They've come?
        Meg.   <u>They're very nice, Stan.</u>
        Stanley.   Why didn't they come last night?
        Meg.   They said the beds were wonderful.
        Stanley.   Who are they?
        Meg.   <u>They're very nice, Stanley.</u> (p. 34)

(25)   McCann.   Were you going out?
        Stanley.   Yes.
        McCann.   On your birthday?
        Stanley.   Yes, why not?
        McCann.   But they're holding a party for you tonight.
        Stanley.   Oh really? That's unfortunate.
        McCann.   Ah no. <u>It's very nice.</u> (pp. 37–38)

Each time "very nice" is repeated, its meaning changes, with the audience reinterpreting the new layer of meaning.

In *The American Dream*, Albee gives us an unnerving portrait of the dull conversation that occurs between spouses when one does not care about what the other is saying. Mommy expects Daddy to pay attention to her. To do that, Daddy must continuously respond to her queries. If he doesn't respond as she expects him to, she accuses him of not paying attention.

(26)   Mommy.   All right, now. I went to buy a new hat yesterday and I said, "I'd like a new hat, please." And so, they showed me a few hats, green ones and blue ones, and <u>I didn't like any of them, not one bit</u>. What did I say? What did I just say?

Daddy.   <u>You didn't like any of them, not one bit</u>.

Mommy.   That's right; you just keep paying attention. And then they showed me one that I did like. It was a lovely little hat, and I said, "Oh, this is a lovely little hat; I'll take this hat; oh my, it's lovely. What color is it?" And they said, "Why, this is beige; isn't it a lovely little beige hat?" And I said, "Oh it's just lovely." <u>And so, I bought it</u>.

Daddy.   <u>And so you bought it</u>.

Mommy.   <u>And so I bought it</u>, and I walked out of the store with the hat right on my head, and I ran spang into the chairman of our woman's club, and she said, "Oh, my dear, isn't that a lovely little hat? Where did you get that lovely little hat? It's the loveliest little hat; I've always wanted a wheat-colored hat myself." And, I said, "Why, no, my dear; this hat is beige; beige." And she laughed and said, "Why no, my dear, that's a wheat-colored hat . . . wheat. I know beige from wheat." And I said, "Well, my dear, I know beige from wheat, too." What did I say? What did I just say? (pp. 59–60)

As Tannen has reported (1989, p. 61), speakers show listenership by repeating the words of the previous speaker. Mommy is never quite certain whether or not Daddy is listening and so keeps prodding him to give her signs of participation in the conversation. Albee foregrounds this process by setting Daddy's short, perfunctory replies against Mommy's droning, repetitive tale of the lovely little beige or wheat-colored hat.

In *The Zoo Story*, the dialogue begins with Jerry, a transient, trying to get the attention of Peter, a middle-class gentleman sitting on a park bench.

(27)   Jerry.   <u>I've been to the zoo</u>. (Peter doesn't notice.) I said, <u>I've been to the zoo</u>. MISTER, <u>I'VE BEEN TO THE ZOO!</u> (p. 12)

With the repetition of these lines, Albee sets up the prime movement for the play; Jerry wants Peter to know why he went to the zoo and what happened there. But in the play's dialogue between the two characters, what is foregrounded for the audience is the continual evasion of the subject by both characters, Jerry because what he learned at the zoo is so painful and Peter because he is afraid to learn what happened to Jerry and how it might encroach on his nicely ordered world. This evasion is manifested in the repetition of lines about the zoo. The characters take turns bringing the dialogue back to the subject of the zoo, but each time Jerry gets close, either he or Peter moves the conversation's center away.

(28)   Peter.   What? Whose face? Look here; is this something about the zoo?
       Jerry.   The what?
                     (distantly)
       Peter.   The zoo; the zoo. Something about the zoo.
       Jerry.   The zoo?
       Peter.   You've mentioned it several times.
       Jerry.   The zoo? Oh, yes; the zoo. I was there before I came here.
                     (pp. 19–20)

At the end of Jerry's long monologue several pages later, which on the surface seems to have nothing to do with his trip to the zoo, Jerry says, "But I imagine you'd rather hear about what happened at the zoo" (p. 27). Peter enthusiastically, as Albee's notes tell us, replies, "Oh, yes; the zoo," repeating Jerry's exact lines from seven pages earlier. But Jerry, who now has another opening initiated by Peter, starts by saying, "Let me tell you why I went," and then changes the subject to the seedy roominghouse he lives in. What underlies the tension of the play is Jerry's disturbing visit to the zoo, in which he discovers how close his life is to an animal's existence. The continual repetition of "the zoo" phrases affects both Peter and the audience. The tension in the play mounts each the phrase recurs.

The evasion of communication cued by repetition in these plays occurs for different reasons. With the responses of Petey toward Meg in *The Birthday Party* and Daddy toward Mommy in *The American Dream*, the characters are, as Goffman (1967) terms it, contriving to show involvement. Their responding in such routine, repetitive ways makes us uneasy about their failure to show a deeper level of interest in what is being said. Pinter and Albee are foregrounding the same kind of uncomfortable conversations that take place every day between members of households who really don't want to listen to each other. In *The Zoo Story* the conversation is uncomfortable from the first line of the play because Jerry is forcing Peter to talk to him. Peter would like to withdraw from the conversation, but Jerry keeps the conversation moving. Goffman (1967) again provides insight into Peter's predicament by pointing out that once individuals enter a conversation such as this, "they are obliged to continue until they have the kind of basis for withdrawing that will neutralize the potentially offensive implications of taking leave of others" (p. 120).

These obligations are certainly in full force for the very middle-class Peter, who keeps looking for ways out of the conversation. Jerry keeps bringing up the subject of the zoo to keep Peter on the conversational hook; Peter brings it back to the front of the conversation, partially to force Jerry to get on with the story so he (Peter) can get out of this uncomfortable situation, and also because Jerry has piqued his interest in what happened at the zoo.

In this chapter, I have suggested that repetition in dramatic discourse takes the same forms as repetition in everyday conversation. Both same speaker and second speaker repetition in the Pinter and Albee plays follow repetition patterns for conversation. In this respect then, repetition in dramatic discourse in these plays is modeled on conversational features the audience is familiar with. The repetitions in these plays from the Theater of the Absurd, however, do not show us positive models for involvement in conversation. Instead, they represent failed conversational attempts, presenting participants who have little desire to share themselves with conversational partners.

REFERENCES

Albee, E. (1959 and 1960). *The American dream and the zoo story: Two plays by Edward Albee.* New York: Signet.

Anderson, M., & Ingersoll, E. (Eds.). (1988). Living on the precipice: A conversation with Edward Albee. In P. Kolin (Ed.), *Conversations with Edward Albee* (pp. 158–172). Jackson, MS: University of Mississippi Press.

Burton, D. (1980). *Dialogue and discourse.* London: Routledge and Kegan Paul.

Esslin, M. (1987). *The theater of the absurd.* Middlesex, UK: Penguin.

Friedrich, P. (1986). *The language parallax: Linguistic relativism and poetic indeterminacy.* Austin, TX: University of Texas Press.

Goffman, E. (1967). *Interaction ritual: Essays on face-to-face behavior.* New York: Pantheon Books.

Goffman, E. (1974). *Frame analysis.* Boston: Northeastern University Press.

Kawin, B. (1972). *Telling it again and again: Repetition in literature and film.* Ithaca, NY: Cornell University Press.

Keenan, E. (1977). Making it last: Repetition in children's discourse. In S. Ervin-Tripp & C. Mitchell-Kernan (Eds.), *Child discourse* (pp. 125–138). New York: Academic Press.

Norrick, N. (1987). Functions of repetition in conversation. *Text, 7* (3), 245–64.

Ochs, E. (1979). Planned and unplanned discourse. In T. Givon (Ed.), *Discourse and syntax* (pp. 51–80). New York: Academic Press.

Pinter, H. (1961). *The birthday party and the room.* New York: Grove Press.

Pinter, H. (1964). Writing for the theatre. *Evergreen Review, 33,* 80–82.

Pinter, H. (1984). *One for the road.* London: Methuen.

Sherzer, D. (1978). Dialogic incongruities in the theater of the absurd. *Semiotica, 22*(3/4), 269–285.

Tannen, D. (1987). Repetition in conversation: Toward a a poetics of talk. *Language, 63*(3), 574–605.

Tannen, D. (1989). *Talking voices: Repetition, dialogue, and imagery in conversational discourse.* Cambridge, UK: Cambridge University Press.

Zindel, P., & Yerby, L. (1988). Interview with Edward Albee. In P. Kolin (Ed.), *Conversations with Edward Albee* (pp. 11–19). Jackson, MS: University of Mississippi Press.

Chapter 8
Lexical Parallelism in the Nonfiction of Joan Didion

Dennis Rygiel

Department of English
Auburn University

In her nonfiction, Joan Didion often makes use of the kind of patterned repetition of words that traditional rhetorical treatises place in the category of schemes and catalogue under such names as *anaphora*, *epistrophe*, and *anadiplosis*. This is the kind of repetition that has been distinguished by Leech (1969) as *verbal parallelism*—"exact verbal repetitions in equivalent positions" (p. 79)—and that can be classified more precisely as *lexical parallelism* (Berlin, 1985, pp. 80–83). Didion's use of lexical parallelism is interesting, not only because of its frequency in her nonfiction, but also because such parallelism is not usually associated with contemporary nonfiction, especially the essay. In fact, the presence of much lexical parallelism, which has traditionally been associated with rhetorical artifice and formality, would seem to run counter to what Anderson (1987, p. 139) identifies as one of Didion's characteristic strategies—"the rhetoric of process," which creates in her prose an impression of spontaneity, of exploration, of a mind in the act of thinking. Here I would like to do two things: first, to determine how much Didion actually uses lexical parallelism in her nonfiction, especially in comparison to other writers; and second, to try to explain what it is about Didion's use of lexical parallelism that makes it compatible with "the rhetoric of process."

THE FREQUENCY OF LEXICAL PARALLELISM

For the quantitative part of the study, I have used a classification of lexical parallelism into distinct types, a classification derived ultimately from traditional rhetoric, but adapted for greater precision and completeness along lines suggested by modern stylistics (Leech, 1969, pp. 73–86; Hiatt, 1975). In this classification seven types of lexical parallelism are distinguished (*underlining added in examples throughout*):

Initial-final (epanalepsis)
1. Decree 207 had been the source of considerable confusion and infighting during the weeks preceding my arrival in El Salvador, <u>suspended</u> but not <u>suspended</u>. (Didion, 1983, p. 91)

Initial and final (symploce)
2. <u>They</u> have not <u>been</u>, and <u>they</u> probably never will <u>be</u>. (Didion, 1968, p. 171)

Initial (anaphora)
3. <u>We would</u> make a separate peace. <u>We would</u> do graduate work in Middle English, <u>we would</u> go abroad. <u>We would</u> make some money and live on a ranch. <u>We would</u> survive outside history. (Didion, 1979, p. 207)

Medial
4. They were paying <u>the familiar</u> price for it. And they had reached <u>the familiar</u> season of divorce. (Didion, 1968, p. 9)

Final (epistrophe)
5. Vultures of course <u>suggest the presence of a body</u>. A knot of children on the street <u>suggests the presence of a body</u>. (Didion, 1983, p. 19)

Final-initial (anadiplosis)
6. They took it <u>twice</u>. <u>Twice</u> the girl offered John Wayne the tattered Bible. (Didion, 1968, p. 40)

Crossing pattern (chiasmus)
7. <u>Your</u> notebook will never help <u>me</u>, nor <u>mine you</u>. (Didion, 1968, p. 140)

To supplement this basic classification, I have taken into account several of the factors that affect the relative prominence of any particular instance of lexical parallelism. The most important of these is syntactic parallelism, which is so typically an accompaniment to lexical parallelism that it does not make sense to treat lexical parallelism apart from syntactic parallelism (Leech, 1969, p. 82). Thus I focus on those instances of lexical parallelism that involve syntactic parallelism as well. But two qualifications need to be made. First, initial-final lexical parallelism (epanalepsis) precludes syntactic parallelism in the usual sense. Second, the more common the type of lexical parallelism, the more stringent is the requirement for syntactic parallelism. With initial lexical parallelism (anaphora), by far the commonest type, the syntactic parallelism must be moderate to strong, and the units in which the parallelism occurs must be of the same grammatical rank and type. With initial and final (symploce), medial, and final lexical parallelism (epistrophe), the units need not be of the same rank and type. And with final-initial (anadiplosis) and the crossing pattern (chiasmus), even weak syntactic parallelism is sufficient. As for other factors affecting prominence, I have included the following: semantic parallelism, the presence of asyndeton or polysyndeton, the level on which the parallelism occurs, and the number of members.[1]

To get a sense of how much Didion uses lexical parallelism, I have studied three of her works: *Slouching towards Bethlehem* (1968), *The white album* (1979), and *Salvador* (1983). To get a sense of how Didion compares in her use of such parallelism to other 20th-century writers of nonfiction, I have studied six additional works, all essay collections. Two works are by writers who were influenced by the repetition-rich tradition of Black preaching, and who therefore might be expected to use lexical parallelism more than Didion: James Baldwin, in *Notes of a native son* (1955), and Martin Luther King, Jr., in *Why we can't wait* (1964). Four works are by writers who wrote in genres (the informal essay, the New Journalism feature article) where lexical parallelism is not usually prominent, and who therefore might be expected to use lexical parallelism less than Didion: George Orwell, in *A collection of essays* (1954); E. B. White, in *Essays of E. B. White* (1977); Lewis Thomas, in *The lives of a cell* (1974); and Tom Wolfe, in *The kandy-kolored tangerine-flake streamline baby* (1968). From each work I have taken a sample of 3,500 words, based on seven 500-word cuts chosen according to a random number table.[2] Two samples have been taken from *Bethlehem*, one for journalism and one for essays.

---

[1] Semantic parallelism includes both pleonasm and antithesis (Hiatt, 1985, pp. 58–59). Asyndeton is defined here as omission of a coordinating conjunction in a sequence of two or more parallel units.

[2] My sampling technique is based on Cluett (1976, p. 16). Each cut begins with the first full written sentence on the page and ends with the 500th written word (because the focus is on self-repetition, quotations are excluded from the count). The pages on which the cuts begin are as follows: Didion (1968): 39, 104, 83, 79, 68, 9, 5 (journalism); Didion (1968): 171, 191, 175, 140, 148, 217, 207 (essays); Didion (1979): 122, 37, 207, 168, 191, 147, 111; Didion 1983: 75, 42, 90, 47, 17, 65, 56; Baldwin (1955): 154, 31, 144, 45, 74, 65, 102; King (1964): 140, 75, 144, 110, 83, 165, 116; Orwell (1954): 251, 45, 143, 54, 75, 104, 217; White 1977: 11, 263, 184, 49, 147, 116, 53; Thomas (1974): 45, 12, 71, 143, 63, 92, 54; and Wolfe (1968): 21, 273, 35, 208, 243, 11, 106.

The quantitative results appear in Tables 8.1 and 8.2. As the lines labeled "Totals" show, the Didion samples include, respectively, 58, 55, 50, and 43 instances of repetition, the Baldwin sample 43, Orwell 35, King 34, White 32, Thomas 23, and Wolfe 19. It is apparent, then, that Didion does in fact use lexical parallelism more than all the other writers studied except Baldwin, and that exception holds for only one of Didion's four samples. With respect to the individual types of lexical parallelism, Didion equals or exceeds all the other writers in every category except initial-final and medial. Moreover, in almost every factor affecting prominence, Didion tends to exceed the others as well. She uses semantic parallelism more: 8x, 13x, 10x, and 11x, compared to King's 6x, the next highest. She uses asyndeton more: 23x, 32x, 21x, and 21x, compared to the next highest frequency of 11x in Baldwin and King. She has more in-

Table 8.1   Frequency of Lexical Parallelism in Selected Samples: Joan Didion

	Didion 1968 (journalism)	Didion 1983	Didion 1968 (essay)	Didion 1979
Frequency by type				
Initial-final	3	2	1	2
Initial & final	2	3	2	0
Initial	42	38	38	32
Medial	3	5	0	3
Final	2	5	6	3
Final-initial	6	2	2	2
Crossing pattern	0	0	1	1
TOTALS	58	55	50	43
Other parallelism				
Syntactic	55	53	49	41
Semantic	8	13	10	11
Co-occuring devices				
Asyndeton	23	32	21	21
Polysyndeton	1	1	0	1
Level of parallelism				
More prominent				
Sentence	20	16	6	11
Main clause	11	6	17	10
Totals	31	22	23	21
Less prominent				
Subordinate clause	3	4	7	3
Phrase	21	27	19	17
Number of members				
Doublet	50	44	42	33
Triplet	4	7	6	5
Series	1	2	1	3

Table 8.2   Frequency of Lexical Parallelism in Selected Samples:
Other Authors

	Baldwin (1955)	Orwell (1954)	King (1964)	White (1977)	Thomas (1974)	Wolfe (1968)
Frequency by Type						
Initial-final	2	2	3	4	4	1
Initial & final	1	1	0	0	0	0
Initial	27	27	26	25	15	15
Medial	8	2	4	1	1	1
Final	5	2	0	2	3	2
Final-initial	0	0	0	0	0	0
Crossing pattern	0	1	1	0	0	0
TOTALS	43	35	34	32	23	19
Other Parallelism						
Syntactic	41	33	31	28	19	18
Semantic	5	3	6	3	2	0
Co-occurring Devices						
Asyndeton	11	10	11	9	6	9
Polysyndeton	0	0	0	0	0	0
Level of parallelism						
More prominent						
Sentence	5	1	7	5	3	6
Main clause	9	11	5	6	5	3
Totals	14	12	12	11	8	9
Less prominent						
Subordinate clause	11	6	7	7	5	1
Phrase	16	15	12	10	6	8
Number of members						
Doublet	40	32	25	26	18	14
Triplet	1	0	2	1	1	2
Series	0	1	4	1	0	2

stances of lexical parallelism at the most prominent levels, namely, sentence and main clause: 31, 22, 23, and 21 instances, compared to Baldwin's 14 as the next highest. And she has more triplets (4, 7, 6, 5) than the other writers, none of whom has more than two. In short, Didion uses prominent lexical parallelism more frequently than the other writers studied, typically far more frequently.

LEXICAL PARALLELISM AND THE RHETORIC OF PROCESS

I want to look now at how and why Didion's frequent use of lexical parallelism is compatible with the rhetoric of process that character-izes her prose. A good place to start is with the limits of purely quantitative study: as Lanham (1983) says about Tom Wolfe's use of anaphora, "You won't necessarily find out how Wolfe uses anaphora by counting them" (p. 155). The same holds true for Didion's use of the various types of lexical parallelism. For though lexical parallelism is usually associated with certain general effects (e.g., hammering a point home), such parallelism actually can have many different effects. Wright (1965) puts it well with regard to the figures of repetition in general: "the figures, as is the case with 'sound symbolism,' have no intrinsic force; they are differing means of emphasis, and what they emphasize depends on their context" (p. 94).

A full treatment of context would include both the macrocontext and microcontext. But here I want to focus on just the macrocontext. For Didion, three aspects of that context (and their interpenetration) are particularly important: genres of writing, spoken conversation, and the individual writer.

In terms of genre, Didion's nonfiction consists of essays and journalism (mainly feature articles). Anderson (1987) claims, rightly I believe, that Didion's "most important and representative work falls into the category of the essay" (p. 142). However, he also argues that there is not much difference between Didion's essays and her journalism: "Her work is an important hybrid of the essay and journalism; her journalism is essay-like; her essays are journalistic" (p. 144). While I would not go quite this far—there are differences in the mixture of the two genres in her writing[3]—I believe that Anderson is correct in finding in much of Didion's nonfiction "the quality of reflective/exploratory writing" (p. 142), a quality associated with the tradition of the essay, especially the personal essay, deriving ultimately from Montaigne.[4] Personal essays usually have a tentative quality, are based on personal experience and observation, assume a tone of intimacy, are self-revelatory, and have a structure that is not systematic but organic, reflecting a mind in the act of thinking (Holman & Harmon, 1986, pp. 186–190; Good, 1988, pp. 1–25; Klaus, 1989, pp. 155–175). Much of Didion's nonfiction has just these characteristics. Didion prefers the particular to the general, the concrete to the abstract, so that whatever meaning she finds or constructs has a tentative, provisional quality, rooted in and depen-

---

[3] While most of Didion's nonfiction does indeed represent a fusion of the essay and journalism, some of it is essentially in the tradition of the personal essay, and some of it is essentially journalistic (Henderson, 1981, pp. 92–93, 121).

[4] Essays are usually divided into two major types, formal and informal; the personal essay is a type of informal essay. However, Klaus (1989) argues persuasively that essayists think in terms of the essay as a genre without giving much attention to such distinctions as formal versus informal essays.

dent on the specific circumstances of her experience, her thinking, her writing (Anderson, 1987, pp. 133–141). The content of Didion's nonfiction tends to be, not just particular, but personal, or made personal (Taylor, 1983, p. 138). Didion's tone, except in her pure reportage, tends to be intimate; Winchell (1989, p. 12) remarks that "she comes perilously close to being the journalistic equivalent of a confessional poet." This is not surprising, since Didion (1976) says, "I write entirely to find out what I'm thinking, what I'm looking at, what I see and what it means. What I want and what I fear" (p. 2). And she has found the most congenial forms for this self-exploration to be association and juxtaposition (Anderson, 1987, pp. 134–140).

The essay, especially the personal essay as characterized above and as practiced by Didion, has obvious affinities with spoken conversation: the exploration of matters of personal concern, the assumed relationship of friendship or even intimacy, the strong element of self-revelation, and the seemingly spontaneous structuring related to the unfolding topics and individual response. Moreover, critics typically draw implicitly if not explicitly on a comparison of the essay to conversation, most notably in discussing an essayist's voice (Elbow, 1989, pp. 211–234).[5] The tradition starts with Montaigne, who "gave the death of his friend Etienne de La Boétie as his main reason for beginning essay-writing as a substitute for their conversations" (Good, 1988, p. 13). But an affinity with conversation is not the same as an impression of conversation, and essays can and do differ greatly in the extent to which they convey such an impression. What is crucial here is that Didion is much more insistent and consistent in creating an impression of conversation (particularly in her essays) than the other writers included in this study. The devices she uses to achieve this effect are mainly those Anderson (1987, pp. 133–41) associates with Didion's three characteristic strategies: the rhetoric of particularity (reliance on images and details), the rhetoric of gaps (reliance on juxtapositioning without subordination, transitional words, interpretation, or commentary), and the rhetoric of process (use of statement followed by modification or qualification, parentheses, repetition of predicates, polysyndeton, cumulative sentences, simple coordination, deictics, and qualifiers). Most of these devices are usually associated with conversation or the impression of conversation (Wardhaugh, 1986, p. 287;

---

[5] Elbow (1989) connects the sense of voice partly to how sayable the prose is, which is connected in turn partly to the degree to which the prose has the rhythms and cadences of speech. Didion's prose has those rhythms and cadences to a high degree, but that point merits a separate study.

Leech & Short, 1981, pp. 228–233). Perhaps the most salient is Didion's frequent use of *I, we,* and especially *you* to create conversation-like involvement. Here is a good example:

8.   <u>You</u> might protest that no family has been in the Sacramento Valley for anything approaching "always." . . . In fact that is what <u>I</u> want to tell <u>you</u> about: what it is like to come from a place like Sacramento. If <u>I</u> could make <u>you</u> understand that, <u>I</u> could make <u>you</u> understand California. (Didion, 1968, p. 172)

Moreover, many of Didion's other favorite devices are among the involvement strategies Tannen (1989, p. 17) lists as ones "that researchers have identified in conversation [and] which literary analysts have independently identified as important in literary discourse": repetition and variation, style figures of speech, tropes, dialogue, and narrative. The presence of style figures on the list is particularly significant, since that category includes lexical parallelism. It is a point that needs to be stressed: Though lexical parallelism is typically associated with rhetorical artifice and, by an easy progression, with artificiality, such parallelism does in fact turn up in naturally occurring conversation.[6]

More to the point, it turns up in Didion's conversation, at least in the serious conversation of an interview. Here are two of the many instances of prominent lexical parallelism that occur in recent published interviews:

9.   When I'm working I don't read much. <u>If it's a good book it will depress me because mine</u> isn't as good. <u>If it's a bad book it will depress me because mine's</u> just as bad. (Davidson, 1984, pp. 18–19)
10. <u>I am</u> not only small, <u>I am</u> too thin, <u>I am</u> pale, <u>I</u> do not look like a California person. (Stamberg, 1984, p. 27)

Finally, it is worth noting that Didion uses prominent lexical parallelism several times as well in the brief preface to *Bethlehem* (1968, pp. xi–xiv), which she has said was written quickly and "rather in my own voice" (Stamberg, 1984, p. 25).

---

[6] Tannen (1989, pp. 71, 22) provides several examples, including example 11 below and the following: "*then it works, then it's* a good idea" (anaphora); *It's a good idea in terms of eating, it's not a good idea in terms of* time" (anaphora); "if I don't prepare and *eat* well, I *eat* a LOT" (medial); "And so if I'm just eating like *cheese and crackers,* I'll just STUFF myself on *cheese and crackers*" (epistrophe); "CAMP was LIFE! My whole *life* was *camp!*" (chiasmus).

With the notion of Didion's own voice comes the third aspect of context I want to discuss, the individual writer. In Didion's case it is not easy to distinguish between the voice of the living writer and the voice that comes through the writing. Much of her nonfiction is an effort at self-definition; as Winchell (1989) says, "her writing seems to be a search for identity, an attempt to create a fictive persona with which to impose artistic coherence upon the randomness of life" (p. 1). In this way the expressing of self becomes the making of self. The self Didion expresses/creates in her nonfiction has certain characteristics that seem relevant to her frequent use of lexical parallelism. One is seriousness: the psychological seriousness of a woman who often sounds on the edge; the artistic seriousness of a professional craftsman for whom every word counts; the moral seriousness of a culture critic who has a rigid sense of right and wrong, even if she claims to apply it only to herself (Stamberg, 1984, pp. 23–24). Traditionally, lexical parallelism has been the language of seriousness: of religious writing and preaching, political oratory, high literature. Another, related Didion characteristic is a powerful attraction to ritual, where lexical parallelism typically has had a prominent role. Didion "was brought up Episcopalian," and though she stopped going to church, she has said, "I like the words of the Episcopal service, and I say them over and over in my mind" (Davidson, 1984, p. 18). Didion's attraction to ritual is not only deep and wide-ranging (extending to "little compulsive rituals" like cooking and sewing, as well as to going back to Sacramento to finish each of her books), but also is seemingly part of an attraction to the formal and the aesthetic, symbolized nicely by Didion's predilection for "using good silver every day" (Davidson, 1984, p. 19). It is not surprising, then, that Didion seems fond of the formal patterning of lexical parallelism, or that she puts it to everyday use. Finally, Didion is a perfectionist, and perfectionism often involves repetition in the effort to get something exactly right. She has said that Henry James was important for her "in trying to come to terms with the impossibility of getting it right" (Davidson, 1984, p. 18). But she has also associated the dread of going into her office each morning with the "fear you're not going to get it right. You're going to ruin it. You're going to fail." (Davidson, 1984, pp. 15–16). And anyone who spends "most of a week writing and rewriting and not writing a single paragraph" (Didion, 1979, p. 171) has yet to come fully to terms with the impossibility of perfection. The important point, though, is that Didion's frequent use of lexical parallelism can be connected in part to the effort to get it right, whether that effort is a function of

neurotic perfectionism, conscious craftsmanship, moral seriousness, or all three.

So far I have stressed that Didion's use of lexical parallelism needs
to be interpreted in context, and that three aspects of context are
especially relevant: the personal essay as the genre Didion charac-
teristically writes in; spoken conversation, an impression of which
she is usually at pains to convey; and the serious self she projects in
that "conversation," one attracted to ritual, the formal, and the
aesthetic—and a perfectionist. I want to take the next step now and
try to relate Didion's use of lexical parallelism to these aspects of
context, and particularly to their interpenetration. Of the many
points that could be discussed, I will focus on just two: the types of
lexical parallelism Didion uses, and the way Didion often blends
lexical parallelism and apposition.

Just as the other writers studied, Didion mainly uses anaphora
and makes much less use of the rarer types of lexical parallelism.
What anaphora offers is a frame for producing discourse fluently
and spontaneously, and in this respect it is quite consonant with
and useful in spoken conversation. As Tannen (1989, p. 48) says,
"repetition . . . enables a speaker to produce fluent speech while
formulating what to say next," as in the following example of anaphora, which Tannen gives from an oral narrative (transcription
altered):

11. And he knows Spanish, and he knows French, and he knows English,
     and he knows German, and he is a gentleman.

Many of Didion's instances of anaphora, especially at the level of
sentence or main clause, have a similar effect—as if she is using
anaphora as a frame to recollect or think something through. Sometimes the frame involves a repeated pronoun and verb, as in examples 3, 10, and the following:

12. I remember driving up Wilhemina Rise to look for Alma's house and I
     remember walking out of the Royal Hawaiian Hotel and expecting to
     see Prewitt and Maggio sitting on the curb and I remember walking the
     Waialae Country Club golf course, trying to figure exactly where Prew-
     itt died. (Didion, 1979, p. 147)

Sometimes the frame involves a repeated subordinating conjunction, infinitive marker, or preposition:

13. A few days ago someone just four years younger than I am told me that
     he did not see why a sunken ship should affect me so, that John

Kennedy's assassination, not Pearl Harbor, was the single most indelible event of what he kept calling "our generation." (Didion, 1968, pp. 192–193)

14.   I am interested in the folklore of Howard Hughes, in the way people react to him, in the terms they use when they talk about him. (Didion 1968, p. 68)

In any event such uses of anaphora are compatible with the impression both of a mind in the act of thinking and of one person talking to another.

The other point I want to make about Didion's use of lexical parallelism is that there is frequently an appositional quality to it that reflects a process of thinking. I am using apposition here in the extended sense developed by Dillon (1978):

Basically, apposition is the juxtaposition of two or more like phrases or clauses without a conjunction. Semantically, the difference between coordination and apposition is crucial—coordinated elements are almost always understood as referring to different things, appositives to the same thing. Usually apposition is discussed in terms of noun phrases, but other elements can also be appositively juxtaposed. (p. 90)

As an example of the difference between coordination and apposition, Dillon offers a sentence from Henry James's *The Ambassadors*:

15.   Chad and Miss Gostrey had rummaged and purchased and picked up and exchanged, sifting, selecting, comparing.

The verbs *rummaged, purchased, picked up,* and *exchanged* "refer to different (though closely related) actions" and therefore constitute coordination; the verbs *sifting, selecting, comparing* "refer to the same action" and so constitute apposition. Thus processing an appositive means distinguishing it from coordination, and the main structural clue one looks for is the presence of a coordinating conjunction before the last item: when a conjunction is there, one takes the items as coordinated; when a conjunction is not there, one takes the items as apposed. Dillon goes on to distinguish five semantic types of apposition—synonymous, specifying, generalizing, replacing, and a type he describes as "a mix of coordination and apposition" (p. 99).

Dillon's extended sense of apposition fits Didion's practice well, since Didion frequently juxtaposes parallel phrases or clauses without a coordinating conjunction.[7] Sometimes these phrases or clauses occur without lexical repetition:

16.   Only one person I knew at Berkeley later discovered an ideology, dealt himself into history, cut himself loose from both his own dread and his own time. (Didion, 1979, p. 208)

More frequently, though, the juxtaposed phrases or clauses not only are parallel but also occur with lexical repetition and so constitute both lexical parallelism with asyndeton and apposition, as in examples 10, 13, and 14. Here are a few more examples:

17.   It might have been <u>anyone's</u> bad summer, <u>anyone's</u> siege of heat and nerves and migraine. (Didion, 1968, p. 9)
18.   I happen to know about that trip because I <u>come from</u> California, <u>come from</u> a family, or a congeries of families, that has always been in the Sacramento Valley. (Didion, 1968, pp. 171–172)
19.   Language as it is now used in El Salvador is the language <u>of</u> advertising, <u>of</u> persuasion. (Didion, 1983, p. 65)

Most of the instances are of the specifying type of apposition (examples 14 and 18) or the mix of coordination and apposition, as in example 13 and the following:

20.   There was <u>a trip</u> to pick up a prescription for Nembutal, <u>a trip</u> to a self-service dry cleaner. (Didion, 1968, p. 9)

But instances of the other semantic types of apposition occur as well: generalizing in example 19, synonymous in example in 21, and replacing in example 22:

21.   There had been . . . <u>fewer</u> dead around since the election, <u>fewer</u> bodies, they thought, than in the capital. (Didion, 1983, pp. 47–48)
22.   . . . at <u>night</u>, most <u>nights</u>, I walked outside. (Didion, 1979, p. 208)

Apposition of the sort I have been talking about so far is a grammatical relationship involving elements within a sentence; however, there can be appositive-like relationships between sentences, too. Indeed, many instances of sentence-level lexical parallelism in Didion's nonfiction are juxtaposed, usually short sentences in which the semantic relationships between sentences look much like types

---

[7] Anderson (1987) calls the appositive Didion's characteristic modifier but limits the reference to "a redefining noun phrase" (p. 139).

of apposition. The most frequent relationship is the mix of coordination and apposition, as in examples 5, 9, and 23:

23. <u>Many</u> mean guilts had been recalled and exorcised. <u>Many</u> lessons had been divined, in both the death and the life. (Didion, 1979, p. 147)

But specification also occurs, as in examples 3, 6, and 24:

24. People <u>were missing</u>. Children <u>were missing</u>. Parents <u>were missing</u>. (Didion, 1968, p. 84)

What makes Didion's use of appositive or appositive-like lexical parallelism especially significant is its frequency. Of the 197 instances of lexical parallelism where asyndeton could occur, 97 (49%) have co-occurring asyndeton and are therefore appositive in the extended sense of the term. Moreover, most involve only two units and so do not even fit some definitions of asyndeton, for example, Hiatt's (1975): "omission of conjunctions in triplets and series" (p. 59). In effect this strengthens an appositional interpretation of a great many of Didion's instances of lexical parallelism, anaphora in particular, since so many are doublets without a coordinating conjunction.

Let me end by making explicit how I think Didion's use of asyndetic lexical parallelism contributes both syntactically and semantically to her rhetoric of process. Most of the instances within the sentence occur as what Leech and Short (1981, p. 229) call *trailing constituents* (i.e., final dependent constituents and noninitial coordinate constituents), which are associated with loose structure and the qualities of "easiness, relaxation, informality: the qualities one expects, in fact, in fairly unconsidered use of language." Didion is too serious to seem relaxed and too artful to seem to be using language in an unconsidered way. But the frequent trailing constituents, including those that involve asyndetic lexical parallelism, do suggest the sense of a mind exploring, modifying, refining ideas. The instances of lexical parallelism that occur in sentences juxtaposed without explicit linkage, instances that I have suggested are appositive-like, also convey a similar impression, where connections are implicit, embedded in the flux of experience, and still in the making.

Semantically, all five types of apposition also contribute to a sense of an ongoing process of thinking. Four of the types—synonymous, specifying, generalizing, and replacing—are similar in that, as Dillon (1978, p. 99) says, "the final appositive has the last word—that is, it comes at the end of what often appears to be a process of getting it just right," which, as we have seen, is a preoccupation of Didion's. Dillon adds that "a writer may essentially develop his thinking about something through a string of appositives." Often Didion seems to be doing just that. The other semantic type of apposition—the mix of coordination and apposition—also ties in with a central effect in Didion: the sense she gives that she is still trying to sort things out, still trying to decide if two things are the same thing or two different things, or whether they are so linked that it is not possible to tell if they are one or two, and wrong to suggest that you can tell. Perhaps the frequent mix of coordination and apposition in Didion's nonfiction is meant to be doubly iconic: to embody the way Didion sees things, and at the same time to cause readers to experience for themselves, as they try to process all those juxtaposed parallel items, exactly how difficult it can be to sort things out and get it right.

REFERENCES

Anderson, C. (1987). *Style as argument: Contemporary American nonfiction.* Carbondale, IL: Southern Illinois University Press.

Baldwin, J. (1955). *Notes of a native son.* Boston: Beacon Press.

Berlin, A. (1985). *The dynamics of biblical parallelism.* Bloomington, IN: Indiana University Press.

Cluett, R. (1976). *Prose style and critical reading.* New York: Teachers College Press.

Davidson, S. (1984). A visit with Joan Didion. In E. G. Friedman (Ed.), *Joan Didion: Essays and conversations* (pp. 13–21). Princeton, NJ: Ontario Review Press.

Didion, J. (1968). *Slouching towards Bethlehem.* New York: Farrar.

Didion, J. (1976, December 5). Why I write. *New York Times Book Review,* pp. 2, 98–99.

Didion, J. (1979). *The white album.* New York: Simon.

Didion, J. (1983). *Salvador.* New York: Simon.

Dillon, G. L. (1978). *Language processing and the reading of literature: Toward a model of comprehension.* Bloomington, IN: Indiana University Press.

Elbow, P. (1989). The pleasures of voice in the literary essay: Explorations in the prose of Gretel Ehrlich and Richard Selzer. In C. Anderson (Ed.), *Literary nonfiction: Theory, criticism, pedagogy* (pp. 211–234). Carbondale, IL: Southern Illinois University Press.

Good, G. (1988). *The observing self: Rediscovering the essay.* London: Routledge.

Hiatt, M. P. (1975). *Artful balance: The parallel structures of style.* New York: Teachers College Press.

Henderson, K. U. (1981). *Joan Didion.* New York: Ungar.

Holman, C. H., & Harmon, W. (1986). *A handbook to literature* (5th ed.). New York: Macmillan.

King, M. L., Jr. (1964). *Why we can't wait.* New York: Harper.

Klaus, C. H. (1989). Essayists on the essay. In C. Anderson (Ed.), *Literary nonfiction: Theory, criticism, pedagogy* (pp. 155–175). Carbondale, IL: Southern Illinois University Press.

Lanham, R. A. (1983). *Analyzing prose.* New York: Scribner's.

Leech, G. (1969). *A linguistic guide to English poetry.* London: Longman.

Leech, G. N., & Short, M. H. (1981). *Style in fiction: A linguistic introduction to English fictional prose.* London: Longman.

Orwell, G. (1954). *A collection of essays.* Garden City, NY: Doubleday.

Stamberg, S. (1984). Cautionary tales. In E. G. Friedman (Ed.), *Joan Didion: Essays and conversations* (pp. 22–28). Princeton, NJ: Ontario Review Press.

Tannen, D. (1989). *Talking voices: Repetition, dialogue, and imagery in in conversational discourse.* Cambridge, UK: Cambridge University Press.

Taylor, G. O. (1983). *Chapters of experience: Studies in 20th century American autobiography.* New York: St. Martin's.

Thomas, L. (1974). *The lives of a cell: Notes of a biology watcher.* New York: Viking Press.

Wardhaugh, R. (1986). *An introduction to sociolinguistics.* Oxford: Blackwell.

White, E. B. (1977). *Essays of E. B. White.* New York: Harper.

Winchell, M. R. (1989). *Joan Didion* (rev. ed.). Boston: Twayne.

Wolfe, T. (1968). *The kandy-kolored tangerine-flake streamline baby.* New York: Farrar.

Wright, K. (1965). Rhetorical repetition in T. S. Eliot's early verse. *Review of English Literature, 6*(2), 93–100.

Chapter 9
Repetition and Text-Building in Classical Thai Poetry

Thomas John Hudak

Department of Anthropology
Arizona State University

For over 700 years Thailand has had a rich literary heritage, much of it unknown in the West. Until 1932, most of this literature was composed in one of five classical verse forms: *râay, khlooŋ, kàap, chăn,* and *klɔɔn.* Buddhist birth stories, didactic tales, royal ceremonies, and imaginative romances filled with the fantastic provided topics for poetic compositions. In Thailand, literary analyses of this body of work have been primarily concerned with biographical summaries and attempts to determine when and where many of the poems were composed. Other studies have aimed at duplicating the traditional versification textbooks, the *chănthálák,* in which the verse forms are meticulously described. In the West, critical analyses of Thai poetics have begun to appear only in the past two decades. Most of these studies examine the historical development of the meters (Gedney, 1978; Bickner, 1981; Hudak, 1990). Only Bofman (1984) and Bickner (1989) have provided examinations of text-building strategies involved in extended narratives. Other studies have concentrated on specific genres (Chitakasen, 1972), rhyming patterns (Hudak, 1986, 1987), and poetic devices (Hudak, 1985, 1988).

In 1767, the ancient Thai capital of Ayutthaya was completely destroyed by the Burmese. Then, in 1782, the capital was reestablished on the present site of Bangkok. Without a doubt, these political events represent a major division between ancient Thailand and the beginning of the modern nation. Interestingly, along with these political changes there seems to have been a concurrent change in the literary practice. That is, much of the poetry produced up until the destruction of Ayutthaya can be characterized by specific structural components that appear over and over again. On the other hand, the poetry produced after the founding of Bangkok seems to be characterized by a different group of components, even though the literary topics remain the same as those of the Ayutthaya period (1351–1767). No major examination of this theory has yet been conducted. The brief analysis of *Sàmùtthákhôot kham chăn* ("The Story of Samutthakhoot") in this chapter is an attempt to delineate components characteristic of the literature of Ayutthaya, all of which involve patterns created by repetition, and repetition of these patterns.

As a composition attributed to the Ayutthaya period, *Sàmùtthákhôot kham chăn* is unique both for its length (2,221 stanzas, while most others are only 100–200 stanzas) and for the history of its composition. Begun by the court astrologer and teacher Maharatchakhru during the reign of King Narai (1656–1688), it was inexplicably left unfinished. Literary history holds that King Narai himself then composed a portion but also failed to complete it. Finally, in the mid-19th century, Prince Paramanuchit Chinorot (1790–1853), the Supreme Patriarch and a renowned Indian classicist, took up the task of finishing the poem. An indigenous Buddhist birth tale, *Sàmùtthákhôot kham chăn* depicts the adventures of the Buddha in one of his former lives, that of Prince Samutthakhoot. His adventures in the heavenly realms and upon the earth provide the opportunity to illustrate and teach the morals and precepts associated with Buddhism. Even though it was composed by three separate authors, the poem is considered one of the best poetic compositions of the classical Thai period. The structural components used to build this text, as well as other texts during this period, are easily delineated. All are based on different types of repetition. These components are of two types: those predetermined and requisite for the formal construction of a poem, and those created and used freely by the poets.

PREDETERMINED STRUCTURAL COMPONENTS

Thai poets and scholars have always claimed that, for a poem to exist, rhyme must be present. While this statement is certainly true for Thai poetics, it does not go far enough, for meter and stanzaic organization are also required. All three components are given, in the sense that these were the structures with which the poets worked. The classical poets did not create new meters or stanzaic forms, although they were free to rearrange the required patterns of rhyme.

The creation of a meter represents the simplest use of repetition. As Fussell (1979, pp. 4–5) notes, "meter is what results when the natural rhythmical movements of colloquial speech are heightened, organized so that pattern—which means repetition—emerges from the relative phonetic haphazard of ordinary utterance." In Thai, colloquial speech tends to fall into natural groups of two or three syllables in phonological or syntactic phrases:

phîan	khǎw	yùu	thîi	bâan
friend	he	be	at	house

His friend is at home.

In classical poetry, groups such as those in the above example have been formalized into a variety of different meters. In some cases, as in *kàap* and *chǎn*, the final forms taken by the meters were influenced not only by the structure of the Thai language but also by the language from which the meter was borrowed, Khmer for *kàap* and Sanskrit and Pali for *chǎn*.

The classical poets worked with a fixed set of verse forms. They did not introduce new meters into the corpus or develop new stanzaic forms. Nevertheless, the original formation of the metric lines into patterns designated as stanzas did involve the use of repetition. In the case of Thai, the minimal stanza is one determined by the presence of a couplet, that is, two lines linked together by two end syllables with the same final vowel or vowel + consonant. The length of each line, of course, had already been predetermined by the metrical pattern. With the basic stanza set at two lines, a variety of different stanza types were created by adding additional couplets or variations on the couplets. Thus some stanzas were formed by adding lines in which another couplet was defined, the end syllable of one line rhyming with one of the first three syllables (generally) in the following line. Still more complicated stanzas resulted from the combination of several different couplets. All of the various types of stanzas possible in classical poetry are described in accurate detail in the versification textbooks known as *chănthálák*, and occasionally in literary anthologies. These discussions are largely prescriptive with no analytical or historical discussion of their development. (For an in-depth discussion of the development of the *chăn* meters, see Hudak, 1990; and for the five classical meters in general, see Gedney, 1978.)

The third area of poetics determined by patterns of repetition is rhyme. Like meters and stanzaic patterns, patterns of rhyme are in many cases predetermined. Two types of rhyme exist, external and internal. *External rhyme* occurs between syllables at the end of lines and is required for the formation of the stanzaic couplets. *Internal rhyme* occurs between syllables within a line and is considered necessary for a composition to be aesthetically pleasing. Any examination of classical poetry reveals all of these patterns. Classical poetry, however, also exhibits a large variety of other rhyming patterns not identified by the poets but nevertheless present in the very best of the compositions. It seems to be the case that the very best poetic compositions incorporate the required patterns as well as the others. By contrast, mediocre compositions only attempt to use the required patterns.

Thai versification textbooks list two types of internal rhyme, vocalic and consonantal (alliteration). *Vocalic rhyme* requires the repetition of the same final vowel or the same final vowel + consonant. These rhymes are then grouped into different patterns of two rhyming syllables, three rhyming syllables, two different sets of rhyming syllables, two rhyming syllables with one intervening syllable, and two rhyming syllables with two intervening syllables. *Consonant rhyme* involves the reduplication of initial consonants arranged into patterns similar to the vocalic ones: two paired syllables, three contiguous syllables, four contiguous syllables, two sets of paired syllables, two paired syllables with one intervening syllable, and two paired syllables with two intervening syllables. Other reduplicative techniques include *consonance*, the reduplication of a final consonant with a different vowel preceding it; *pararhyme*, the reduplication of the initial and final consonant with a different intervening vowel; *reverse rhyme*, the reduplication of the initial consonant and vowel with a different final consonant; *semialliteration*, the reduplication of initial consonants which are the same except for some phonetic feature(s); *semiconsonance*, the reduplication of final consonants which are the same except for some phonetic feature(s);

assonance, the reduplication of the vowel with different final consonants; and *semiassonance*, the reduplication of vowels which are
the same except for some phonetic feature(s).

Meters, stanzas, and rhyme patterns were also used in the poetry
composed after the establishment of Bangkok. What had shifted,
however, was the preference for specific meters. Whereas *khlooŋ*,
kàap, and *chăn* dominated the Ayutthaya period, *klɔɔn* became the
preferred meter of the Bangkok era.

VARIABLE STRUCTURAL COMPONENTS

In the classical poetic compositions, the emphasis is upon story and
the formal techniques of producing *phayrɔ́?*, the pleasing sound
quality so important to Thai poetry. While most scholars and analy-
sists see *phayrɔ́?* as the sole result of the rhyme patterns, longer
poetical works such as *Sàmùtthákhôot kham chăn* demonstrate
that the aesthetic cohesiveness of the poems results from the use of
a variety of different devices, all a result of different repeated patterns. Moreover, it appears that these devices are not only essential
to the idea of a poem but are also essential to the building of an
extended text. These devices do not have any required order of appearance but appear as dictated by the plot of the story.

Three components help determine the overall structure of the
poem. First and foremost, each poem is begun with a section that
praises the three gems—the Buddha, the Sangha, and the Dharma;
the Hindu deities; the king; and the poet's teachers. While the meter
employed is not important, the presence of the section is. A second structural component is the summary. In the case of *Sàmùtthákhôot kham chăn*, a summary of the entire poem is placed before
the start of the poem. Similar units of summary appear throughout
the poem. Thus when Samutthakhoot locates his lost wife by recognizing their lives depicted in a frieze, the poet retells the entire story
up until that point. The purpose of these summaries remains open
to conjecture; however, if the poem were meant to be recited or to be
used as the text for a shadow puppet show, the summaries may have
been incorporated to remind the audience of what has occurred,
which seems entirely reasonable given the informality with which
these shows were presented, the audience moving about or chatting
in a highly informal atmosphere. In the poem under examination,
these summaries are signaled with the repetition of the lexical item
paaŋ "then, at that time" at the start of each stanza in the summary. A third component, based on the structure of the Buddhist birth

tales, completes *Sàmùtthákhôot kham chăn.* That is, there is a section that identifies the characters with the individuals that occur in the Buddha's life.

Within the body of the poem proper, certain devices occur so repeatedly that it must be said that they characterize, not only the poem under study, but also the poetry produced during the Ayutthaya period. As noted above, these devices appear when needed in the plot. They are not so much methods of advancing the plot as means of elaborating it. The first of these devices is the *descriptive passage*, a passage used to describe a person, place, or thing. In general, descriptive passages all have the same structure: a prelude that locates the description within the story, a body that is the description proper, and a coda that forms a transition back to the story. Within the body, the description generally follows a specific overall arrangement that may be arranged spatially, chronologically, or by means of some other mode of organization. For a temple, the description begins at the finials, then moves to the roofs, the eaves, the walls, the doors, the inside walls, the interior of the temple, the stairs leading out of the temple, the surrounding grounds, and finally the forest. For a city, the description begins outside the city walls, moves to the doors and ramparts, then to each of the encircling walls and moats, then to the city proper and its streets and buildings, and finally to the palace which forms the center of the city. Chronological descriptions simply summarize an event from its inception until its conclusion.

The structural arrangement of each of these different types of descriptions is roughly the same. Each stanza forms a single semantic unit that may consist of a single topic and comment. Other stanzas may have two topics and two comments, or some stanzas may consist solely of topics in which case the stanzas form part of a catalogue (for an in-depth discussion of descriptive passages, see Hudak, 1988).

Closely aligned to the descriptive passages are the *catalogues*. Catalogues appear in the text generally in conjunction with one of the characters, the accumulation of the objects in the catalogue helping to suggest or emphasize the character's mood. Thus, when Prince Samutthakhoot sees the birds and fish with their mates, he is propelled into a melancholy that is highlighted by the sheer number of birds and fish enumerated. In another instance, when a heavenly deity has lost his wife in a battle, he mourns her loss. The agony is emphasized by the listing of each of the features of the lost love and how they remind him of her. In contrast, in the justly famous erotic passages of classical Thai poetry, each of the beauty's features is listed, but in this case each feature helps to excite the prince.

The structural arrangement of catalogues tends to have one of five forms. The first is a catalogue of items from a single semantic group. That is, the catalogue items are of a single type but have no internal organization. Examples include a list of flowers, or birds, or fish. The second type is organized by consonantal or vocalic rhyme, although the consonantal seems more common, as with the alliterating *k* in the following example:

kûŋ	kâŋ	kùmáphin	mákɔɔn	kràchɔn	chon	kɔ̂	wâay
shrimp	fish	fish	fish	shake	water	then	swim

kòt	kaa	lɛ́	krim	kraay
fish	fish	and	fish	fish

kràtràp
fish

Kung, kang, kumaphin, makorn shook the water swimming
With the kot, ka, krim, kray
And kratrap.

The third variety is a mixture of the first two. In the following catalogue of animals, a variety of different vocalic and consonantal patterns dominate:

kwaaŋ	saay	lámâŋ	kàp	tháŋ	kàthiŋ
deer	deer	deer	with	all	bison

kɔ̂	waaŋ	wîŋ	ná	phraywan
then	release	run	at	forest

khǎnkhaa	wáraahà	kháná	phan
rhino	boar	group	group

chámót	mêen	chàmǎn	mǐi
civet	skunk	stag	bear

Deer, antlered and without, bison,
Ran about the forest.
Rhinos, boars in packs,
Civets, skunks, stags, and bears.

The fourth incorporates punning as the organizational principle. For example, as the prince walks through the woods he looks at the trees and flowers, the name of each having a secondary meaning that describes his emotions at the moment.

sàwàat	phrít	rálìk	pràlêe	sàwàat
tree type	tree	remind	as	love, pleasure

wárárâatcháswǎamii
royal husband

máy	rák	mǐan	rák	nárábɔ̀diisǔan
tree	tree type	like	love	king

ráaŋ	sànèe	naan
abandon	love	long time

The sawat tree reminds me of the love and pleasure (sawat)
Of my noble royal husband.
The rak tree is like the king's love (rak),
His love now long absent.

The last catalogue type also fits the requirements for a descriptive passage, for it describes something, usually a woman, listing each of the features and how it affects the speaker. Another example of a descriptive catalogue is the description of the ancient army with its four divisions: the elephant battalions, the horse battalions, the chariot battalions, and the infantry. In this catalogue, the unit being described is listed in the first hemistich of the stanza with the remainder of the stanzas completing the description. Army catalogues run for numerous stanzas, with each of the four units treated to a lengthy description. In the case of the descriptions of the army written in the *chǎn* meters during the Ayutthaya period, the same meter is repeatedly used so that its appearance is almost always associated with this type of catalogue.

phon	khóchá	kháná	hǎanhàk
force	elephant	group	brave, bold

kàreenthɔɔn	pàk
elephant trunk	party, group

pràap	pràlay
subdue	destroy

Elephant forces, very brave;
Elephant trunks
Subduing and destroying.

phon	khóchá	kháná	sə̀ək	kàsǎy
force	elephant	group	enemy	end

chìaw	sàmâat	chay
skilled	capable	victory

chamnaan   ron
proficient   battle

Elephant forces eliminating enemies:
Skilled in victory,
Skilled in fighting.

Other components are more directly associated with the characters and their actions. Thus, certain actions of the royal character always appear, even though they may be extraneous to the development of the plot. With a king or prince, there is always a royal bath, a ceremonial dressing in the royal regalia, and a departure scene that frequently moves into a descriptive catalogue of the army. In most cases, these sections appear in one of the forms already discussed, descriptive passages or catalogues.

With royal characters, conversations are handled in a manner that characterizes the whole of the poetry produced during the Ayutthaya period. Specifically, conversations are very stylized. Each interchange begins with a set phrase that is repeated throughout the conversation with a slight variation. For example, in a conversation between the prince and his beloved, the conversation may begin with a vocative, a pronoun or kinship term appropriate to the addressee, and occasionally an epithet that provides information about the addressee. Only after the formalized means of address have been completed does the conversation proceed. These stylized exchanges continue until the conversation has been completed:

ʔâa   mɛ̂ɛ   càk   mɨa   khlay
oh   mother   will   go   walk

thít   day   kɔ̂   daan   chàŋǒn
direction   which   then   create   confusion

Oh, my beloved, where'll we go?
In which direction? I'm lost and confused.

ʔâa   phrá   cà   dəən   dàt
oh   noble   will   walk   make a path

phánát   sɨ̂ŋ   khánɨŋ   khànǎaŋ
forest   which   think   doubt

Oh, my beloved noble one, if we go
Into the forest, I'm unsure.

In another exchange, a repeated formalized question and answer form the cohesive factors.

khŭn	day	ʔan	khìi	sùwan	rót
noble	which?	which	ride	gold	vehicle

Which noble rides in the golden chariot?

khŭn	nán	chïi	tháaw	mákhɔɔnrâat
noble	that	name	prince	(name)

That noble's called Prince Makhornrat.

Returning to the meters reveals a further organizational principle. That is, a close examination of the particular meters used and their content shows that specific meters are used with specific topics, a concept occasionally mentioned by critics in the versification textbooks. In *Sàmùtthákhôot kham chăn*, the *chăn* meters are used in the following manner: *wàsăntàdilòk chăn 14*—stylized dialogues and actions of the royalty; *ʔintháráwíchian chăn 11*—descriptive passages and catalogues; *maalínii chăn 15*—descriptions of the army; *sàttháraa chăn 21*—a single climactic point; *tòdòkkàʔ chăn 12*—a single climactic point. Besides the *chăn* meters, the poets of *Sàmùtthákhôot kham chăn* have employed the *kàap* meters which also have specific functions: *kàap chàbaŋ 16*—general narration; *kàap sùraaŋkhánaaŋ 28*—rapid conversation between nonroyalty and summaries.

The striking feature of the variable components is the regularity with which all of them appear in the poetry of the Ayutthaya period. As noted earlier, *Sàmùtthákhôot kham chăn* was composed by three different poets, with the final portion not completed until well into the 19th century, when the style of poetry had already changed radically. However, Prince Paramanuchit, the author of this part, rigorously followed the conventions and devices used by the poets who wrote during the 17th century, including the characteristic use of the meters for specific topics. If the *chan* poetry written during the 20th century were examined, the same conventions and devices would most likely be found.

CONCLUSION

Repeated patterns provide the building blocks for the construction of all poetry. The repetition of individual sounds, of syllables, and of syllabic organization form the required structural components for any poem, pre- or post-Ayutthaya. Further elaboration, rearrangement, and repetition of phonological and syntactic patterns provide the basis for the variable components which contribute to a far more complex structure and which characterize Ayutthayan poetry. Given a plot, the poets expanded and embellished its various elements so that an elaborate structure was formed. With such treatment, the plot line appears to have a series of peaks, each peak representing one of the elaborated conventions. In the poetry of Bangkok, repetition also plays a role, the most obvious case being in the formation of the meters, stanzas, and rhyme patterns. What remains for investigation, however, is the manner in which the variable components have changed, for even a casual examination of a poem from the Bangkok period must strike the reader as something new and completely different.

REFERENCES

Bickner, R. J. (1981). *A linguistic study of a Thai literary classic.* Unpublished doctoral dissertation. The University of Michigan.

Bickner, R. J. (1989). Directional modification in Thai fiction: The use of 'come' and 'go' in text building. In D. Bradley (Ed.), *South-east Asian syntax* (Series A–No. 77, Papers in South-east Asian linguistics No. 11, pp. 15–79). Canberra: Pacific Linguistics, The Australian National University.

Bofman, T. H. (1984). *The poetics of the Ramakian.* DeKalb, IL: Northern Illinois University, Center for Southeast Asian Studies, Monograph Series in Southeast Asia, Special Report No. 21.

Chitakasem, M. (1972). The emergence and development of the *nirāt* genre in Thai poetry. *Journal of the Siam Society, 60/2,* 135–68.

Fussell, P. (1979). *Poetic meter and poetic form* (rev. ed.). New York: Random House.

Gedney, W. J. (1978, August). *Siamese verse forms in historical perspective.* Paper presented at the Conference on Southeast Asian Aesthetics, Cornell University. (Reprinted in Gedney, W. J., *Selected papers on comparative Tai studies* (R. J. Bicker, J. Hartmann, T. J. Hudak, & P. Peyasantiwong, Eds.). (1989). Ann Arbor, MI: Michigan Papers on South and Southeast Asian Studies, The University of Michigan, No. 29.)

Hudak, T. J. (1985). Poetic conventions in Thai *chan* meters. *Journal of the American Oriental Society, 105/1,* 107–117.

Hudak, T. J. (1986). Meta-rhymes in classical Thai poetry. *Journal of the Siam Society, 76,* 38–61.

Hudak, T. J. (1987). Internal rhyme patterns in classical Thai poetry. *Crossroads, 3(2–3),* 94–105.

Hudak, T. J. (1988). Organizational principles in Thai *phannánaa* passages. *Bulletin of the School of Oriental and African Studies, 51(1),* 95–117.

Hudak, T. J. (1990). *The indigenization of Pali meters in Thai poetry.* Athens, OH: Ohio University, Monographs in International Studies, Southeast Asia Series, No. 87.

Chapter 10
Education by the Use of Ghosts: Strategies of Repetition in Effi Briest

Rebecca S. Gault

Department of German
American University

INTRODUCTION

Many discourse analysts have noted that repetition is a cohesive device that gives meaning to discourse. Norrick (1987), for example, proposes a taxonomy for self- and allo-repetition in oral discourse, finding that textual coherence results from speaker strategies. In her analysis of four approaches to current research on repetition, Johnstone (1987) refers to the "ubiquitous phenomenon" of repetition and (quoting Halliday and Hasan, Tannen, Labov, and Ochs) discusses repetition as a cohesive device. Tannen (1987) describes four purposes of repetition that together create coherence (and interpersonal involvement). The functions she cites are accompanied by linguistic "sound and sense" patterns that require audience (hearer, reader) participation in inferring meaning from instances of repetition.

In this chapter, I discuss the novel Effi Briest, by the 19th-century German writer Theodor Fontane (1967). Known for his depictions of society in Berlin before the turn of the century, he portrays his

characters in everyday situations in which dialogue figures promi-
nently. My analysis of *Effi Briest* concentrates on repetition as an
interactive device that occurs, not only in conversations between
characters in the novel, but also in the "conversation" between author and reader. I show how the strategies of repetition employed by
the author contribute to the reader's understanding of the text and
point to reader participation in creating meaning.

The title for the study is taken from a line in a conversation
between two of the novel's characters. The line "education by the use
of ghosts" (Fontane, 1967, p. 125),[1] uttered in question form by the
character Effi, takes on significance in its allusions to relationships
among the three main characters in the novel. In addition, the ghost
signifies Fontane's use of repetition as a didactic tool to educate the
reader. Acting as a social critic, he makes use of the special properties of repetition—to remind of the past, and, through the establishment of a pattern, to refer to the future. The uncanny ability to
allude backward and forward is what I call the "ghost" of discourse.
The ghost in this novel is the reminder of a deceased Chinese man
whose presence caused controversy and whose grave still evokes
associations in the world inhabited by the novel's characters. But
the ghost is also the ineffable, ghostly presence that exists in associations and meanings of words and phrases in the dialogic interchange between author and reader.

Using the theoretical framework for the novel suggested by Mikhail Bakhtin (1981) in *The Dialogic Imagination*, I see the interaction in this novel, *Effi Briest*, as inherently dialogic. *Heteroglossia*
is the manifestation of the dialogic principle in the novel; it makes
possible the multiplicity of meanings of any utterance. Bakhtin describes it this way:

> Heteroglossia, once incorporated into the novel (whatever the forms
> for its incorporation), is *another's speech in another's language*,
> serving to express authorial intentions but in a refracted way. Such
> speech constitutes a special type of *double-voiced discourse*. It serves
> two speakers at the same time and expresses simultaneously two
> different intentions: the direct intention of the character who is
> speaking, and the refracted intention of the author. In such discourse
> there are two voices, two meanings and two expressions. And all the
> while these two voices are dialogically interrelated, they—as it were—
> know about each other (just as two exchanges in a dialogue know of

---

[1] For the sake of convenience, I have used the English translation of the German
novel; all excerpts in this chapter are from the English edition.

each other and are structured in this mutual knowledge of each other);
it is as if they actually hold a conversation with each other. (p. 324)

The ghost of the Chinese man assumes importance in many conversations within the novel *Effi Briest*—between Effi and her husband,
between Effi and her maid, between the maid and Effi's husband,
between Effi and her lover, and in the written monologic "conversation" of a letter from Effi to her mother. Seldom is the ghost described in authorial exposition, but rather in the words of the particular characters. But I submit that the author's voice, and his
implicit social commentary, can be heard as an echo surrounding
the voices of the individual characters as they attempt to educate the
young Effi into the ways of society.

To use the musical metaphors preferred by Bakhtin, any novel is
a symphonic work constituted from the polyphony of many inter-
mingling voices. It is not only the characters' voices that are heard in
the work, but also the voice of the author, who gives nuances and
shades of meaning to tones of the notes or words. In addition,
strains of other works, like familiar melodies, enter the symphony,
lending echoes of their voices. The presence of a multitude of voices
gives the novel a rich texture, but there must be something that
prevents it from being a cacophony of dissonant voices. In order to
make sense, to be aesthetically pleasing, there must be a unifying
principle at work. In *Effi Briest*, one such principle is structural.
The novel has the developmental ternary structure of a sonata:
theme, development, and recapitulation. In addition, I propose that
the presence of the ghost is a leitmotif which unifies and provides
coherence (and thereby meaning) in the work as a whole.

REPETITION IN *EFFI BRIEST*

I will discuss two strategies of repetition employed by Fontane in the
novel: (a) structural repetition, in connection with which I use the
musical terms *ternary form* and *leitmotif*; and (b) psychological
repetition, which includes allusions and associations of words said
and *not* said that convey meaning to conversational participants
and to the reader. Following my analysis of three examples of dialogue from the text, I concentrate on the paradigmatic and didactic
function of the story to which the dialogues refer and towards which
they build, pointing to the interactive role of the reader in decoding
the author's message. I show that, just as Effi's husband and her

lover use repeated allusions to a ghost story to educate Effi, Fontane uses strategies of repetition to educate the reader as to the nature of society in 19th-century Prussia.

Structural Repetition

Ternary Form. The overall form of the narrative that constitutes the novel *Effi Briest* is that of the musical sonata (ternary) form: exposition—development—recapitulation, or ABA form. Reduced to its simplest elements, the novel tells the story of the young woman Effi Briest, who, barely past childhood, is persuaded by her parents to marry a man 17 years her senior. The story of her life before, during, and after her marriage is in three sections that correspond to the ABA form of the sonata: (a) *Exposition* [A]: Effi is introduced as an energetic child of nature passing time with friends and playing on the country estate that is the family's home in Hohen-Cremen, in an edenic pastoral existence. (b) *Development* [B]: Effi begins her married life with Baron Geert von Innstetten in the far-away northern seaport town of Kessin. Here she learns truths about herself, her husband, and about the world that surprise and dismay her. She has difficulty living up to society's expectations of her and, in an attempt to escape from her role, she succumbs to the temptation offered by the attentions of a seductive charmer, Major Crampas. Although her affair is not discovered until 7 years later, her transgression has tragic consequences. Her husband challenges Crampas to a duel in which he kills him; Effi must live alone, now in Berlin, trying in vain to support herself, alienated from her husband and daughter, as well as from the rest of society. (c) *Recapitulation* [A]: At first rejected even by her parents because of her transgression, she is invited to return home only after developing tuberculosis; here in her girlhood home she comes back to die in a state of grace. She is buried in the family plot under her girlhood name, her true identity: Effi Briest.

Effi's story begins and ends in the town of Hohen-Cremen. But is the end really a return to the beginning? Is the recapitulation a return to the original innocence of the primary section? Recapitulation in music is a special type of repetition:

> Recapitulation will rarely be a literal repetition of the exposition. If it were, it could at best function only as a way of achieving a symmetrical, formal, balanced design. The danger in a literal recapitulation lies in its psychological falsification or dramatic untruth. . . . A literal recapitulation implies that nothing really has happened to alter one's

perspective with respect to the original presentation. (Fleming & Veinus, 1958, p. 122)

In traditional readings of this "realistic" novel, Effi's end, especially her deathbed "confession," was seen as her acceptance and understanding of her fate, a type of resignation that implied acceptance of her guilt. Recent literary criticism has called this ending into question; however, Greenberg (1988) claims that Effi's narrative resists closure, and that her death is in fact not an ending. Whether or not Effi achieves closure is open to speculation precisely because of the apparent repetition. On the surface level, her birth place and resting place are the same. The recapitulation of the exposition inherent in the sonata-like form is a type of repetition that encourages the reader to raise questions about the meaning of the text.

Leitmotif. The most compelling factor in the development (B section) of the novel of Effi's life is the recurring motif of the Chinese man and his lingering ghost. Mentions of the man and allusions to the spirit recur again and again in conversations in the development section that corresponds to Effi's married life, contributing to the formal (as well as thematic) coherence. In his discussion of motifs and symbols in *Effi Briest*, Reinhard H. Thum (1979) describes literary *leitmotifs* as "variations on a set phrase, or as constantly recurring objects which are connected with a figure time after time, subtly varied, so that the phrase or object becomes emotionally charged, capable of calling forth a number of associations" (p. 117). The German word, meaning "leading motive," is adopted from the musical world, primarily from Richard Wagner's use in his operas. *Leitmotifs* are defined as:

> short, aphoristic fragments [that] may vary in length from motive to melody and are designed to characterize individuals, aspects of personality, abstract ideas . . . . Motives by no means are static entities and they undergo constant symphonic development. (Fleming & Veinus, 1958, p. 373)

In Wagnerian opera, the orchestra often acts as interpreter of the actions on stage, giving musical clues via leitmotifs as to the motivations, states of mind and feelings of the characters. In *Effi Briest*, the reader is the interpreter. Each time the leitmotif of the ghost occurs, it occurs with a slightly different overtone, a shade of meaning colored by its place in the narration. The significance of the motif changes according to the events and feelings in Effi's life; as she reacts to the mention of the Chinese man and his ghost, the reader interprets and reinterprets the meaning of the motif.

The Chinese man is first mentioned as a possibility, as an example of the exotic realm Effi will be exposed to in the new seaport town in which she will begin her marriage. In response to her question about what kind of people populate the town, guessing Turks or even Chinese, Innstetten replies that there indeed once was a Chinese man, and that someday he'll show her the grave and tell her the story. Effi's active imagination is fueled by the possibility of a ghost in her own house, once owned by a sea captain. Stirred by both excitement and fear, left alone at home one evening when her husband is out of town, she "sees" a Chinese man at her bedside. From this moment on, the Chinese man becomes a ghost that will haunt her in one way or another for the rest of her married life. It hovers in many conversations in the novel, not only providing the thematic link caused by its appearance, but also giving the reader clues as to the relationships between the characters in those conversations. The words of the characters themselves, rather than a direct authorial or narrative commentary, carry the author's implicit social commentary.

Fontane undoubtedly intended the Chinese man figure and/or his ghost to be central to Effi's story; in a well-known letter he refers to the ghost as "der Drehpunkt für die ganze Geschichte" (Keitel & Nürnberger, 1982, p. 506). Critics have interpreted the ghostly leitmotif politically, psychologically (as representing incipient sexuality, repression, guilt), and thematically; it stands for the disintegrating marriage of Effi and her husband and can be seen as a paradigm for the love triangle of Effi-Innstetten-Crampas. Greenberg (1988) notes that "the critical response suggests that Fontane created a device as evocative and elusive as literature itself" (p. 773). Another critic, claiming that a ghost is really a "nonthing," poses the question: "What is a ghost but the apparition of what once was, a phenomenon presupposing death, the pastness of the original, and therefore equally a representation of absence?" (Subiotto, 1985, p. 141). Based on Fontane's own words in his correspondence, however, it is clear that this novel does not rest on absence; the pivotal ghost, however elusive, is a real presence. Its meaning changes for Effi and the other characters, just as its meaning varies according to who, at what time, is reading and interpreting its appearance(s). Given the quantity and variety of interpretive literature regarding the Chinese ghost, it seems it means everything—or nothing. The ghost leitmotif, its occurrence and recurrence, manifests the presence of the author in the work. Though he speaks mainly through the zones surrounding his characters, using their words, Fontane's voice and social criticism can still be heard as an echo around the voices of the individual characters, especially the males, as they attempt to educate the young Effi into the ways of society.

Psychological Repetition

With the strategy of repetition on the psychological level, we enter the ghostly realm of allusions and associations, for the main character Effi and for the reader. Geert von Innstetten tells his wife a story about a Chinese man that affects her imagination and psyche to the extent that the ghost of the man informs and reflects her actions for much of the novel. The story is not told until the tenth chapter in the novel, after Effi has begun to settle into her new life. Even before she hears the story, however, Effi has begun to be unnerved by the spectre of a deceased Chinese man. In conversation with his wife, Innstetten discusses the Chinese man, alluding to his significance even before he has told her the story. He seems to play on her helplessness, curiosity, and attraction to fear, as well as her isolation and alienation in the new city and total dependence on him, as he uses the ghost in their conversations.

The conversation that provides the later "Chinese ghost" frame takes place just as Effi prepares to enter her new home in the town of Kessin. During a carriage ride, she talks of her excitement to her husband (I have identified the speakers in brackets):

". . . There's a whole new world to discover. All sorts of exotic people. That's right, isn't it? You meant something like that?" [Effi]

(Geert nods.)

"A whole new world, then, perhaps a Negro or a Turk or perhaps even a Chinaman." [Effi]

"Even a Chinaman. How clever you are at guessing. It's possible that we may still have one, but in any case we did have one. Now he's dead and buried on a little plot of earth enclosed by an iron fence, right beside the cemetery. If you're not scared, I'll show you the grave when we have the chance. It's among the sand-dunes, with nothing but wild oats all around and a few everlasting flowers here and there, and you can hear the sea all the time. It's very lovely and very awe-inspiring." [Innstetten]

"Yes, that's the word and I should quite like to know more about it. But perhaps I'd better not, because I'll immediately have dreams and visions, and as I hope to sleep well tonight I shouldn't like to see a Chinaman heading for my bed straightaway." [Effi]

"Nor will he." [Innstetten]

"Nor will he. Do you know that sounds strange, as if it were possible all the same. You want to make Kessin sound interesting for me, but there you're going a bit too far." [Effi] (Fontane, 1967, p. 48)

This conversation provides the context in which the Chinese ghost assumes such importance later in the novel. By engaging in this interchange, the participants have established the fact that there is an exotic element in the town of Kessin, that one of these elements is in the past, in the character of a Chinese man, that there is a reminder of his presence in the small grave, and that this figure could cause fear in Effi. Geert prefaces his offer to show his young bride the grave by saying, "if you're not scared"; his negative formulation with the qualifier *if* implies that she *should* be frightened. Effi adopts a fearful stance when she says she'll have dreams and visions, and that she doesn't want to see a Chinese man[2] heading for her bed. Geert gives her more cause for fear when he replies to her use of the noun preceded by indefinite article ("a Chinaman"), with his use of the pronoun *he*. By referring to the noun antecedent in this way, Geert acknowledges that it is a possibility that the Chinese man could come toward his wife's bed. Effi notices that he has, in fact, substantiated her fears, but this observation does not rid her of them. Geert's attitude toward the possibility of a Chinese ghost actually exacerbates Effi's fears. If her husband-provider, her superior in social matters, puts stock in this idea, then this influences, in turn, what she believes. No matter what Innstetten's words of reassurance and comfort are, Effi knows that he believes in the ghost too, and this unnerves her. Their shared knowledge of the possibility of a ghost creates a frame of reference that influences later actions and informs their relationship to one another.

Set up by the preceding conversation about exotic possibilities, and further confused by Innstetten's serious reaction to a tiny sticker-like picture of a Chinese man found stuck to the back of a chair in the attic, Effi's fears culminate in an episode during her husband's absence in which she sees the Chinese man rushing by her bed. The vision has become a reality that haunts her. Fed by her own fears and fantasies and insecurity in her new situation, as well as her husband's belief in the ghost (despite his disclaimers), Effi has created an image that is at odds with the society in which the Innstettens live. The following conversation takes place the day after Effi's nightmare or sighting of the Chinese man. When she tells her

---

[2] The word *Chinaman*, used in the Parmee translation, is somewhat pejorative in English; I therefore refer to *der Chinese* as *the Chinese man*.

husband about the events of the previous night, Geert says it was all a dream or a hallucination. He then reminds her of his societal expectations and standing:

> I can't have people here in the town saying: Governor Innstetten is selling his house because his wife saw beside her bed the ghost of a little Chinaman whose picture had been stuck up on a chair back. It would be fatal, Effi. I should never recover from the ridicule. (Fontane, 1967, p. 78)

Innstetten refuses to entertain the idea of moving from the house at Effi's suggestion. His concern is for himself and his social position, as seen from the use of the first person singular pronoun *I* and his fear of being talked about or ridiculed by the townspeople. At the same time, he ridicules his wife for her fears and, in an ironic turn, uses the word *ghost* to validate Effi's vision. He thus intimidates her into thinking that she is irresponsible for believing in the ghost, while in fact encouraging the belief; this intimidation reinforces their asymmetrical power relationship. Effi learns from this conversation that to give in to fantasy is not proper and that it is very important what people think.

The relationship between Effi and her husband is further illustrated by their short conversation just before Innstetten begins the narrative that explains the place of the Chinese man in the history of the town. The immediate impetus for the dialogue (as well as for Innstetten's ensuing monologic narrative) is the sight of a small fenced plot opposite the churchyard during a sleigh ride around the town of Kessin. Effi initiates the conversation by asking a question about the site:

> "Is someone buried there, too?" asked Effi.
> "Yes, the Chinaman." [Innstetten]
>
> Effi gave a violent start, as if she had been stung, but she still had the strength to control herself and with apparent indifference asked:
>
> "Ours?" [Effi]
>
> "Yes, ours . . ." [Innstetten] (Fontane, 1967, p. 82)

Geert's answer to the first of the two questions posed by his wife shows that he and his wife share knowledge about the term *Chinaman*. The definite article before the noun indicates a familiarity, that the Chinese man is someone (or something) known to both of them. Indeed, as the authorial description of Effi's reaction to her husband's words shows, the words are cause for alarm. Not only is the Chinese man a known quantity to both parties in this conversation, it is also something they in a sense "own," indicated by the use of the first-person plural possessive *ours* used by Effi and repeated by Geert. In both interchanges, Effi poses a question, asking for clarification or reassurance, and Geert answers with authority. These two minimal exchanges characterize the relationship shared by the couple; she, the young, inexperienced bride, is dependent on her husband to provide her with the answer she needs to function in her new life. His role is to educate her, and one of the ways he performs this role is by the use of the story of the Chinese man.

When Innstetten finally tells the story of the Chinese man, it is already overlain with associations, for Effi and for the reader. The tale begins with Captain Thomsen, a sea-captain who had traveled to many foreign ports, including China. When he retired as a wealthy man, he bought the house in which the Innstettens now live. With Captain Thomsen were a young woman of whom he was guardian (his niece or granddaughter), and a Chinese man who worked for him but who was more a friend than a servant, At the arranged marriage of the young woman, heavily attended by all the well-born families in the town, the bride danced with everyone present, including the Chinese servant. But right after the wedding, the Chinese man mysteriously died. The town pastor would have allowed his burial in the community cemetery in the churchyard, but the community would have protested. Captain Thomsen then purchased the small plot of land opposite the churchyard and had his friend buried there.

The story has a firm place in the collective memory of the townspeople; it is not the property of Geert Innstetten, nor is it a narrative of his own personal experience; what makes it important in the context of the novel is the manner in which it is told, and the intended and received effect. No doubt Innstetten has heard and has told this story many times; in this case, the narrative corresponds to the type of discourse Michael Macovski refers to as "textual recursion" (1990). Important is not only the story itself but what the repetition represents to the speaker and its effect on the hearer. Macovski states that the act of repetition signifies a didactic relationship; in the case of the narrative told by Innstetten within the greater narrative of the novel, this is especially true. Geert's purpose in telling the story is to elucidate, to provide background for the previous allusions, but most of all to educate his wife, just emerging from her protected parental environment, on the manner and ways of life in the adult world.

The story also performs a broader function within the novel; it is a means of informing or educating the reader. The reader who reads Innstetten's tale as Effi hears it is similarly educated in interaction with the writer. The writer (Fontane or Fontane's authorial voice) uses the tale as a paradigm for the relationships within the novel, and it foreshadows the outcome of the plot. Innstetten has told a story about an event in Kessin with essentially three characters—Captain Thomsen, the young woman reputed to be his niece, and the Chinese man, against the backdrop of the town and its people. Similarly, the writer tells in *Effi Briest* the story of three characters and their fates—Geert Instetten, his young wife Effi, and the interloper who becomes her lover, Major Crampas. The interplay of the characters in the novel, acting in accordance with their personalities and their society, culminates in a tragic ending. Just as in the story, the novelistic triangle is dissolved at the end; Crampas is killed in a duel, and Effi dies at home with her parents, thus disappearing from adult society. The informed reader who has made the connection between Captain Thomsen and Baron von Innstetten, and the niece and Effi, is prepared for the entrance of the intruder, Major Crampas, into the textual world.

In a conversation with Major Crampas long after Effi has heard the story of the Chinese man from her husband, she is reminded of Innstetten's pedagogic bent. Crampas has just finished telling Effi of Innstetten's predilection for storytelling, especially about ghosts, a trait he had noticed while under his command in the army. He continues in his analysis of Innstetten's character as he explains what he sees as Innstetten's passions:

> "In addition to his ardent desire to further his own career at all costs, even to the extent of dragging in a ghost if need be, Innstetten has a second passion: he always wants to be educational; he's a born pedagogue . . ."

> "And so he wants to educate me, too? Education by the use of ghosts?" [Effi]

> "Educate is perhaps not the right word. But educate indirectly . . . A young wife is a young wife and a governor is a governor. He often has to travel all over the district and then the house is deserted and empty. But a ghost like that is a good as a cherub with a sword . . ." [Crampas] (Fontane, 1967, p. 125)

If Crampas is correct, Effi now draws the conclusion that her husband has been trying to educate her by the use of ghosts. Using the fears and associations surrounding the Chinese man, he has reinforced her belief in something which no longer exists, except in her mind. When he told her the story, ostensibly to clarify and explain, or perhaps even to entertain, as in a mystery, he was attempting to perform a pedagogic function. The role of pedagogue fell naturally to him by virtue of his age and experience; Effi's inexperience and dependence on him made her a suitable pupil. The story's effect on Effi was based on the world of shared knowledge they had about the Chinese ghost, a shared world created through repeated allusion.

CONCLUSION

Using structural and thematic "psychological" strategies of repetition which include the devices of recapitulation, recurrence, inference and allusion, Theodor Fontane has, in *Effi Briest*, written a novel in which meaning is created in interaction. The dialogic nature of the novel makes possible a "double-voiced" discourse, to use Bakhtin's words, that simultaneously expresses both the character's and author's intentions. The instances of repetition create a "sense" pattern that requires hearer (that is, a character within a conversation) and reader participation in inferring meaning. Just as the character Effi is educated by the character Innstetten, the reader is also educated by the author through the use of repetition. Successful interpretation of Fontane's depiction and indictment of society in 19th-century Prussia depends on appreciation of strategies employed by the author. The ghostly presence of allusion and association as strategies of repetition provides coherence in the text and creates, through its required interaction, the meaning of the discourse.

REFERENCES

Bakhtin, M. M. (1981). *The dialogic imagination*. Austin: The University of Texas Press.

Fleming, W., & Veinus, A. (1958). *Understanding music*. New York: Holt, Rinehart and Winston.

Fontane, T. (1967). *Effi Briest* (Douglas Parmee, Trans.). Harmondsworth, UK: Penguin Books.

Greenberg, V. (1988). The resistance of *Effi Briest*: An untold tale. *PMLA*, *103*(5), 770–782.

Johnstone, B. (1987). An introduction. In B. Johnstone (Ed.), *Perspectives on repetition*. *Text*, 7(3), 205–214.

Keitel, W., & Nürnberger, H. (1982). *Theodor Fontane: Werke, Schriften und Briefe. IV*. München: Carl Hanser Verlag.

Macovski, M. (1990, May 25–27). Retelling, recoverability, and reinterpretation: Hermeneutics of literary interpretation. Paper presented at conference on *Repetition in discourse*. College Station, TX.

Norrick, N. R. (1987). Functions of repetition in conversation. *Text, 7*(3), 245–64.

Subiotto, F. (1985). The ghost in *Effi Briest. Forum for Modern Language Studies, 21*, 137–50.

Tannen, D. (1987). Repetition in conversation: Toward a poetics of talk. *Language, 63*(3), 574–605.

Thum, R. H. (1979). Symbol, motif and leitmotif in Fontane's *Effi Briest. Germanic Review, 54*, 115–24.

Part III

Repetition and Learning: Cooperation, Cohesion, Cognition

Chapter 11
Repetition in Language Development: From Interaction to Cohesion

Tina L. Bennett-Kastor

Department of English Language and Literature
Wichita State University

INTRODUCTION

The issue of whether or not children learn language "by imitation" has been so resoundingly put to rest that scholars in child language have been hesitant to examine the large role that more broadly defined repetitive phenomena play in language development. However, works by Tannen (1984, 1987a,b, 1989), and by Ochs and co-authors Schieffelin and Platt (1976) have demonstrated the significance in degree and quality of repetition in language use; it is only reasonable, then, to explore how repetition works in the language produced by caregivers and young children in the typical developmental context. It has been shown that repetition in adult discourse allows participants to achieve conversational coherence in a variety of ways, from the production of fluent talk through automaticity, to the comprehension of discourse which is "semantically less dense" (Tannen, 1987a, p. 582), to the emergent unfolding of propositions and the cooperative establishment of topics that is accomplished by means of reliance of the previous speaker's utterances (Ochs et al., 1976; Ochs & Schieffelin, 1976).

In addition to these overt uses of repetition in which part or all of preceding utterances is reproduced by subsequent speakers, subtler forms of repetition also propel discourse forward and make it cohesive. Pronominalization, some forms of ellipsis, parallelism—the variety of phenomena generally included under the category of "co-indexing"—all depend upon recurrence of semantic or grammatical information. Coherence, in contrast with cohesion, depends upon the reactivation of concepts, scripts, and frames underlying a text. Thus, in studies of adult language use, repetitive phenomena form a continuum from what might be considered the *microphenomena* of cohesive devices, to the *macrophenomena* of full, overt repetition in interactive discourses (most notably conversation). Underlying this is the semantic *megaphenomenon* of reactivated cognitive and social structures that allow language to be representational and conventional.

The line between interactive and discourse-cohesive functions of repetition is impossibly blurry. Although cohesion is achieved primarily through grammatical devices, and interaction through less tangible means, many of them overtly repetitive, the grammatical devices of cohesion apparently emerge out of repetition, which serves interactional purposes. Evidence for this contention comes from a review of already existing analyses, some specific to language development but some not. I will also look briefly at some reanalyses of preexisting corpora, as well as at a small amount of new data I am in the process of collecting and analyzing. The chapter will take this form: (a) a brief review of the evidence that, historically, grammar emerges out of discourse; (b) presentation of some evidence that conversation is the rudimentary form from which discourse of all types develops; (c) discussion of the preverbal underpinnings of conversation in the early interactions of infants and caregivers ontogenetically, which share major structural features of adult conversation, of which repetition is one of the primary defining features; and (d) a look at early conversations that are themselves largely repetitive.

As the child matures, overt repetition is gradually replaced by utterances which are only partially repetitive, and self-repetition comes to play a greater role in the child's language. Increasingly subtle forms of repetition are acquired—pronominalization, ellipsis, and a variety of types of parallelism. Once these are acquired, the child is equipped with the necessary tools to produce formal discourse as literacy is established. In informal situations, however, the fundamental forms of interactive discourse continue to flourish. That is, as repetition becomes grammaticalized, earlier acquired forms are not abandoned but retained and used, along with later acquired forms in appropriate contexts, congruent with Ochs's "retention" model of language development (1979), to which I will refer at greater length subsequently.

FROM DISCOURSE TO GRAMMAR

A number of works in the past 15 years or so have proposed that grammar emerges from discourse, most notably Givon (1979a,b), the latter being a collection of papers focusing on the relationship between syntax and discourse, including a paper by Givon. Givon argued strongly in the earlier work (1979a) that the justification for syntax was discourse-pragmatic functions. In the later paper (1979b) Givon retreats somewhat, but still underscores the belief that syntax must be understood as arising from discourse "and the communicative parameters and principles that govern both its rise out of the pragmatic mode and its selection along the register scale of human communication" (p. 109). Givon presents evidence from the processes of diachronic change, language development, pidginization, and register shifting.

Earlier, Sankoff and Brown (1976) had demonstrated that relativization in New Guinea Tok Pisin was derived from an adverb of place, which was extended to function as a demonstrative and a postposed deictic, and then further extended "for general 'bracketing' use, including topic-comment structures, relativization, and cleft sentences" (p. 663). Also focusing on relative clauses, Fox and Thompson (1990) show that attention by the participants to managing the flow of information in conversation explains many structural choices that speakers make.

Niger-Congo languages have been rich sources for demonstrating the relationships between discourse and syntax. Wald (1979) discusses the development of the Mombasa Swahili object marker as a syntacticization process. More recently, Bresnan and Mchombo (1987) discuss the closely related processes of grammatical subject agreement and anaphoric object agreement in Swahili. Some of my own research has concerned the Bassa language of Liberia. In Bassa, the question marker /kE/ occupies the position of an argument that has undergone Wh-movement. From the standpoint of intrasentential cohesion, /kE/ can be viewed as a grammaticalized expression of the topic under query. (In the Bantu languages, /ki/

often serves a similar function.) Its distribution is similar in some ways to that of resumptive pronouns in Niger-Congo relative clauses, and presumably, /kE/ is co-indexed with the Wh-word, hence "anaphoric" in Government-Binding terms; it is also a repetitive phenomenon, since it is semantically reiterative. Grammatically, it may not appear in nonargument positions. There is, however, a discourse use of /kE/ in which speakers append it to a repetition of a prior utterance, in nonargument position, in order to express doubt or initiate a repair. In other words, /kE/ implies a contingency on prior discourse, just as its anaphoric, grammaticalized appearance is dependent upon (co-indexed with) a pre-existing A-position.

Other advocates of the position that syntax is motivated by, and emerges from, discourse-pragmatic considerations are DuBois (1987), who discusses the discourse basis of ergativity in Sacatulpec Maya, and Hopper and Thompson (1984), who focus on the discourse basis of lexical categories. This by no means exhaustive list of works in this area serves to demonstrate that there is much evidence for viewing syntax as the grammaticalization of discourse-pragmatic features, despite the reservations of scholars such as Comrie (1986).

Ontogenetically, a number of studies have demonstrated that grammar emerges after the child has already begun producing rudimentary discourse. (For some scholars, such as Gelman, 1983, true linguistic development does not begin until the child starts to combine words.) For example, Wells (1985) presents a thorough examination of the development of language in preschool children via carefully collected longitudinal data. He focuses on several systems involved in language development: clause-level syntax, NP syntax and semantics, time, aspect, modality, conjunction, meaning relations, and functions. Pragmatic and semantic levels precede syntactic development in virtually every case and full head NPs precede pronominalized heads. For example, 50% of the children in the study could express a full head NP such as *dog* by 15 months, but not a pronominal head (*it*) until 21 months. Inflected pronouns emerged later: *he* at 33 months, but *him* at 42 months. Content questions emerged functionally at 24 months, through the use of two constituents; their grammaticalization as *wh-* + *copula* + *S* does not emerge until 27 months (and *wh-* + *aux* + *S* + *V* not until 36 months). Thus are children able to express, in the conversational context, meanings which do not manifest themselves in full grammatical regalia until several months later.

One might ask, for what reason does grammar exist? That is, what motivates the child's development of a complex grammatical system along with lexical development? The simplest answer is that grammar allows the interlocutors to communicate better: grammatical morphology provides redundancy, in some cases disambiguates vague references, and frees consciousness to focus on the substance of talk while backgrounding the mechanics of keeping track of topics. An examination of child language data reveals that, in the early months, an enormous amount of talk is aimed at establishing mutuality, for which grammar is not prerequisite, but it is from this function that information sharing and topicality in general emerge. Once topics are established, child and caregiver move on to the joint establishment of predication or, if predication is the topic, to the establishment of arguments. Only later do children come to rely more on their own generative abilities to produce novel forms and functions; still later, in the third year, repetition and the mutuality it brings declines as the child is capable of articulating more complex topic-comment structures which require such "modulations of meaning," in Brown's (1973) words, as pluralization, pronominalization, tense and aspect, and other grammatical markers.

THE ORIGINS OF DISCOURSE IN CONVERSATION

Most discourse occurs under conditions of spontaneous, unplanned, face-to-face interaction. These conditions are mitigated, however, by a conventionalized structural organization (Goffman, 1974, 1981; Gumperz, 1982; Gumperz & Hymes, 1972; Sacks, Schegloff, & Jefferson, 1977). Thus, many aspects of conversation within a given community are routinized, that is, conventional (and thus repeated over time). The organizational pattern of conversation allows it to proceed relatively smoothly, even though participants may have no prior knowledge of the topics to be addressed.

Once topic is established in conversation, interlocutors continue to rely on a number of strategies which ease the uncertainty of spontaneous discourse. Turn taking, of course, is the dominant structural feature of conversation, and it shapes the way that participants contribute to talk. Participants collaborate through the turn-taking mechanism to establish propositions and to articulate topics (Ochs et al., 1976; Ochs & Schieffelin, 1976). The tension of having to generate utterances spontaneously is thus considerably abated by the participatory nature of conversations, in which propositions are often presented and reworked over many turns by both interlocutors. Throughout, a speaker may use a previous speaker's utterance either overtly, through full or partial repetition of form or content, or the previous speaker's utterance may be incorporated in the subsequent speaker's as a presupposition or as now given information. Developmentally, this former "topic collaboration" emerges prior to the latter "topic incorporation" (Ochs & Schieffelin, 1976, pp. 340–342).

However, the type of language characteristic of conversation also mitigates the pressure of spontaneity. As Ochs (1979) has shown, in unplanned discourse speakers rely on a number of devices that are cognitively less complex than those that characterize planned and/or formal discourse: immediate context, morphosyntactic structures acquired in the first 3 or 4 years of language development, repetition and replacement of lexical items, and similarity in the form and content of sequential acts. Participants are also more tolerant in conversation than in formal discourse of such features as afterthought phenomena and continual confirmation and feedback eliciting.

If conversation is typically unplanned and dyadic, and if it relies so heavily on conventionalized structural organization and on features typically acquired early in a child's life, prior to any formal education or even before a great deal of socialization has occurred, it is reasonable to assume that it is developmentally prior to any other form of discourse. Some other genres have been investigated in young children's language use, most notably narrative, but these do not develop until rudimentary conversational skills have been established. Moreover, there is some evidence that a child's narrative ability develops only after he or she is able to describe individual events (Berman, 1988, p. 493). Other types of discourse, such as expository and hortatory genres, are dependent upon logical rather that temporal linkages (Hinds, 1979). Research demonstrates that children acquire temporal connectives before logical ones (Bennett-Kastor, 1986) and thus are able to produce narrative and procedural discourse earlier than other forms. Conversation itself, however, is characterized by much less use of connectives. The most common conversational connective is a nontemporal, nonlogical "and," which assumes various connective functions (Laubitz, 1987). Because early acquired structures and patterns are not discarded as later ones are learned, logically based genres retain many features of narrative and of prenarrative discourse which unfolds in the conversational-interactive context (Bennett-Kastor, n.d.; Umiker-Sebeok, 1979). Thus the entire range of discourse genres can be seen to evolve from the interactional language of conversation.

THE DEVELOPMENT OF CONVERSATION

Quite some time ago, child psychiatrist Margaret Mahler described "mutual cueing" between infants and mothers as "a circular process of interaction established very early . . . by which they 'empathetically' read each other's signs and signals and react to each other" (Mahler, Pines, & Bergman, 1975, p. 290). Mutual cueing is a primary means by which mothers learn to care for their newborn infants. Stern, Jaffee, Beebe, and Bennett (1975) extended a similar concept into the arena of early vocalizations. Facial and gaze behaviors by infant and mother (or other primary caregiver) also evolve into a dyadically structured ritual by about the third month (Stern, 1974). Typically, these preverbal "conversations" contain identifiable opening and closing sequences. The infant, for example, may seek to initiate the interaction through eye-gaze, or, not succeeding, by kicking and smiling. The end of the interaction is signalled by aversion of eye-gaze. Toward the end of the third of fourth month, the infant vocalizes in response to the utterances which the mother directs toward him or her. The interaction will proceed turn by turn until tension builds to a certain point when simultaneity takes over (Kaplan, 1978, p. 112).

Once the infant's ability to vocalize in a variety of ways is well established, he or she may summon the mother to an interaction (other than by crying). The mother may respond by imitating the child's vocalization or, later, by reinterpreting it linguistically; the infant will in turn reiterate the mother's utterance or attempt an approximation of it. Once words are acquired, the infant–caregiver pair retain many of the same features in their interactions, including the structure of turn taking (which comes to dominate over unison vocalizing), opening and closing sequences, and full and partial repetitions. Such organizational patterns dominate even when verbal children resort to sound-play dialogues; thus, the overall structural organization of conversation is not limited to actual linguistically driven interactions but is established far prior to the development of language per se.

THE ROLE OF REPETITION
IN INFANT–CAREGIVER TALK

What do early conversations look like, and what role does repetition play in them and in the later development of other types of discourse? The earliest conversations, that is, those which occur in the second year of a child's life, are extraordinarily repetitive in nature.

That is to say, both the child and the caregiver, notably the mother, engage in large amounts of full and partial repetitions of one another's utterances. The functions of repetition in early dialogues are numerous, and distributed across speakers, although self-repetition is frequently viewed in the literature separately from other-repetition, sometimes referred to, often erroneously, as "imitation."

It is difficult to find estimates of the degree to which children and mothers repeat one another, primarily because there are so many methodological problems involved in identifying what "counts" as repetition. Some people are willing only to accept full or partial repetitions of lexical items with heavy semantic content, but not, for example, pronouns or grammatical morphemes (R. S. Tomlin, personal communication, May 27, 1990). Others feel that even reiteration of phrase structure, as in parallelism, or of sound sequences, must be included if repetition is to be fully appreciated. Bennett-Kastor, Ochs, and Tannen, for example, take this position. Also, there is disagreement concerning how the "distance" between items affects their status as repetition. Bennett-Kastor (1986) found that the majority of parallel clauses in children's narratives occurred within two clauses, although occasionally they appeared to occupy a longer domain. Yet another problem arises because researchers in child language tend to focus on children older than the age at which repetition may dominate.

These problems aside, some figures have appeared in the literature. Bloom, Hood, and Lightbown (1974) found that the extent of "imitation" of a caregiver's utterances by a child varied from a minimum of 4% to a maximum of 42%. Also, the same child would not necessarily be consistently repetitive across interactional occasions. Repetition of the caregiver's utterances by the child also appears to decline with age, so that, by age 3, in the absence of some disorder interfering with hearing or comprehension, there is much less of it.

Caregivers also engage in repetition of the child to a great extent. Mothers especially will repeat themselves when talking to 2-year-olds four times more frequently than when talking to 10-year-olds (Snow, 1972), for example. Fathers are reported to self-repeat somewhat less than mothers when talking to children, according to Friedlander, Jacobs, Davis, and Whetstone (1972). A more recent study put the number of modeled, expanded, or directly repeated utterances of normal 2-year-olds by mothers at 22% (Schodorf, 1981), although direct and full repetition occurred rarely (3%).

An examination of the transcripts found in the appendix of Bloom (1973) reveals a pattern of increasing self-repetition by the child and decreasing self-repetition by the mother, accompanied by increasing other-repetition by the mother. Self- and other-repetition by the mother both equalled 30% when Allison was 16 months, 3 weeks; Allison repeated herself 23%. At 20; 3, Allison's self-repetitions increased to 52%, while Mother's self-repetitions declined to 19% and her other-repetitions dropped to 23%. At 22 months, Allison repeated herself 45% of the time, Mother repeated herself only 7%. Other-repetitions increased for Mother, however (42%), and dropped considerably for Allison (6%). It is notable that these early dialogues are virtually devoid of pronominal reference by Allison, although her mother uses deictic pronouns freely and occasionally follows full nominal reference with a third-person pronoun. Alison avoids even deictic reference, referring to herself as "baby" and to her mother as "Mommy" at 22 months, which gives her utterances an oddly disembodied texture. My son Patrick developed use of the possessive pronoun *my* prior to 2 years. However, it coexisted in alternation with the (unmarked) possessive form of his name. The latter was used of objects not in his physical possession, whereas *my X* referred to objects actually held in his hand. This strongly suggests that deictic pronominal usage emerges along with, and is often complicated by, the child's own individuation process and his or her sense of existence as an autonomous person.

Examination of data from another of my own children, who at 2 years, 9 months, still used repetition extensively, also reveals a gradual decrease in other-repetition by the child, an increase in his self-repetition (see below), and a decrease in my self-repetitions. The picture that emerges is one of increasing autonomy by the child in the contributions to the conversation, an autonomy which parallels the increasing grammatical competence of the child to refer to previous acts, events, and utterances through other means besides direct repetition. Conversational autonomy also parallels, surely not coincidentally, individuation and increasing social and emotional autonomy on the part of the child.

Concerning the relationship between repetition and one aspect of its grammaticalization, namely, pronominalization, one might note the relationship between the two in a sample from the dialogues of Bloom and her daughter Allison at 22 months. For references to self and other in the dyad, 72% of Allison's initial references were full nominals; 28% were characterized by the absence of any lexical item. All of the latter were references to self. In contrast, Bloom's initial references to herself were 50% pronominal, 25% full and 25% null, while her initial references to Allison were entirely pronominal. Subsequent references by M, interestingly enough, were more likely to be full NPs, of which two-thirds were full repetitions of Allison's prior utterance, with or without expansion. Allison's subsequent references, on the other hand, were primarily full or partial self-repetitions incorporating full NPs. For Allison, prior to 2 years, the alternative to overt repetition is null reference rather than (deictic) pronominal reference, although, oddly enough, this is more likely to appear in initial reference, and only to self.

More important than frequency, however, are the forms and functions of repetition in early dialogues and how these change as the child's linguistic skills develop. The picture is considerably complicated by the fact that adults do continue to utilize repetition in its full and overt forms at given times in certain situations, that males and females may differ considerably in their use of repetition, both in function and frequency, and that repetition and its forms are most assuredly sensitive to discourse genre and to values within the community to which speakers belong. Space does not here permit articulation of the implications of all these variables for language development, so what is offered is a general view of the forms and functions of repetition in language development, beginning with the acquisition of the first word around the child's first birthday.

Repetition as Teaching and Learning Strategy

An obvious function of repetition is the overt teaching by the caregiver of lexical items, or of conventional uses of language, or, less clearly, of grammatical skills. Some of these are accompanied and possibly facilitated by repetition of the item by the child. Bloom et al. (1974) concluded that, for children whose imitation (i.e., other-repetition) rate was above .15, the repetition appeared to assist in the acquisition of new lexical items (p. 394). It is unclear what the role of the caregiver's repetition may be in the child's lexical development. Much research has reported that frequency of occurrence of lexical items in a mother's speech to her child is not necessarily related to rate or order of acquisition. However, a recent study by Hampson and Nelson (1990) indicates that certain features of maternal input to 13-month-old early talkers are related to the child's language development at 20 months. This is the case primarily with children who are considered "referential" rather than "expressive" in their linguistic style. These authors maintain that the failure of some previous studies to show a facilitating effect of maternal speech, one apparently universal aspect of which is repetition (Ferguson, 1977; Snow, 1972), were probably focusing primarily on children who were later-talkers, examining maternal input to children 18 to 24 months old rather than 13 months, and not taking into account individual stylistic differences. (For a review of the controversy which still rages regarding the efficacy of maternal language for child acquisition, see Bennett-Kastor, 1988, chap. 1).

Caregivers routinely elicit repetition from the child and repeat themselves as well, in the course of socializing children through language. Schieffelin and Ochs's (1986) volume contains several articles relevant here. For example, Watson-Gegeo and Gegeo (1986) report examples from Kwara'ae children of "calling out" and "repeating" routines in which the adult prompts the child's repetition of an object name or other linguistic item by saying "lia" (look) or " 'uri." Not only are names taught in this manner, but also such conventions as greeting and requesting. It is also suggested that such routines may assist children in analyzing the language which occurs around them. Demuth (1986) looks at prompts by Basotho parents which are designed to teach children the appropriate context in which to utter certain responses. Of course, one need not examine cultures so far away from our own to find caregivers prompting their children in order to teach them socially appropriate responses ("Say 'Please,' " "Tell him 'Thank you,' " or, of a telephone conversation, "Say 'This is Patrick,' " and so on).

Of syntactic development some of the same can be said as for lexical development, although frequency has a much clearer effect on the latter. Bloom et al. (1974) also found that repetition of the mother's utterances was developmentally progressive for syntactic-semantic aspects of language, for some children at least, although by and large children tended to repeat structures with which they were already somewhat familiar (pp. 412–413). The majority of reports examining the role of so-called "imitation" in language development, most of which were published in the seventies, lead one to the conclusion that nonelicited other-repetition by the child is developmentally progressive provided that the structures are only slightly in advance of the child's current grammatical competence (see, for example, Bohannon, 1975, and Love & Parker-Robinson, 1972). However, the mechanisms that would enable repetition to contribute to development have not been described in an acceptable way by authors whose main interest is grammatical development. It is the role of repetition in the larger sense of discourse development, of socialization-individuation, and of what might be called the pragmatic aspects of repetition, which have allowed us to see the relationship between the child's and the adult's language most clearly, and to begin to understand how the difficult problem of identifying transitional mechanisms bridging the two might be solved.

Repetition and Pragmatic Development

When utterances are viewed in the context of conversations, repetitions by the child and the caregiver clearly serve a variety of purposes, some of which can also be served by nonrepetitions. Ochs (1977), for example, has identified the following functions of repetition: agreement, attitudinal commenting, query, self-informing, matching claims or making counterclaims, returning greetings, reversing the direction of a question, requesting or making a repair, and, of course, imitating (pp. 132–133). While these functions hold for children and adults, some uses of repetition, such as imitation, agreement, and repair functions, emerge earlier than others. The "imitation" function emerges especially early and may serve the additional purpose of allowing the child to practice articulation as well as mutuality. In my observations, for example, I have noted such interactions between a 12-month-old girl and her mother. While changing the baby's diaper, the mother utters a word which she knows the baby will recognize. The baby's gaze is locked onto the mother's while the baby repeats the word *sotto voce*, carefully matching the shaping of the mother's mouth. The mother repeats the name, the baby again matches it, and this goes on for several turns. Since the word is the name of a nonpresent older sibling, and the mother offers no further comment about it except to grin widely at the baby's reproductions, the function of these repetitive episodes seems to be articulatory practice, made more interesting by the mutuality of focus by mother and child. At this point, the baby is quite incapable of making additional comments about the topic, which is thus engaged in simply for its own sake. Scollon (1976) reports a similar case in which a 1-year-old appears to be "practicing" articulations with her many repetitions of a word.

Aside from the teaching functions, which account for much use of self-repetition by the caregiver to the child in the early stages of language development (and even prior), a great deal of repetition on the part of the caregiver is devoted to "checking" or confirming the child's utterance. Not only is this necessary because young children often articulate differently from adults, but the child's utterance must be confirmed before the caregiver can make any further contribution to the conversation. Early other-repetitions uttered by the caregiver also serve to check on the communicative intent of the child's utterance, and these are often partial repetitions with expansions, under the category of collaborating discourse topics.

Prior to achieving much grammatical competence, some children may repeat, or attempt to repeat, nearly everything the caregiver says. Because the caregiver may also repeat the child's last contribution, early conversations consequently consist at times of the same utterance being recycled extensively over several turns before information can be established as given. After imitation, this "checking" function seems to emerge in the child's speech as he or she will repeat the caregiver's utterance (which is often a repetition of the child's), as if to "confirm" that the utterance was received. Later, the child may add a lexical affirmation ("yeah," "okay") preceding the repetition. By age 3, however, substitutions come to replace full repetitions in the child's language, substitutions which themselves rely upon background knowledge without overtly repeating it (Ochs Keenan & Klein, 1975, p. 85). In this way, overt repetition becomes increasingly "out of focus" and frees the consciousness of participants for new information which builds upon established presuppositions and discourse-given information.

For example, in one exchange between Bloom and her daughter Allison at 16;3, "down" is repeated 15 times over the course of 31 turns. Several repetitions seem to be the mother's efforts to understand not that Allison is saying "down," but what she means by it. In my own data of conversations with one of my sons, then 2, I have observed five or six full repetitions by me of what I thought was his utterance, alternating with repetitions by him of my own attempts to repeat his original utterance. Once I have established what he is saying, I then go on to utilize part of his utterance in my attempt to determine his intention, for example, "Yes, that's the bathtub. Do you want to take a bath in the bathtub?" Note again the avoidance of pronominal reference. Once my son's other-repetitions had declined but his self-repetitions had increased, that is, his language use showed somewhat more autonomy, both of us used pronouns more frequently, where before we would have used full nominal reference even to something just mentioned in the previous clause.

CONCLUSIONS

This admittedly sketchy review of the development of discourse has focused on the roles that repetition plays, first in the early preverbal interactive routines of infants and caregivers, then in their early conversations, then in less overt forms (substitutions) such as presupposed information or pronominalization which nevertheless reiterate semantic content. Repetition as cohesive device, as the least cognitively complex form of utterances, and as symbol of relational symbiosis is a dominant feature of child language, but one which also predominates in adult conversation. It is suggested that repetition becomes increasingly grammaticalized as competence develops, so that, although the young child has recourse primarily to overt repetition to achieve grammatical and discourse goals, the adult repertoire contains both full, overt forms of repetition and the more broadly defined repetitive phenomena which take the subtler forms associated with co-indexing. Although both extremes can be utilized simultaneously by the adult, different discourse situations typically rely on different manifestations of repetition. Language development might thus be viewed within the context of social development as the increasing differentiation of repetitive phenomena.

REFERENCES

Bennett-Kastor, T. L. (1983). Noun phrase coherence in child narrative. *Journal of Child Language, 10*, 135–149.

Bennett-Kastor, T. L. (1986). Cohesion and predication in child narrative. *Journal of Child Language, 13*, 353–370.

Bennett-Kastor, T. L. (1988). *Analysing children's language. Methods and theories.* Oxford: Basil Blackwell.

Bennett-Kastor, T. L. (n.d.). *Elaborative structures in children's narratives.* Unpublished manuscript, Wichita State University Department of English.

Berman, R. (1988). On the ability to relate events in narrative. *Discourse Processes, 11*, 469–497.

Bloom, L. (1973). *One word at a time.* The Hague: Mouton.

Bloom, L., Hood, L., & Lightbown, P. (1974). Imitation in language development. *Cognitive Psychology, 6*, 380–420.

Bohannon, J. N., III. (1976). Normal and scrambled grammar in discrimination, imitation, and comprehension. *Child Development, 47*, 669–681.

Bresnan, J., & Mchombo, S. A. (1987). Topic, pronoun, and agreement in Chichewa. *Language, 63*, 741–782.

Brown, R. (1973). *A first language.* Cambridge: Harvard University Press.

Comrie, B. (1986). Review of F. Klein-Andreu (Ed.), *Discourse Perspectives on Syntax. Language, 62*, 163–166.

Demuth, K. (1986). Prompting routines in the language socialization of Basotho children. In B. Schieffelin & E. Ochs (Eds.), *Language socialization across cultures* (pp. 51–79). Cambridge, UK: Cambridge University Press.

DuBois, J. W. (1987). The discourse basis of ergativity. *Language, 63*, 805–855.

Ferguson, C. (1977). Baby talk as a simplified register. In C. Snow & C. Ferguson (Eds.), *Talking to children. Language input and acquisition* (pp. 209–235). Cambridge, UK: Cambridge University Press.

Fox, B. A., & Thompson, S. A. (1990). A discourse explanation of the grammar of relative clauses. *Language, 66,* 297–316.

Friedlander, B., Jacobs, A., Davis, B., & Whetstone, H. (1972). Time sampling analysis of infants' natural language environment in the home. *Child Development, 43,* 730–740.

Gelman, R. (1983). Reconsidering the transition from prelinguistic to linguistic communication. In R. M. Golinkoff (Ed.), *The transition from prelinguistic to linguistic communication.* Hillsdale, NJ: Erlbaum.

Givon, T. (1979a). *On understanding grammar.* New York: Academic Press.

Givon, T. (Ed.). (1979b). *Syntax and semantics. Vol. 12. Discourse and syntax.* New York: Academic Press.

Givon, T. (1979c). From discourse to syntax: Grammar as a processing strategy. In T. Givon (Ed.), *Syntax and semantics. Vol. 12. Discourse and syntax* (pp. 81–112). New York: Academic Press.

Goffman, E. (1974). *Frame analysis: an essay on the organization of experience.* New York: Harper & Row.

Goffman, E. (1981). *Forms of talk.* Philadelphia: University of Pennsylvania Press.

Gumperz, J. (1982). *Discourse strategies.* Cambridge, UK: Cambridge University Press.

Gumperz, J., & Hymes, D. (Eds.). (1972). *Directions in sociolinguistics: The ethnography of communication.* New York: Holt, Rinehart & Winston.

Hampson, J. & Nelson, K. (1990, April). *Early relations between mother talk and language development: Masked and unmasked.* Paper presented at Stanford Child Language Research Forum, Palo Alto, CA.

Hinds, J. (1979). Organizational patterns in discourse. In T. Givon (Ed.), *Syntax and semantics. Vol. 12. Discourse and syntax* (pp. 135–157). New York: Academic Press.

Hopper, P. J. & Thompson, S. A. (1984). The discourse basis for lexical categories in universal grammar. *Language, 60,* 703–752.

Kaplan, L. (1978). *Oneness & separateness: From infant to individual.* New York: Simon & Schuster.

Laubitz, Z. (1987). Conjunction in children's discourse. *Papers and Reports on Child Language Development, 26,* 64–71.

Lewis, D. (1969). *Convention: A philosophical study.* Cambridge, MA: Harvard University Press.

Love, J. M. & Parker-Robinson, C. (1972). Children's imitating grammatical and ungrammatical sentences. *Child development, 43,* 309–319.

Mahler, M., Pines, F., & Bergman, A. (1975). *The psychological birth of the human infant.* New York: Basic Books.

Ochs (Keenan), E. (1977). Making it last: Repetition in children's discourse. In S. Ervin-Tripp & C. Mitchell-Kernan (Eds.), *Child discourse* (pp. 125–138). New York: Academic Press.

Ochs, E. (1979). Planned and unplanned discourse. In T. Givon (Ed.), *Syntax and semantics. Vol. 12. Discourse and syntax* (pp. 51–80). New York: Academic Press.

Ochs (Keenan), E., & Klein, E. (1975). Coherency in children's discourse. *Journal of Psycholinguistic Research, 4,* 365–380.

Ochs, E., & Schieffelin, B. (1976). Topic as a discourse notion: A study of topic in the conversations of children and adults. In C. Li (Ed.), *Subject and topic* (pp. 335–384). New York: Academic Press.

Ochs, E., Schieffelin, B., & Platt, M. (1976). Propositions across utterances and speakers. *Papers and Reports on Child Language Development, 15*, 127–143.

Sacks, H., Schegloff, E., & Jefferson, G. (1974). A simplest systematics for the organization of turn-taking in conversation. *Language, 50*, 696–735.

Sankoff, G. & Brown, P. (1976). The origins of syntax in discourse. *Language, 52*, 631–666.

Schegloff, E., Jefferson, G., & Sacks, H. (1977). The preference for self-correction in the organization of repair in conversation. *Language, 53*, 361–382.

Schegloff, E., & Sacks, H. (1973). Opening up closings. *Semiotica, 7*, 289–327.

Schieffelin, B. & Ochs, E. (Eds.). (1986). *Language socialization across cultures*. New York: Cambridge University Press.

Schodorf, J. (1981). *A comparative analysis of parent-child interactions of language-delayed and linguistically normal children*. Unpublished doctoral dissertation, Wichita State University.

Scollon, R. (1976). *Conversations with a one-year-old: A case study of the developmental foundation of syntax*. Honolulu: University of Hawaii Press.

Snow, C. (1972). Mother's speech to children learning language. *Child development, 43*, 549–565.

Stern, D. (1974). Mother and infant at play: The dyadic interaction involving facial, vocal, and gaze behaviors. In M. Lewis & L. Rosenblum (Eds.), *The effect of the infant on its caregiver* (pp. 187–214). New York: John Wiley & Sons.

Stern, D., Jaffee, J., Beebe, B., & Bennett, S. (1975). Vocalizing in unison and in alternation: Two modes of communication within the mother-infant dyad. In D. Aaronson & R. Reiber (Eds.), *Annals of the New York Academy of Sciences. Vol. 263. Developmental psycholinguistics and communication disorders* (pp. 89–100). New York: New York Academy of Sciences.

Tannen, D. (Ed.). (1984). *Coherence in spoken and written discourse*. Norwood, NJ: Ablex Publishing Corp.

Tannen, D. (1987a). Repetition in conversation: Toward a poetics of talk. *Language, 63*, 574–605.

Tannen, D. (1987b). Repetition and conversation as spontaneous formulaicity. *Text, 7*, 215–243.

Tannen, D. (1989). *Talking voices: Repetition, dialogue, and imagery in conversational discourse*. Cambridge, UK: Cambridge University Press.

Umiker–Sebeok, D. J. (1979). Preschool children's intraconversational narratives. *Journal of Child Language, 6*, 91–110.

Wald, Benji. (1979). The development of the Swahili object marker: A study of the interaction of syntax and discourse. In T. Givon (Ed.), *Syntax and semantics. Vol. 12. Discourse and syntax* (pp. 505–524). New York: Academic Press.

Watson-Gegeo, K. & Gegeo, D. (1986). Calling out and repeating routines in Kwara'ae children's language socialization. In B. Schieffelin & E. Ochs (Eds.), *Language socialization across cultures* (pp. 17–50). Cambridge, UK: Cambridge University Press.

Wells, G. (1985). *Language development in the preschool years*. Cambridge, UK: Cambridge University Press.

Chapter 12
Repetition In Second Language Acquisition*

Russell S. Tomlin

Department of Linguistics
Yamada Language Center
Institute for Cognitive and Decision Sciences
University of Oregon

INTRODUCTION

The NEH conference on repetition in discourse provided its participants an unusual interdisciplinary opportunity to consider repetition from two related perspectives. First, we examined the nature
and function of repetition in particular discourse settings: in conversation, in the classroom, in literature, in the cockpit, in ritual.
Second, we considered how one might develop a theory of repetition
suitable to embrace the disparate kinds of discourse we each had
examined individually. In this chapter I discuss both of these perspectives as they pertain to second language acquisition.

---

* This research was supported by a grant (G008541129) from the Fund for the
Improvement of Postsecondary Education (FIPSE). This chapter represents a particu-
lar product derived from the work of a group of people, including Sarah Douglas,
David Novick, Kyra Carroll, Suzanne Shroyer, and Gary Smithrud. I have also bene-
fited from discussions and criticisms offered by Hartmut Burmeister, Larry Selinker,
Matthew Dryer, John Henderson, and Michael Dawson.

General Issues

Among the general issues about repetition raised during the conference, many of which are examined in other contributions to this volume, there are two of importance to this chapter:

1. Are structural conditions alone sufficient to identify instances of repetition?
2. What does it mean to say that there are different kinds of repetition?

These issues center on the problem of identifying those linguistic behaviors which are to be called repetitions. Without some explicit treatment of these issues no coherent theory or model of repetition is possible. While it is clear that there must be structural congruence between an initial utterance and a repetition, I will claim that structural congruence alone is not adequate to define or identify repetition. The second issue has to do with the range of variation in linguistic behavior we call repetition and requires a clear indication of how distinct types are to be properly distinguished.

Issues Concerning Second Language Acquisition

The issues of importance to *second language acquisition* (SLA) derive from earlier work on input and interaction in SLA discourse. Within the SLA literature an important distinction is drawn between the primary linguistic data to which the learner has access, called *input*, and that portion of the input which is in fact processed by the learner, called *intake* (Ellis, 1980, 1986; Gass, 1985; Gass & Madden, 1985; Hamayan & Tucker, 1980; Hatch, 1983; Larsen-Freeman, 1983; Long, 1985; Scarcella & Higa, 1981). In general, it is argued that input which is *comprehensible* to the learner (Krashen, 1977, 1982; Krashen & Terrell, 1983) facilitates intake and thus acquisition. Input can be modified to increase its comprehensibility through three general strategies: (a) exploit the immediate physical context, the so-called "here-and now" principle; (b) modify the structural features of the input; and (c) modify the interactional characteristics of the input. Repetition represents one kind of tactical action an interlocutor can take to implement these three principal strategies.

While repetition has always been seen as important to second language learning and teaching, relatively little research has been conducted on its role in SLA discourse interactions. There are four issues which should be considered.

1. What functions does repetition realize in SLA discourse?
2. Under what conditions does repetition occur in SLA discourse?
3. What kind of input is repetition in SLA discourse?
4. What can the study of repetition contribute to our understanding of input and interaction in SLA?

On the surface, repetition in SLA appears trivial, even uninteresting: one interlocutor, say a language tutor, provides an additional token of some input utterance or some part of it. Sometimes repetitions are complete; sometimes they are partial. Sometimes utterances are repeated in conjunction with further actions taken by the tutor or the learner; sometimes there seems to be repetition with no associated action on either participant's part. Repetition in SLA looks like nothing more than random or unconstrained redundancy. It appears to provide additional input tokens, but exactly when, where, or why is unclear.

The position developed here is that repetition in SLA is a social act with cognitive consequences. As a social act, repetition represents an attempt by the tutor to help the learner comprehend an immediately preceding utterance; but this social act has clear cognitive consequences for the learner in helping transform L_2 input into intake. In the tutorial protocols we examined, we can identify four distinct kinds of repetition, each with a distinct role to play within the second language discourse.

THE FLATLAND PROTOCOL

The FlatLand protocol permits the consistent collection of comparable interactive discourse data from a variety of learner–tutor pairs. It provides a means, congruent with task-based, communicative language teaching theory, of examining the earliest development of listening comprehension abilities in nil proficiency learners.

In the FlatLand protocol we set a simple, observable teaching–learning problem before two participants. A second language tutor must help a nil proficiency learner construct two-dimensional configurations of geometric shapes, using the new second language. The configurations are constructed piece by piece from a restricted inventory of eight objects, all visible to both participants: large and small, black and white, circles or squares. Participants are further

Before   After

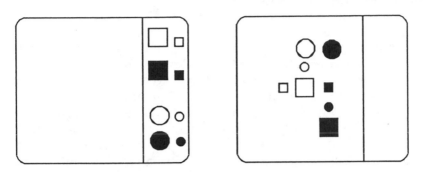

Tutor Utterances

Take the large white square and put it in the center of the screen.
Put the small black square to the left of the large white square.
Put the small black circle below the small black square.
Put the large black square below the small black circle.
Put the small white square to the left of the large white square.
Put the small white circle above the large white square.
Put the large white circle above the small white circle.
Put the large black circle to the right of the large white circle.

Figure 12.1   Before and after a FlatLand protocol

restricted to the use of a set of five spatial relations: above, below, left, right, and between, and their counterparts in languages other than English. We asked the tutor to use only L_2, and the learner not to speak during the interaction, though both participants were free to manipulate the objects as each chose to. Some protocols were collected face-to-face using matte board counters. Others were collected through a computer-mediated arrangement in which the participants could see and manipulate the same set of objects displayed on different monitors and could freely speak and hear each other but could not see each other.[1] Figure 12.1 illustrates the beginning state

[1] These data were originally collected as part of a FIPSE-supported project in computer-assisted second language instruction. We needed to compare how tutors interacted face to face, where visual access to hand, eye, and facial movements were freely accessible, with how they interacted without visual access, simulating the kind of environment found in a computer-based tutor, which can neither see nor send such cues.

of the display, a subsequent state at the end of a protocol, and a sample discourse leading to it.[2]

The FlatLand data collection protocol offers some advantage to the study of second language acquisition. It gives the researcher a very complete record of the initial stages of acquisition. At the beginning of the interaction, the learner knows nothing of L_2. In fact, for the Indonesian data considered here we know that the learner had never before heard uttered a word of Indonesian. At the end of the session we know also that the learner had acquired some measure of listening ability in L_2, albeit limited ability, because the learner could build configurations of geometric shapes in response to near native-like instruction in L_2[3]. After a single 40-minute session, subsequent testing on the same task, as long as 18 months later, still showed the learner capable of building these simple configurations in response to oral instructions in L_2, even though the learner had invested no additional effort to learn L_2, or be exposed to L_2, or even to practice at all what she had encountered. By videotaping the interaction, we record virtually all of the input and interaction leading to the limited acquisition we witness.

The data discussed in this chapter come from one of 11 FlatLand protocols recorded, an interaction between an experienced teacher of Bahasa Indonesia (Indonesian) and a nil proficiency learner.

A SOCIOCOGNITIVE MODEL OF TASK-BASED INTERACTIONS IN SLA

Second language acquisition is an individual-based process of socially mediated cognitive development (Tomlin, 1990).[4] The details

---

[2] It is not possible in a printed format to convey the dynamic nature of these interactions. For the reader to appreciate better the protocol, one might start with the left-hand picture and then read the first line of the discourse. Imagine not just the end state of the display but the act of selecting the object and the path it takes through space to its proper goal location. Proceed with this for the remaining lines in the discourse. The information the participants work with during the interaction includes all of the temporal and directional information inherent in the physical procedure along with the linguistic evidence and the initial and final states of the display.

[3] The main difference is one of pace or speed of production on the part of the tutor.

[4] The term *development* is sometimes restricted to maturational changes in children. I will use the term in a less restricted sense to convey adult changes from lacking any knowledge of L_2 to acquiring some knowledge of L_2.

of the L_2 grammar are developed in a particular individual through interaction within the social environment. At the most microscopic level of analysis one would like to know precisely what sort of social acts contribute to the development of the grammar, and how they operate to do so. Both the goals and the methods of SLA research must ultimately target the individual learner.

Repetition represents one useful window for examining the socio-cognitive bases of SLA. Repetition, at least as it will be conceived here, represents one general sort of social act encountered by the learner specifically to support comprehension in the learner; it is a social act engaged in by participants in second language discourse. The significance of repetition as a social act in second language discourses derives not at all from its social consequences alone but from its cognitive consequences on the developing grammar of the L_2 learner. To be of importance to a theory of SLA, acts of repetition must contribute new cognitive states in the learner in some explicit manner.

The model of task-based discourse interaction in SLA used here derives from earlier FlatLand work described by Tomlin (1989). In that model the behavioral task placed before participants is represented as a network of *events*, where each event in the network represents some behavioral act which must occur in order for some overall *general task* to be completed. In the FlatLand protocol the general task is building the simple two-dimensional configurations described above. In order to do so, the learner, or anyone else for that matter, must be able to work through the network of related subtasks displayed in Figure 12.2.

In order to construct the two-dimensional configuration shown in Figure 12.1, the learner must maneuver through this event network eight times. Each time the learner must (a) identify the object to be placed, the *target object*; (b) identify the intended location for its placement, the *target location*; which is identified through (c) identification of a landmark, the *landmark object*. With these subtasks completed, the learner can then move the target object to its required location.

How the tutor and the learner proceed to accomplish the general task in the new L_2 is managed rather neatly. The tutor provides input utterances congruent with the earliest event in the network the tutor believes the learner cannot manage in L_2, what we call the *primed* event. Similarly, the learner construes input utterances provided by the tutor as attempts to deal with that earliest event as well (Tomlin, 1989). The participants continue with that earliest primed

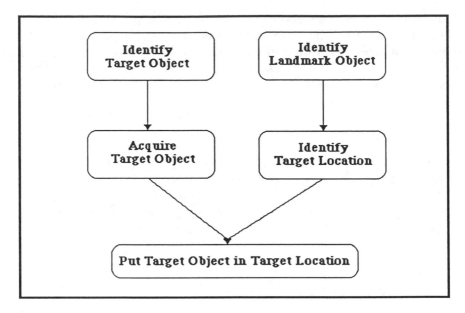

Figure 12.2   The FlatLand event network

event until the tutor is satisfied that the learner can now manage the event in the new language.[5]

In the FlatLand task setting, the learner cannot accomplish either the general task or any of its component iterations without comprehending oral instructions from the tutor. What the tutor says is also well constrained. The tutor selects events estimated to be *essential* to the learner's efforts to build an appropriate event representation for the general task at hand. An event is essential if the tutor believes that:

1. the learner will fail in the general task without its express presentation,
2. the learner cannot already access the event, and
3. the learner cannot infer the event.

Under the circumstances of the FlatLand protocol all of the component events turn out to be essential events.[6] Events estimated by

---

[5] Difficulties encountered by the participants derive from erroneous estimates by one or the other participant about (a) the details of the event network, (b) the current location in the event network, (c) the "next" event, and so on.

[6] The distinction between essential and nonessential events is useful for capturing the difference between utterances like *Put the small black square below the large white circle* and *Get the small black square. Now put it below the large white circle.*

the tutor to be essential to the learner require the tutor to take overt action to ensure their representation in the learner. When that action involves communication, the acts are *rhetorical acts*.

Rhetorical Acts

The rhetorical act represents a basic linguistic action taken by an individual in a given discourse context. It represents an attempt by the speaker to direct some action on the part of the listener. The Indonesian protocol considered here can be viewed as a hierarchically organized rhetorical structure. The structure seen represents the outcome of dynamic rhetorical processes, decisions taken and acted out by the discourse participants. The model of rhetorical organization adopted here follows the general outline of earlier work (Grimes, 1975; Hinds, 1979; Levy, 1979; Mehan, 1979; Sinclair & Brazil, 1982; Sinclair & Coulthard, 1975; Wells, 1981a,b,c) in that it:

1. treats discourse as composed of hierarchically organized rhetorical components,
2. identifies a basic organizational composite, the rhetorical act, as the basic unit of rhetorical activity.

In the discourse fragment in (1), four distinct rhetorical acts can be identified.

In the transcripts which follow the following conventions are used. Bold-faced material describes the state of the computer display. X refers to the cursor. The three-letter code (e.g., **SWS**) captures the size, color, and shape of some object (Small, White, Square). Tutor or Student Control refers to the participant currently controlling the cursor. All utterances are by the tutor except those in italics (none in this example). A single slash indicates the end of an utterance. All capitals indicates stressed items.

In the first case, the speaker assumes that identifying the target object requires no overt action on his part. The utterance deals only with the terminal event on the network, and the speaker leaves it to the hearer to satisfy any earlier events. In the second case, congruent with what we see happen in the beginning stages of FlatLand protocols, the speaker assumes that the hearer cannot routinely identify the target object and so takes an explicit step to assist the hearer in doing so. *Essential* deals only with estimates by the speaker of what the hearer may need; it does not deal with whether a component of the behavioral event network itself is necessary.

(1) Indonesian

		Tutor Control
	02:52	**X →**
	02:56	**X on SWS**
	02:56	**SWS →**
DESC OBJ–	02:57	Ko:tak/
	02:58	**SWS upper-right screen**
	03:01	**reset screen**
VOC———	03:02	Molly
MAN REQ—	03:03	ko:tak/
		Student Control
	03:03	**X →**
	03:06	X on SWS
	03:06	SWS →
	03:06	SWS upper right screen
AFFIRM ——	03:09	Ba:ik/

These four rhetorical acts represent distinctive tactical actions taken by the tutor during the FlatLand interaction. The DESCRIBE OBJECT (DESC OBJ) is used to assist the learner formulate a lexical hypothesis for *"kotak,"* which is required in order to deal with the first event in the FlatLand network (identify target object). The VOCATIVE (VOC) serves to attract the attention of the learner to a change in the current task. The MANIPULATION REQUEST (MAN REQ) permits the tutor to test the presence and strength of L_2 hypotheses in the learner by requiring learner manipulation of the world in response to L_2 utterances. Finally, the AFFIRM act serves to signal to the learner satisfactory closure on the current task.

The FlatLand tutorials are composed of networks of exactly nine rhetorical act types. Adapting insights in Searle (1969, 1976, 1979), a rhetorical act in our framework consists of three criterial components:

1. An intentional construct, or simply Intention,
2. Behavioral content,
3. Preparatory conditions.

The *intention* of a rhetorical act represents the underlying motive precipitating performance of the act. It is, following Brand (1984), a mental event, the immediate and proximate cause of particular actions engaged in by the tutor. It is also the principal defining characteristic of particular rhetorical acts. In some cases, it is only a difference in intention that distinguishes one rhetorical act from another. For the rhetorical act DESCRIBE OBJECT (DESC OBJ) the intention is to establish a lexical hypothesis (i.e., a link between a lexical item and some mental representation of the world) in the learner.

The *behavioral content* represents the set of actions, mental or physical, which the tutor carries out due to the intention. The behavioral content of a rhetorical act includes a description of the generally desired outcome (goals) of the rhetorical act and of the means of achieving this outcome (methods). For the rhetorical act describe object, the behavioral content includes:

1. Goal$_1$: Tutor directs learner attention to some part of the environment.
2. Method$_1$: Tutor points to object.
3. Goal$_2$: Learner links attended object to linguistic input.
4. Method$_2$: Tutor utters object-name after attention is allocated to object by learner.

Preparatory conditions represent tutor assumptions regarding preliminary or ongoing states of affairs in the tutor, in the learner, or in the world which must be present in order for a given rhetorical act to be executed. For the act of describe object, the preparatory conditions include:

1. tutor believes learner does not have lexical hypothesis,
2. tutor assumes object is available to the learner,
3. tutor assumes learner is familiar with the concept of the object,
4. tutor wants learner to include lexical item in learner model.

All of the tutorial interactions we observed can be described in terms of patterns of these nine rhetorical act types:

1. DESCRIBE OBJECT (DESC OBJ),
2. DESCRIBE RELATION (DESC REL),
3. MANIPULATION REQUEST (MAN REQ),
4. REPEAT EXPRESSION (REP EXP),
5. REPEAT FOCUS (REP FOC),
6. REPEAT ACT (REP ACT),
7. AUGMENTED REPEAT (REP AUG),
8. AFFIRM (AFFIRM),
9. VOCATIVE (VOC).

A complete description of this inventory cannot be presented here, but it may be useful to consider one example. In the following

DESC OBJ, the tutor directs learner attention to a square by dragging it out into the central screen area and then utters *kotak* "square" with the completion of the movement.

(2) INDONESIAN

All objects in home position

Tutor Control

DESC OBJ	02:42	**X →**
	02:44	**X on LWS**
	02:44	**LWS →**
	02:46	**LWS lower-right screen**
	02:46	Ko:tak/

The preparatory conditions for this rhetorical act are met in that: (a) the tutor wants the learner to link *kotak* to "square," (b) the tutor knows the learner has not yet made this connection, (c) the tutor knows the object is available to the learner, and (d) there is no doubt the learner is familiar with squares, and so on. These conditions set up activation of the intention to help the learner formulate a specific lexical hypothesis, which in turn leads to execution of the behavioral conditions of (a) drawing attention to the object by moving it, and (b) uttering the input expression *kotak*. The repetition acts seen in the FlatLand protocols can be explicitly described in the same kind of terms.

FOUR KINDS OF REPETITION IN SLA

In these FlatLand data we see four distinct kinds of repetition acts, distinguished from one another by differences in their components and by the contribution each makes to the developing grammar. The four types of repetition are:

1.   REPEAT EXPRESSION (REP EXP)
2.   REPEAT FOCUS (REP FOC)
3.   REPEAT ACT (REP ACT)
4.   AUGMENTED REPEAT (REP AUG)

Repeat Expressions (REP EXP)

REP EXP acts display the following structural characteristics. A REP EXP consists of the verbatim repetition of an immediately preceding utterance. REP EXP's exhibit no significant differences from their preceding utterances in lexical items selected, nor in the grammatical construction used, nor in the intonational pattern selected. In addition, one sees no change in the associated visual display. The tutor does not move any objects nor does the tutor point to any particular object. Further, the learner performs no action of any kind. Finally, REP EXPs occur principally, but not exclusively, with DESC OBJ or DESC REL acts, actions which introduce lexical items to the learner.

Examples (3) and (4) illustrate two instances of REP EXPs.

(3) INDONESIAN PROTOCOL

Tutor control

	┌00:00	**X on LBS**
DESC OBJ┤	00:06	**LBS →**
	00:08	**LBS lower-right screen**
	00:08	Ko:tak/
REP EXP—└	00:11	Ko:tak/

(4) INDONESIAN PROTOCOL

	┌24:51	**SWS →**
	24:54	**SWS upper screen (above other shapes)**
DESC REL┤	24:55	**X moves erratically (trying to drag?)**
	25:02	**SWS →**
	25:06	**SWS r LBC /l LWC**
	└25:08	Ko:tak (.11) pu:tih KE:CIL (.84)
		DI:(.11)ANTARA (.21) ling:karan/
REP EXP——	25:16	Ko:tak pu:tih KE:CIL (.60) DI:ANTARA (.84)
		DI:ANTARA lingkaran/

Functionally, REP EXPs are produced by the tutor with no explicit or overt action on the part of the learner. They appear to come early in the formation of lexical hypotheses, and they are offered very quickly. For the 26 instances of REP EXPs in the Indonesian sample, the mean latency between end of the first utterance and the start of the repetition is 2.248 seconds with a standard deviation of about 1 second.

In example (3), the objects are all located in their original home positions. The tutor selects the large black square and moves it into the lower right-hand quadrant of the display, uttering *kotak* "square." About 3 seconds later, with no action displayed or taken by the learner and none requested or expected, the tutor repeats *kotak* again. In example (4), occurring 24 minutes into the protocol, the tutor selects the small white square and moves it to a position between the large white circle and the large black circle (placed earlier). His utterance at 25:08 constitutes a description of the resulting display: the small white square is between the circles. Again, 1.92 seconds later, the tutor repeats his first utterance. And, again, he does so without overt action by the learner of any kind.

Interestingly, it turns out that the ability of an individual to sustain a phonological representation without further rehearsal or input is about 2 seconds (Cowan, 1988). In addition, learners who participated in the FlatLand protocol report severe difficulty sub-vocalizing the utterances of the tutor, even though they are uniformly able to comprehend those utterances well enough to complete the overall task. It appears then that the tutor provides REP EXPs to help the learner sustain a phonological representation of the utterance to work on. This is not to say that the tutor knows that the learner needs an additional token of input for any specific cognitive reasons; in fact, it is very unlikely that any tutor would even suspect such a thing. On the other hand, it seems also unlikely to be accidental that the conditions under which the tutor provides this additional input should so closely match the cognitive conditions associated with the privileged phonological loop.

REPEAT EXPRESSIONs represent the simplest and in some sense purest kind of repetition in these SLA data. An exact replica of an immediately preceding utterance is produced without any associated change in the current context. The timing and distribution of these acts suggest strongly that they help the learner sustain a phonological representation the learner may otherwise be incapable of sustaining in the earliest stages of SLA. If this is true, we see a clear instance in which a rhetorical act, under the conscious control of the tutor, may have consequences which neither the tutor nor the learner is directly aware of but which aid directly in the cognitive processing of L_2 speech by the second language learner.

Repeat Focus (REP FOC)

REP FOC acts display structural characteristics distinct from those of REP EXPs. A REP FOC consists of the verbatim repetition of just one part of an immediately preceding utterance. One sees no change in the associated visual display. The tutor does not move any objects nor does the tutor point to any particular object. Further, the learner performs no action of any kind. Finally, REP FOCs occur principally, but not exclusively, with MAN REQ acts. That is, they occur in association with actions that test the strength of hypotheses in the learner.

Examples (5–7) illustrate three instances of REP FOC's.

(5) INDONESIAN PROTOCOL

MAN REQ	34:25	Ko:tak hitam kecil (1.02) DI:ANTARA (.81) KO:TAK pu:tih/
	34:29	**X → (tries to drag SBS)**
REP FOC	34:31	DI:ANTARA (.15) KO:TAK pu:tih/
	34:32	**SBS →**
	34:36	**SBS a LWS/u SWS**
AFFIRM	34:36	Baik/

(6) INDONESIAN PROTOCOL

Student Control

MAN REQ	23:28	Ko:tak hi:tam kecil (2.04) DI:KANAN (.66) lingkaran (.11) pu:tih (.11) be:sar/
	23:36	**X → (tries to drag SBS)**
REP FOC ——	23:36	Di:kanan?/
	23:37	**SBS →**
AFFIRM ——	23:39	Baik/
	23:40	**SBS r LWC /l LBC**
AFFIRM ——	23:41	Baik/

(7) INDONESIAN PROTOCOL

	08:09	**X →**
	08:16	**X on SWS**
	08:16	**SWS →**
	08:20	**SWS upper screen**
	08:25	**X on LWS**
	08:25	**LWS →**
	08:36	**LWS u SWS (circuitous route)**
DESC ——	08:40	Ko:tak (.93) ke:cil PU:TIH (1.65) DI:ATAS (.63)
REL		kotak (.39) besar (.27) putih/
REP FOC	08:51	DI(.15)ATAS/

In (5) the tutor asks the learner to place the small black square between the white squares. The learner attempts to pick up the small black square but drops it. At this point the tutor repeats the locative portion of his prior utterance. The learner then picks up the small black square and places it in the correct target location, between the white squares. The tutor confirms this with an AFFIRM act, realized by the utterance *baik* "right."

In (6) the tutor follows very much the same pattern. He asks the learner to put the small black square to the right of the large white circle. The learner tries to move the small black square but drops it. The tutor then repeats just a portion of his prior utterance, the preposition *di:kanan*. The learner reacquires the target object and begins to move it to the target location, receiving an AFFIRM. At 34:36 the learner places the target object in its targeted location, receiving another AFFIRM from the tutor.

In (7) no MAN REQ is involved. Instead, the tutor moves the small white square onto the screen and follows this by placing the large white square below it. He follows these actions with the utterance at 8:40 that describes the resulting state of the display: the small white square is above the large white square. About 3 seconds later the tutor repeats a portion of the preceding utterance, the preposition *di:atas* "above."

In each of these cases the tutor repeats only a portion of the preceding utterance. The repeated segment is not randomly determined, nor is it structurally determined, despite the illustrative examples all displaying locative prepositions. To see how the selection is made, we need to reconsider the model of SLA discussed earlier.

In that model the general task of building these configurations is composed of a network of events, represented by the directed graph in Figure 12.2. The learner cannot complete events later in the graph until he or she has completed events earlier on. This constrains the participants' interaction in important ways. It constrains the tutor to provide input utterances congruent with the earliest event located in the graph that the learner cannot yet manage. There is no point trying to deal with identifying target locations if the learner cannot yet deal with identifying objects in L_2. Similarly, the learner is constrained to interpret incoming input utterances, consistent with the Gricean principle of relevance (Grice, 1975), as efforts to provide input congruent with the earliest event the learner cannot yet manage in L_2.

Such an event is an *essential* one, since the learner cannot complete the task without its explicit communication, but it will also be called a *primed* event to indicate its status as the earliest event the learner cannot yet manage in L_2. Whenever the identity and structure of the primed essential event are clear to the learner and the input provided by the tutor congruent with that event, the input will be comprehensible to the learner and it will be processed as data for the developing grammar, that is, treated as intake.

REP FOCs repeat just the portion of the preceding utterance that deals with the critical primed event. By the time of the utterances presented in each of the examples, the tutor and learner have already dealt with the earlier events associated with the identification of objects. The learner has already demonstrated that she can select particular objects from the given inventory by comprehending utterances in L_2. However, she has not yet demonstrated that she can manage utterances dealing with the identification of target locations, meaning that it is this event which is the current primed one during each of the example cases.

It is, of course, logically possible that other parts of a given utterance might be repeated. For example, in example (4) there are seven lexical items and there is no a priori reason why any one of them should not be repeated. Yet in virtually every case in the Indonesian protocol, it is the portion of the preceding utterance which deals with the primed essential event which is repeated in the REP FOC.

Up to this point we have considered *what* is repeated; we need also to consider when this kind of repetition occurs. Clearly, it does not occur on every occasion of a MAN REQ or a DESC REL. The preponderance of cases of these acts do not have corresponding REP FOCs. This means that it is not the presence of another rhetorical act that prompts the occurrence of the REP FOC.

Instead, it appears that REP FOCs occur when the tutor has some reason to believe that the learner is having trouble with the most recent input utterance. In our SLA model, the tutor monitors two different learner behaviors: *uptake* and *hesitancy*. Uptake is the latency between the end of a tutor action and the beginning of an expected learner action. It can be measured by noting the time between the end of an input utterance requiring learner action and the movement of the cursor by the learner. Hesitancy is the directness with which the learner performs an expected action. It can be measured by directness or smoothness of the movement of an object along a path from the current location of an object to the requested location. In general, both uptake and hesitancy are taken to be normal when the time and effort it takes for the learner to complete an action does not exceed significantly the time it would take the tutor or another native speaker to carry out the requested task.

Most REP FOCs occur when the tutor sees the learner make an error, where the error is either slow uptake or hesitant movement. In examples (5) and (6), the learner drops the target object and must pick it up again, an instance of hesitant behavior. Of the 23 instances of REP FOCs in the Indonesian protocol, all but four involve MAN REQs. Of those, 11 involve overt hesitancy on the part of the learner, usually dropping the target object, sometimes moving it slightly without any indication of a particular path or destination. Seven involve uptake, with the median latency at about 7 seconds, considerably longer than the 2- to 3-second delays on MAN REQs without associated REP FOCs. The remaining case involves an overt learner mistake selecting the target object. The tutor targets the small black square, but the learner selects the small black circle. This error triggers a REP FOC which repeats identification of the intended target object.

Functionally, the purpose of the REP FOC is to provide additional input to offset an error made by the learner, reflected in the uptake and hesitancy with which the learner responds. The REP FOC selects that portion of the preceding utterance which deals most directly with the critical primed essential event at the moment in the tutorial interaction.

Repeat Act (REP ACT)

REP ACT acts display the following structural characteristics. A REP ACT consists of the verbatim repetition of an immediately preceding utterance coupled with an identical repetition of the immediately preceding nonverbal action. There are only a few instances of REP ACTs in the protocol, represented well by (8).

(8) INDONESIAN PROTOCOL

	⌐01:10	**X on SBS**
	│ 01:10	**SBS →**
	│ 01:12	**SBS upper-right screen**
DESC OBJ —└ 01:12		Ko:tak/
REP AUG —— 01:13		Ko:tak HITAM/
	01:18	**SBS →**
	01:19	**SBS slightly to right**
REP ACT —— 01:19		Ko:tak HITAM/

Unlike the previous kinds of repetition, REP ACTs do involve tutor manipulation of the visual display. Initially, the tutor moves the small black square into a position in the upper right corner of the display, and produces a DESC OBJ coupled with an augmented repetition (see below). The function of this combination of acts is to help the learner develop initial hypotheses for the lexical item *hitam*, "black." Immediately afterward, the tutor again moves the same small black square in virtually the same position and repeats his last utterance. Thus, the tutor has repeated the complete action begun at 1:10.

It is not at all clear what the function of this kind of repetitive act might be. There are only five cases of REP ACTs in the entire protocol. They all occur after rhetorical acts which introduce lexical items for color or shape or location, DESC OBJs or DESC RELs. But they seem to add little to the tutorial interaction. They do not narrow down the hypotheses the learner might be entertaining about some lexical item, as do ordinary DESC OBJs or DESC RELs. Nor do they seem to provide an additional input token for memorial purposes as do REP EXPs; otherwise there would be no reason to move the target object. It seems most likely that the tutor believes that the learner simply missed the original act or that the tutor has botched his own effort and offers a second effort to make up for the mistake, but there is no evidence recoverable from the transcript to easily sustain such a view.

Augmented Repetition (REP AUG)

REP AUGs are the final kind of repetition seen in the FlatLand protocols. Its structural characteristics distinguish it from the other three kinds of repetition, though it is most similar to simple REP EXPs. A REP AUG involves the verbatim repetition of an immediately preceding utterance but with additional information provided. Like REP EXPs, a REP AUG displays no delay between the initial utterance and the repetition itself. And, it is restricted to early segments of the protocols, the time during which lexical hypotheses are generated and tested. The added information targets a new component to object identification, and this component information is typically stressed. Example (9) illustrates a REP AUG.

(9) INDONESIAN PROTOCOL

		Tutor control
	03:50	**reset screen**
	03:53	**X →**
	03:54	**X on SWS**
	03:54	**SWS →**
	03:56	**SWS upper-right screen**
DESC OBJ	03:57	Ko:tak/
REP AUG	03:59	Ko:tak (.45) PU:TIH/
	04:01	**SWS →**
	04:03	**SWS upper right screen (slightly lower)**
	04:03	**X →**
	04:07	**X on LWS**
	04:08	**LWS →**
	04:09	**LWS lower-right screen**
DESC OBJ	04:09	Ko:tak/
REP AUG	04:10	Ko:tak (.21) pu:tih/

At this point in the protocol, the participants have completed work sufficient to have established the meaning and use of *kotak*, "square." The tutor now begins to work on color as a second variable in the identification of targeted objects. After resetting the screen, which moves all of the objects to their original positions to the right of the work area, the tutor selects the small white square, moves it to the upper right quadrant of the work area, and provides the input utterances at 3:57 and 3:59. The delay between the end of the initial utterance and the beginning of the REP AUG is only .84 seconds.

The first utterance is not needed to establish or sustain a hypothesis about the lexical item *kotak*; that has already been established in earlier interaction. It is the second utterance which does the new work in this interaction, introducing the lexical item *putih*, "white." What, then, is the relationship between the first and second utterances in such a pair?

The most reasonable hypothesis is that the first utterance sets up the conceptual framework against which the second utterance is construed. The second utterance then provides crucial elaborative information that must be incorporated into the current learner model. The speed with which the REP AUG is offered is very fast, always within a second of the initial utterance and in one instance a mere .11 second later. This quickness almost suggests that the utterance pairs are really a kind of topicalization structure, except that the initial utterance does display the falling intonation and closure of an utterance boundary and the delay is just a bit too long to sustain that view.

DISCUSSION

Thus far, we have described a general framework for examining task-based tutorials, focusing on the notion of an event network coupled with a set of rhetorical acts to maneuver through it. We have also identified four distinct types of repetition as specific rhetorical acts used by the tutor during the tutorial interaction.

1. REP EXPs duplicate exactly and quickly the preceding utterance and appear to help the learner sustain a phonological representation of the input utterance.
2. REP FOCs duplicate the portion of the preceding utterance associated with the currently primed essential event to help the learner manage uncertainty revealed by hesitancy or uptake delay.
3. REP ACTs duplicate an entire preceding tutorial event, language and behavior, apparently as self-correction by the tutor.
4. REP AUGs duplicate a preceding utterance quickly and add an additional bit of information needed to address a newly addressed essential event.

We should consider now the issues raised at the beginning of this chapter in light of the observations made here about repetition on SLA discourse.

With regard to the issues specific to repetition in SLA, there are three main points to be made. First, the four distinct repetition acts identified and described here provide input to the learner which helps to make other L_2 utterances more comprehensible to the learner. Each type represents a tactical act providing very immediate support to the dynamic unfolding of the discourse interaction. The support provided in each case is a kind of cognitive support, a localized assist to the learner as she tries to build a complete mental representation of the geometric configuration being built. Each repetition seen in the protocol data seems directed to helping the learner develop a mental representation of the next step in the geometric structure, reflected in the observable, step-by-step actions taken, which is clear and explicit and complete.

Second, the repetition acts described here occur only when the tutor estimates the learner may be having trouble dealing with some immediate L_2 utterance. Those estimates are made in terms of how the learner is managing a general task whose components can be described explicitly as a network of interrelated events. The selection of particular repetition acts, the clearest perhaps being REP FOCs, is conditioned by the immediate and local success in maneuvering through that network. It seems to me important theoretically to emphasize that the selection of repetition acts is not conditioned by the co-occurrence of other rhetorical acts, despite superficial appearances to the contrary. REP FOCs do not occur as a consequence of having been preceded by MAN REQs, even though most REP FOCs in fact do follow MAN REQs. They occur only because the proper local cognitive conditions hold: that the learner has evidenced hesitancy or slow uptake on a particular primed essential event, a situation which occurs most frequently after MAN REQs.

In principle, then, we can define or describe such event networks explicitly, and we can see more precisely where and when the learner encounters difficulties and what the tutor does to assist. L_2 discourse is thus viewed, not simply as a cohesive set of utterances, as text per se, but as a dynamic interplay between uttering and doing in real, dynamic time. And our theories of how discourse works, especially the union of the cognitive with the social dimensions of communicative interaction, must more directly deal with this kind of dynamism.

Finally, the study of repetition in SLA discourse can add to our general understanding of input and interaction in SLA in two main ways. One, we can see that structural analyses of repetition without accompanying functional analysis will yield a very incomplete picture of repetition. Despite the apparent objectivity of structural analysis, one cannot see clearly the role that repetition plays in SLA without a careful examination of how and when repetitive acts come into play during SLA interactions. For example, without the descriptive detail accompanying the transcriptions produced for this study, the Indonesian protocol looks distressingly . . . repetitive. Here are the first input utterances of the protocol, with no additional information:

Kotak/
Kotak/
Kotak/
Kotak/
Kotak/
Molly/
Kotak/
Kotak/
Kotak hitam/
Kotak/
Kotak hitam/
Kotak hitam/
Kotak/
Kotak hitam/

The structural analysis invites us to conclude that there were seven repetitions of the lexical item *kotak*, three of the NP *kotak hitam*, and one repetition of the vocative *Molly*. Under a simplistic structural analysis acquisition is associated with the frequency with which items are presented to the learner, leading to overly simplistic views that it is through sheer frequency of encounter that lexical items or other aspects of grammar are learned. But the repetition we see contributes much more to the interaction than simply increasing the frequency of exposure to input utterances.

Two, the kind of model offered here can help make more explicit the dynamic nature of discourse and grammar. By examining the microscopic organization of discourses whose associated tasks are transparent to the analyst, especially where we have an explicit understanding of what the L_2 learner is currently capable of doing, we have a good chance to see the contribution made by each utterance to the learner as it is presented in dynamic, real time. Since the goal of our SLA efforts must be to understand the development of an L_2 system in the individual learner, we must look for ways to examine learning happening on an individual basis.

With regard to repetition in more general terms, there are also two conclusions to be drawn. One, if we are to claim that there are distinct types of repetition or that repetition realizes distinct functions, we must provide some explicit means of differentiating repetition types and their associated functions. In this chapter this was done by developing a general model of L_2 discourse interactions in terms of a general event network coupled with a theory of rhetorical action. The differences among the four types of repetition described here can be captured in terms of such an explicit framework.

Two, a theory of repetition must treat repetition as rhetorical action of one kind or another. While all of the acts identified here involve structural congruence between the repetition and a preceding utterance, strict congruence alone is an inadequate means of identifying repetitions, unless repetition is to be reduced trivially to simple structural congruence. In treating repetition as rhetorical action, one recognizes that intention in general and attention to cognitive models in particular are central components of a more general theory of repetition.

REFERENCES

Brand, M. (1984). *Intending and acting: Toward a naturalized action theory.* Cambridge, MA: MIT Press.

Cowan, N. (1988). Evolving conceptions of memory storage, selective attention, and their mutual constraints within the human information-processing system. *Psychological Bulletin, 104* (2), 163–191.

Ellis, R. (1980). Classroom interaction and its relation to second language. *Regional English Language Centre Journal, 11*(2), 29–48.

Ellis, R. (1986). *Understanding second language acquisition.* Oxford: Oxford University Press.

Gass, S. M. (1985). Task variation and nonnative/nonnative negotiation of meaning. In S. M. Gass, & C. Madden (Eds.), *Input in second language acquisition* (pp. 149–161). Rowley, MA: Newbury House.

Gass, S. M. & Madden, C. G. (1985). *Input in second language acquisition.* Rowley, MA: Newbury House.

Grice, H. P. (1975). Logic and coversation. In P. Cole & J. L. Morgan (Eds.), *Speech acts* (pp. 41–58). New York: Academic Press.

Grimes, J. (1975). *The thread of discourse.* The Hague: Mouton.

Hamayan, E. V., & Tucker, G. R. (1980). Language input in the bilingual classroom and its relationship to second language achievement. *TESOL Quarterly, XIV* (4), 453–468.

Hatch, E. (1983). Simplified input and second language acquisition. In R. W. Andersen (Ed.), *Pidginization and creolization as language acquisition* (pp. 64–68). Rowley, MA: Newbury House.

Hinds, J. (1979). Organizational patterns in discourse. In T. Givón (Ed.), *Discourse and syntax* (pp. 135–157). New York: Academic Press.

Krashen, S. (1977). *Second language acquisition and second language learning*. Oxford: Pergamon Press.

Krashen, S. (1982). *Principles and practice in second language acquisition*. Oxford: Pergamon Press.

Krashen, S., & Terrell, T. (1983). *The natural approach: Language acquisition in the classroom*. San Francisco: Alemany Press.

Larsen-Freeman, D. (1983). The importance of input in second language acquisition. In R. Andersen (Ed.), *Pidginization and creolization as language acquisition* (pp. 87–93). Rowley, MA: Newbury House.

Levy, D. M. (1979). Communicative goals and strategies: between discourse and syntax. In T. Givón (Ed.), *Discourse and syntax* (pp. 183–210). New York: Academic Press.

Long, M. H. (1985). Input and second language theory. In S. M. Gass & C. Madden (Eds.), *Input in second language acquisition* (pp. 377–393). Rowley, MA: Newbury House.

Mehan, H. (1979). *Learning lessons*. Cambridge, MA: Harvard University Press.

Scarcella, R. C., & Higa, C. (1981). Input, negotiation, and age difference in second language acquisition. *Language Learning, 31*(2), 409–437.

Searle, J. R. (1969). *Speech acts*. Cambridge, UK: Cambridge University Press.

Searle, J. R. (1976). The classification of illocutionary acts. *Language in Society, 5*, 1–24.

Searle, J. R. (1979). *Expression and meaning: Studies in the theory of speech acts*. Cambridge, UK: Cambridge University Press.

Sinclair, J. M., & Brazil, D. (1982). *Teacher talk*. Oxford: Oxford University Press.

Sinclair, J. M., & Coulthard, R. M. (1975). *Towards an analysis of discourse*. Oxford: Oxford University Press.

Tomlin, R. S. (1989, February). *The microanalysis of individual tutorials: the first hour*. Paper presented at the Second Language Research Forum, UCLA, Los Angeles, CA.

Tomlin, R. S. (1990). Functionalism in second language acquisition. *Studies in Second Language Acquisition, 12*, 155–177.

Wells, G. (1981a). Becoming a communicator. In G. Wells (Ed.), *Learning through interaction: The study of language development*. Cambridge, UK: Cambridge University Press.

Wells, G. (1981b). Language as interaction. In G. Wells (Ed.), *Learning through interaction: The study of language development* (pp. 22–72). Cambridge, UK: Cambridge University Press.

Wells, G. (1981c). *Learning through interaction: The study of language development*. Cambridge, UK: Cambridge University Press.

Chapter 13
Repetition and Relevance: Self-Repetition as a Strategy For Initiating Cooperation in Nonnative/Native Speaker Conversations

Laurie Knox

American English Institute
University of Oregon

Since the mid-1970s, language acquisition researchers have been concerned with the role of social interaction in second language learning, and have looked to nonnative/native speaker conversational discourse as a source of insight into the acquisition process. Studies of foreigner talk and foreigner register (Ferguson, 1975; Arthur, Weiner, Culver, Lee, & Thomas, 1980; Hinnenkamp, 1987), and of native speakers' conversational adjustments to nonnative speakers (see Hatch, 1978, for a survey of early work; also Gaskill, 1983; Long, 1983; Day, Chenoweth, Chun, & Leppescu, 1984; Sato, 1986), have sought to describe the language input available to second language learners, and identify its effect on learning. In a related branch of research concerned with language learners' performance rather than the acquisition process, researchers have used methods from conversational analysis to analyze the conversational strategies nonnative speakers and their conversational partners employ to overcome the difficulty in negotiating meaning that their lack of a shared code presents (Schwartz, 1980; Varonis & Gass, 1983, 1985). The role of repetition in nonnative/native speaker discourse has been considered in several of these studies. Repetition has been recognized as a means of reinforcing comprehensible input and providing corrective feedback, and as a way of initiating negotiations over meaning; in general, repetition has been seen as an elementary strategy which can be used to perform a wide variety of communicative acts.

The analysis undertaken here also centers on repetition as a performance strategy in nonnative/native speaker conversations. Successful conversational performance by language learners is not an individual, but an interactive achievement, which depends on learners' ability to engage their conversational partners in cooperative efforts to treat their utterances as part of a coherent text. A conversation's success, in other words, depends less on its linguistic integrity from an outsider's perspective than on the impression of those involved that they have managed, through their joint efforts, to achieve some degree of intersubjectivity. Nonnative/native speaker conversations present a performance challenge for nonnative and native speakers alike. Because neither participant can rely on a shared code or shared norms of interpretation, the achievement of mutual understanding requires from both a heightening of cooperative interpretive efforts. This chapter describes self-repetition as one strategy which participants in such interactions may use to engage each other in cooperative efforts to produce coherent, mutually meaningful conversation.

THE DATA

The examples discussed in this chapter are selected from data collected as part of a larger study designed to identify the strategies by which the nonnative speakers of English and their conversational partners establish discourse coherence in a variety of social settings. The primary data for this study are the audiotaped conversations in English of three young men enrolled in an Intensive English Program for adults at a large American university. The participants in the study taped their own conversations in a variety of social settings, including service encounters, advising interviews, and casual conversations. The selection of conversations to be taped, as well as the interpretation and analysis of the data, were informed by background information gathered in participants' journals, informal interviews with participants, and observation of the participants' activities over a 3-month period.

The nonnative speakers who participated in this study had all recently arrived in the United States when the study began. While all had had some previous classroom exposure to English, none had been in an English-speaking country before. All scored in the low-intermediate range on a test of English proficiency administered by the Intensive English Program at the beginning of the study, and all scored between 380 and 410 on a TOEFL test (Test of English as a Foreign Language) administered by the program during the study. Of the three participants in the larger study, only two are represented in this chapter. Jose is a 30-year-old Colombian who came to the United States to live with his sister, and hoped to gain admission and a teaching assistantship in the Spanish Department at the university after completing his English study. Philippe is a lawyer and diplomat from the French-speaking Congo, who had received a Fulbright scholarship to pursue Ph.D. degree in the United States but needed to learn English before entering a graduate program.

The taped conversations were transcribed in standard orthography, with modifications to indicate significant prosodic and interactional features:

CAPS	for relatively stressed syllables
:	for lengthened syllables
,	for falling-rising intonation, as in listing
?	for rising intonation, as in yes/no questions
.	for falling intonation, as in statements
[ ]	to mark overlapping utterances and interjections
( )	encloses transcriber's notations of laughter, audible breaths, and other noises

THE POETIC EFFECT OF SELF-REPETITION

One function of self-repetition is to direct hearer's attention to the form repeated as a source of heightened or additional meaning. Dan Sperber and Dierdre Wilson (1986) refer to this effect of repetition as poetic, and claim that repetition "[encourages] the hearer to extend the context and thereby add further implicatures" (p. 221). Sperber and Wilson's analysis of repetition is based on their theory of relevance, an elaboration of the Gricean maxim in a cognitive framework. It rests on the assumption that because hearers interpret what they hear in such a way as to attribute to it maximal relevance to the ongoing discourse, a speaker may, in Sperber and Wilson's words, "leave implicit everything her hearer can be trusted to supply with less effort than would be needed to process an explicit prompt" (p. 218). A repetition prompts the hearer to seek implicit meaning in utterances, by indicating that the speaker aims at a meaning different than that conveyed by uttering an expression only once. Thus, when ideas are complex or words are insufficient, speakers may repeat their utterances in order to engage their hearers in interpretive efforts to make more of what is said.

While Sperber and Wilson observe this effect of self-repetition only in native speaker discourse, their analysis has significance for cross-cultural communication as well, because it suggests that difficulties presented by the lack of a shared code in these exchanges can be compensated for by using strategies like repetition to exploit the limited shared code more fully, just as the poetic use of repetition in native speaker discourse allows speakers to give voice to implicit meanings that cannot efficiently be codified. An example of a non-native speaker's poetic use of repetition is found in the exchange below, in which Jose describes to an American friend his feelings on waking up one morning to see snow for the first time in a fluke October storm. Utterances referred to in the analysis are underlined.

(1)
```
 1  Jose:  many people was—stra:n, stra:n, stra:n! very stran this ye-ah
               the ah snow! snow, is not time, is ⎡ no time  ⎤
 2  Jim:                                          ⎣ it's not. ⎦
 3  Jose:  ah! is-
 4  Jim:   it's going to get-
 5  Jose:  is common? is common ⎡ all years?     ⎤
 6  Jim:                        ⎣ it'll be warm. ⎦
 7  Jose:  common all years?
 8  Jim:   no. not-the-this is very uncommon.
 9  Jose:  ah okay. yes.
10  Jim:   it seldom ever snows in October.
11  Jose   ah. uh huh. (breaths) oh! so is: beautiful, is beautiful. I like
               the cold. I like the col'. I like it very ⎡ much. ⎤
12  Jim:                                                 ⎣ oh!   ⎦   I do too.
13  Jose:  yes. I like!
```

While Jose's style of expression here may not be poetic in a literary sense, his repetition of key phrases "stran" (strange), "beautiful" and "I like the cold" do add emphasis to his expressions, heightening the excitement his contribution conveys to Jim, whose response at line 12 reflects this emotion.

At another point in the same conversation, Jose uses repetition again to communicate implicit meaning. Here, repetition serves not simply to emphasize, as above, but to add propositional content: an implicit indication of temporal aspect. Jose's repetition of intonational patterns and phrases in the exchange below indicates the repetitiveness of the activity he is discussing, as well as the monotony he associates with it:

(2)
1   Jose: ah! I don' I don' like the system walk. to CHANGE the classroom, CHANGE the classroom, I don't like.
2   Jim: yeh.
3   Jose: we don' like. de-de students. we don' like walk, to walk, to walk, ⌈ one class, ⌉
4   Jim;   ⌊ that is ⌋   good for you. you need the exercise.
5   Jose: the first class yeh uhm the first an' second class is in business school the this' class is to: ⌈ to: eh to put ⌉
6   Jim   ⌊ so you go from ⌋ business, then you're down here.
7   Jose: okay
8   Jim: then you're back there?
9   Jose: okay. yes. yes. is go back an' ⌈ go back, an' go back- ⌉
10 Jim: ⌊ that's good for you. ⌋ good for your young body.

Jose's repetitions in the exchange above convey several implicit propositions: not only is Jim prompted to understand the fact that students must move from classroom to classroom every hour, but also that, in Jose's opinion, this system of changing classes is burdensome and unnecessary. Jim's response to Jose, a teasing counterpoint that the move from class to class is "good for your young body" is evidence that he understands the complaining attitude implicit in Jose's repetitions.

PROMPTING INTERPRETIVE EFFORTS THROUGH SELF-REPETITION

The examples above show that nonnative speakers may use repetition for poetic effect much as native speakers do, that is, to prompt their conversational partners to greater interpretive efforts and to the understanding of implicit meaning. However, for nonnative speakers with limited proficiency in the second language, the interpretive effort on the part of the hearer that nonnative speakers' self-repetitions can prompt may be crucial to making any meaningful contribution to conversation at all. The contributions to talk of nonnative speakers with limited proficiency are often linguistically ambiguous, because of the learners' lack of control of phonological, syntactic and semantic patterns in the second language. Thus, these nonnative speakers must always rely on hearers to do a great deal of interpretive work to disambiguate their utterances. By repeating, nonnative speakers can let their conversational partners know that the thoughts they intend to convey are more complex than their linguistic ability to codify them. Employing Sperber and Wilson's terminology, one may say that a nonnative speaker's self-repetitions are ostensive gestures indicating a "communicative intention," that is, an intention that one's utterance make a relevant contribution to conversation, thereby prompting hearers to assess on their own the nonnative speaker's "informative intention," that is, exactly what information the speaker is trying to convey (pp. 54–64). The ostensive gesture performed through repetition may encourage a native speaker to read into ambiguous utterances a meaning appropriate to the context, but not conveyed in the linguistic form repeated.

In the exchange below between Philippe and Paul, the director of the Intensive English Program in which Philippe is enrolled, Philippe uses self-repetition in this way in an effort to inform Paul of his professional status. This exchange was part of a routine interview conducted in Paul's office during Philippe's first weeks of study in the Intensive English Program. At the beginning of the interview, the director establishes a pattern of interaction in which he provides information that he believes might be true of Philippe in the form of yes/no questions, and Philippe validates this information with simple confirmations at lines 2 and 6 and a partial repetition of the director's utterances at line 4.

(3)
```
1  Paul:      did you finish high school?
2  Philippe:  yes. I did.
3  Paul:      kay. in: the Congo?
4  Philippe:  in Congo.
5  Paul:      an: have you finished college.
6  Philippe:  yes. I have.
```

The pattern of questions and answers established in lines 1 through 6 above allows the director to control the development of topic and gather the information he needs efficiently and with certainty of its accuracy. It also provides a supportive framework for Philippe: He is able to participate competently and communicate the information which the director needs without having to produce much language at all. However, this pattern places Philippe in the vulnerable position of relying on the director to formulate propositions for which he, himself, is to be held responsible. And, in fact, at line 8 below, the question/answer pattern of topic development breaks down when Philippe, in order to be fully informative, must do more than simply confirm or deny the proposition proffered by the director.

```
 7  Paul:      d'ya have a bachelor's degree? a four year degree?
 8  Philippe:  uh::: I get-a I I got master degree.
 9  Paul:      master's degree.
10  Philippe:  yes. [        ] in law.
11  Paul:                [ah.] in law.
12  Philippe:  yes.
13  Paul:      from the Congo?
14  Philippe:  uhhuh/ license. after license. — — it is a French system.
15  Paul:      French system.
16  Phillipe:  yes.
17  Paul:      ah— —
18  Philippe:  uh-li-uh: license, after li ⌈cense: master⌉ degree ⌈      ⌉
19  Paul:                                 ⌊oh well.    ⌋        ⌊okay⌋
            so after the license.
20  Philippe:  uh hum. after li ⌈cense-⌉
21  Paul:                       ⌊okay ⌋ so you're a lawyer.
22  Paul:      yes. I-I am. (laughs)
```

While Philippe does not have a bachelor's degree, in the American sense, he does have a higher education, and, in fact, a distinguished professional career as a lawyer and diplomat. To communicate this information, which Paul was unlikely to be able to supply on his own, Philippe has to take an active speaking role in the exchange.

When Philippe begins to introduce propositional content into the conversation himself, the native speaker Paul takes on a role which Bublitz (1988) has called a "supportive secondary speaker role" (pp. 225–232). Paul's partial repetitions after each of Philippe's utterances at lines 8 and 10 display his involvement in Philippe's efforts to communicate. They show that he has taken note of Philippe's utterances, has made a positive assessment of their relevance, and has adopted their propositional content as part of the shared background knowledge on which further conversation can be based.

However, more significant for the analysis here is the effect on the interaction of Philippe's self-repetition at line 18, and his partial repetition—interrupted by Paul—at line 20. These self-repetitions are Philippe's way of eliciting even greater cooperative effort from the director. After Philippe's initial linguistically ambiguous attempt to explain his academic background at line 14, the director's response at line 15, "French system" and his failure at line 17 to use his turn to reestablish the pattern of questioning indicate that he has not fully understood Philippe's informative intention. Though Philippe may not have the linguistic ability to clarify his informative intention, by repeating he is able at least to reassert his communicative intention and to signal that he is not satisfied that the director has grasped the intended relevance of the initial utterance. Although the director twice attempts to close the topic at line 19, Philippe sustains the director's attention to the topic and his efforts at interpretation by recycling his utterance, until, at line 21, he elicits from the director a paraphrase that reflects an understanding of his professional status. This information, articulated unambiguously by the advisor in his paraphrase, then becomes part of the shared knowledge on which subsequent text, and, in fact, subsequent interactions between Philippe and Paul could be constructed. Philippe's self-repetitions allow him to prompt Paul not only to greater interpretive effort, but also to an explicit linguistic articulation of the implicatures he has reached through those efforts. Thus, the nonnative speaker's self-repetitions promote a cooperative effort from the native speaker to establish a coherent text which the nonnative speaker, with his limited linguistic skill, could not provide alone.

REPETITION AS A SIGNAL OF SHIFTS IN TOPIC AND PARTICIPANT ROLES

In the example above, the nonnative speaker repeats a linguistically ambiguous utterance in order to draw attention to its intended original relevance. However, repetition may not only heighten original relevance, but also signal a shift in the criteria for assessing relevance. Sperber and Wilson (1986) write that the fundamental effect of any expression whose linguistically encoded propositional content is not apparently relevant, including repetition, is to engage the hearer in an investigation of contextual information which could make that utterance relevant. By directing the hearer's attention to aspects of the context previously ignored, a repetition can change the character of the interaction itself. Repetition can initiate shifts in topic, in key, and in participants' relations to each other. In the exchange below, both the nonnative speaker and the native speaker use self-repetition to manage intricate shifts from code to content as the topic of conversation and to regulate corresponding shifts in participant roles and key.

This exchange comes near the beginning of a casual conversation between Jose and his conversation partner Bert, an American volunteer who has agreed to meet him once a week for an hour of practice in English conversation. The conversation takes place at Bert and Jose's second meeting. Unlike the routine advisor/student relation exemplified above, the conversation partner relationship is negotiable: The American partner may become a friend, a language tutor, an guide to American culture, or an explorer of his partner's culture. At this early stage in their acquaintance, Jose and Bert are still negotiating their relationship. The repetitions which occur in their conversation help Bert and Jose to engage in this negotiation implicitly.

(4)
```
 1  Jose:  the tes' the te-the toefl test ⌈      ⌉ is difficult.
 2  Bert:                                ⌊  um  ⌋                        yes.
 3  Jose:  ah-AL[s]ough, Although?
 4  Bert:  also although although,
 5  Jose:  although I-I:I think is very [   ] very easy for me. [    ] is very
 6  Bert:                               [eh]                    [yeh]

 7  Jose:  easy. I understand. ⌈            I under⌉ stand.
 8  Bert:                      ⌊ you understood      ⌋     you
        understood it.
 9  Jose:  I understood.
10  Bert:  understood. it's past ⌈ tense.              ⌉
11  Jose:                        ⌊ I under ⌋ stood. I understood the test.
12  Bert:  the test,
13  Jose:  the lis-listen:, Listen, an::'
14  Bert:  the listening part?
15  Jose:  writ{ing:: }
16  Bert:     {an'} the writing,
17  Jose:  no. writing is- is no, because I don't have time, time.
18  Bert:  time.
19  Jose:  the time is very short. ⌈            ⌉ shorter? ⌈ shorter?
20  Bert:                          ⌊ um hum,    ⌋          ⌊ short.
21  Jose:  is ⌈ uh:        ⌉ sho- is-is short.
22  Bert:     ⌊ time-um.   ⌋              the time is- was very
        short,
23  Jose:  is very shor- was very shor- was very short. ⌈ ahm, ahm,  ⌉
24  Bert:                                               ⌊ there wasn't-⌋
25  Bert   it's better to say there wasn't much time.
```

In this exchange, there are actually two topics of conversation. On one level the conversation is about Jose's experience with an English test, the International TOEFL, which he had taken the preceding weekend. Jose has the role of the primary speaker with regard to the topic concerning the TOEFL test; He controls the relevant information and carries primary responsibility for developing the topic in a coherent text. Jose's very first utterance here, marked by hesitations and false starts, indicates his insecurity in this role. At line 3, Jose uses a self-repetition to draw his linguistic insecurity into the foreground as a topic of conversation in itself. In a discussion of this exchange later, Jose remarked that he repeated here because he had earlier been misunderstood when using the word *although* and wanted to be sure that his pronunciation was correct. By repeating the expression *although* twice, with rising intonation and variations in its stress pattern and pronunciation, Jose engages Bert in a side sequence in which the form of the word, rather than its meaning, becomes the primary source of relevance. Jose's self-repetition prompts from Bert a response in which he, first, repeats the form Jose has focused on, with two of its possible disambiguations (*also* and *although*) and, second, provides a model for its correct pronunciation, which Jose acknowledges at his next turn, when he uses the form correctly. With regard to this secondary topic concerning linguistic form, it is Bert, rather than Jose, who is the primary speaker, since he controls the information that is its focus: the correct use of English expressions. At lines 8 through 11, the shift to linguistic form as a topic of conversation is sustained by the native speaker. His repetition at line 8 of Jose's utterance "I understand" with a correction of its tense might be understood merely as a supportive move with regard to the main topic, a sign of agreement and understanding, and in fact, Jose initially treats it as such, continuing in this next turn without acknowledging the correction in form. However, when Bert again repeats the expression with a correction of form at line 8, its potential relevance both as an expression of content and an acknowledgement of content has already been exploited. Thus, this repetition can only be understood as relevant with regard to its form. Bert's repetition reasserts the focus of the conversation on form rather than content, and, at line 10, the focus on form as a topic of conversation is made explicit with his statement of a grammatical principle. At line 11, Jose acknowledges that he is aware of Bert's informative intention by incorporating the change in form into his initial utterance, repeating it once again. The shift in topic from a focus on form to a focus on content and the accompanying shift in participant roles also brings about a shift in key. The focus on language forms draws out the teacher–student aspect of Jose and Bert's relationship, thus establishing a context of interaction in which Bert's explicit corrections and evaluations of

Jose's speech are appropriate, as are Jose's requests for correction. Bert's comment later in the conversation, "it's better to say there wasn't much time" (line 25) in response to Jose's question concerning the expression "the time was very short" would be inappropriate in a conversation between friends, but can be expected in a tutorial setting.

CONCLUSION

The analysis above shows that, in the context of use, the formal redundancy of repetition does not imply a poverty of meaning, but instead exposes the rich pragmatic potential of the linguistic form. The effect of repetition is to shift the work of constructing coherent and meaningful text from a codification process to an interpretive process. When, as in nonnative/native speaker conversations, the lack of a shared code makes linguistic codification an unreliable and ineffective source of meaning in itself, this effect of repetition may become crucial to communicative success. However, the uses of repetition described in the analysis above—to heighten and enhance meaning, to engage hearers in interpretive efforts to make more of what is said, and to signal shifts in topic and key—are not peculiar to cross-cultural interactions. Instead, the nonnative/native speaker conversation represents an extreme case of a universal phenomenon: When language becomes insufficient as a bridge between individuals, either because of the complexity of thoughts to be communicated, or the poverty of words, then we are able to compensate for this failure of language with heightened interpretive efforts, motivated by sensitivity to the pragmatic potentialities of linguistic expressions, and by trust in the integrity of each other's informative intentions.

REFERENCES

Arthur, B. Weiner, R., Culver, M. Lee, Y. J., & Thomas, D. (1980). The register of impersonal discourse to foreigners: Adjustments to foreign accent. In D. L. Freeman (Ed.), *Discourse analysis in second language acquisition* (pp. 111–124). Rowley, MA: Newbury House.

Bublitz, W., (1988). *Supportive fellow speakers and cooperative conversation*. Philadelphia: John Benjamins Publishing Company.

Day, R., Chenoweth, N. A., Chun, A. & Luppescu, S. (1984). Corrective feedback in native-nonnative discourse. *Language Learning, 34*, 19–45.

Derwing, T. (1989). Information type and its relation to non-native speaker comprehension. *Language Learning, 38,* 157–172.

Ferguson, C. (1975). Towards a characterization of foreigner talk. *Anthropological Linguistics, 17,* 1–14.

Gaskill, W. (1983). Correction in native speaker-nonnative speaker conversation. In D. Larson-Freeman (Ed.), *Discourse analysis in second language acquisition* (pp. 125–137) Rowley, MA: Newbury House.

Hatch, E. (1978). Discourse analysis and second language acquisition. In E. Hatch (Ed.), *Second language acquisition* (pp. 401–435). Rowley, MA: Newbury House.

Hinnenkamp, V. (1987). Foreigner talk, code-switching and the concept of trouble. In K. Knapp, W. Enninger, & A. Knapp-Potthoff (Eds.), *Analyzing intercultural communication* (pp. 144–180). Berlin: Mouton de Gruyter.

Long, M. (1983). Linguistic and conversational adjustments to nonnative speakers. *Studies in Second Language Acquisition, 5,* 177–197.

Sato, C. (1986). Conversation and interlanguage development: Rethinking the connection. In R. R. Day, (Ed.), *Talking to learn: Conversation in second language acquisition* (pp. 24–45). Rowley, MA: Newbury House.

Schwartz, J. (1980). The negotiation for meaning: repair in conversations between second language learners of English. In D. Larson-Freeman (Ed.), *Discourse analysis in second language acquisition* (pp. 138–158). Rowley, MA: Newbury House.

Sperber, D., & Wilson, D. (1986). *Relevance.* Cambridge, MA: Harvard University Press.

Varonis, E. & Gass, S. (1983). Nonnative/native conversations: A model for negotiation of meaning. *Applied Linguistics, 6,* 71–90.

Varonis, E. & Gass, S. (1985). Miscommunication in native/nonnative conversation. *Language in Society, 14,* 323–343.

Chapter 14
Repetition in Instructional Discourse: A Means for Joint Cognition

Martha S. Bean

San Jose State University

G. Genevieve Patthey-Chavez

UCLA and Los Angeles City College

Repetition has many functions in instructional settings. Both novices and experts use repetition in the negotiation of instructional outcomes. In this negotiation, repetition serves both cognitive and affective ends. By looking at repetition in three very different instructional settings—a computer lab, a writing conference, and a bilingual reading group—we have been able to identify repetition strategies and functions which operate across age, context, and culture–language boundaries. The frequency and similarity of functions in three such diverse settings suggest possible universality for some forms and functions of repetition.

Our discussion will proceed along the following lines: first, we describe the three settings; next, we isolate the cognitive and affective uses of repetition in each setting; and finally, we foreground common threads across settings. We hope to show that repetition is a major sociocognitive resource in instructional settings.

THE SETTINGS

The computer lab data are selected from 6 hours of audiotaped problem-solving consultations collected over a semester in a university computer lab (see Patthey, 1991). The computer consultants were not computer majors, but students skilled in the basic functions of microcomputer use—word processing, spreadsheet, and database. By using noncomputer majors for microcomputer consulting the university attempted to accommodate novice microcomputer users, as computer majors would enter the instructional interaction at a level far above what the general student computer-using public could handle.

The writing-conference data were pulled from a corpus of ten conferences held by five writing teachers as part of a project investigating the influence of conferencing on writing revisions by novice academic writers (see Ferris, Ferris, Hared, Kowall, & Patthey, 1989). Like computer consultations, writing conferences were one on one; the expert and novice could negotiate a joint outcome, and the novice could acquire new knowledge if he or she so chose. Unlike computer consultations, writing conferences involved an instructional and, by extension, an institutional agenda—the teaching of "academic writing." Larger institutional motives were reflected in the interpersonal dynamics between writing teacher and novice writer, and repetition strategies were deployed in ways consistent with these roles.

A small group reading lesson in a bilingual third-grade classroom, audiotaped and transcribed, provided the final instructional data for the project. Like the writing conference setting, the reading lesson involved a power–rank differential among participants. A teacher guided the lesson while three young students worked within her framework. The goal of the reading lesson was likewise an institutional one; namely, for students to learn how to read. However, as the reading lesson constituted a multiparty interaction, it involved much sharing of the expert role. That is, the students themselves took turns being experts at tasks set by the teacher. The fact that the participants were all bilingual added another dimension to the exchange. Sometimes an utterance made in Spanish was repeated in English, while at other times an unrelated utterance was initiated in English. Such instances of code-switching demonstrated, as Merritt, Cleghorn, and Abagi (1988) noted in a similar bilingual setting, that one can repeat the message but change the language, or repeat the language but change the message.

In the analysis which follows, we will show that repetition is an important, multifunctional strategy in instructional discourse, which provides a ground for the cognitive jockeying of novice and expert as they seek to accomplish different but related goals. The novice's goal is to accomplish the task at hand, whatever it may be; the expert's goal is to approach an optimal point of information transfer (neither too much nor too little) so that the novice can make maximal use of it. That is, novice and expert together attempt to construct a "zone of proximal development" (Vygotsky, 1978, p. 86) through the joint negotiation of a task slightly beyond the novice's reach. From this experience, the novice gains insight or ability to tackle the task independently.

In the computer setting, most tasks represent a win–lose situation in which the novice will either succeed or fail in the next step; the writing and reading settings represent more diffuse incremental situations in which novices must build on previous skills to approach a new level of more global expertise.

METHODOLOGICAL ANCHORS

The frequency of parallelisms and repetitions in human discourse has often been noted (cf. Tannen, 1987) and explicitly linked with learning processes (Tannen, 1989, p. 89; Bennett-Kastor, Knox, Tomlin, this volume). In fact, viewed longitudinally, all learning involves repetition—the reproduction and hence repetition through time (and possibly space) of a given repertory of information. That learning inevitably involves repetition suggests once again that the repetition strategies found in instructional discourse are linked to cognitive and affective outcomes in learning activities. These strategies have lent themselves to description along formal lines.

In order to investigate possible relationships between discourse patterns and activity outcomes, methodological "anchors" are necessary (Merritt, this volume). Drawing on the methodology of conversation analysis (Sacks, Schegloff & Jefferson, 1974) and work on the joint production of family dinner-time narratives (Ochs, Taylor, Rudolph, & Smith, 1989), we have distinguished two fundamental strategies on structural grounds. These are: (a) *repetition*, an exact morphosyntactic rearticulation of the initial utterance; and (b) *redraft*, a paraphrasing of the initial utterance.

Participants made strategic use of reduction, expansion, and intonational contouring in their repetition strategies, and these discourse variables have also been noted. What each participant was willing to repeat in a given activity—that is, which activity elicited *self-repetition* and which elicited other- or *allo-repetition* (or echoing)—has also been noted. We also compared types and amounts of repetition in the speech of the experts and the novices. Our primary question has to do with how repetition strategies contribute to the formulation and articulation (i.e., the joint authorship) of knowledge, and this issue constitutes the major focus of the analysis.

FINDINGS

The Computer Consultation

A complete interaction between Kent and Candy, a computer consultant and a young Asian client, illustrates the interlocking functionality of the different repetition and redraft strategies used in the consultation. The interchange is relatively straightforward; she has a question, and he has the answer. Still, it displays problem-solving activity of considerable cognitive and social complexity. Lexical repetitions and utterance-level redrafts across speakers help weave the cohesive and propositional ties through which the final product of the exchange, the solution, is achieved. In the transcript below, all lexical repetitions have been underlined. To the left of the transcription we describe the repetitions.

Candy approaches Kent with a problem which she describes through a short and garbled narrative in lines 03–06 below, concluding with an implied question in lines 07–09. For the consultant (as well as the analyst), the thrust of Candy's request is recoverable. She is asking for information on file-conversions between two different word processors.

Perhaps because Kent is aware of the need for clarity in computer operations, he initially focuses his attention on clarification. He does so by redrafting the entire narrative, starting in line 10. This redraft incorporates the client's story, but "repairs" it at the same time so that the salient information comes out corrected and in the right order. His redraft is acknowledged in lines 11 and 13, where Candy echoes and redrafts the expert re-articulation of her initial narrative. At this point, Kent adopts Candy's words and, in line 14, draws them into an expanded repetition that coordinates his redraft with her words, thereby completing his repaired narrative accompanied by her input. It is not until this point that Candy's question is answered—with a reply that she echoes, using only words that have been uttered before.

STRATEGY	UTT.	SPEAKER	
	01	C	are you working? (2)
	02	K	(go ahead)
Antecedent narrative	03	C	uhm, (I typed it up in original)
	04		software, and then, (1)
	05		okay, then I brought it up in Wordstar,
	06		and then uh, (edit it) and uh,
	07		when you go back to, Wordstar
	08		I mean Microsoft,
	09		you gotta convert again
Redraft of 03	10	K	okay you started it in Microsoft word
	11	C	uh-huh
Redraft of 05	12	K	you converted it, to Wordstar,
Rep of 05 & Redraft of 12	13	C	uh-huh, I brought up in Wordstar.
Rep-Expansion of & Redraft of 05-06	14	K	you brought it up and changed it,
Redraft-Expansion of 07-09	15	K	yeah now in order to go back you have to convert it backwards,
Echoing of 15	16	C	you have to go back

It is not possible to represent visually the overall effect of all these repetitions, redrafts, and shared utterances. When the cohesive links and joint meaning-development moves across utterances and speakers are foregrounded, they yield what might be called the "texture of joint cognition." On the surface of the discourse, consultant and client share words and partial utterances. Below the surface, however, they effectively formulate and negotiate joint knowledge by means of these shared words.

Ironically, repetitions and redrafts like the ones above are sometimes described as redundant and inefficient. Such descriptions miss the essential efficiency of repetitions and redrafts in interpersonal discourse, especially if that discourse is aimed at realizing instructional goals. By reformulating Candy's description, Kent is doing much communicative work. He is adopting her language as his and coordinating his perspective with hers. He gives her the opportunity to reciprocate, and she takes him up on it. By line 14, Kent has adopted Candy's nontechnical vocabulary, which he then expands in the crucial explanatory utterance of line 15. Through repetition strategies like the ones above, the consultant achieves maximal integration between the client's words and his expertise. This verbal dance between novice and expert results in a shared understanding of both the problem and the solution, an understanding from which the novice can extract the information needed to perform the task at hand.

These strategies are also satisfying in the affective domain. The expert proves willing to take up and work from a technically flawed narrative and continues to accept novice contributions as he reformulates the narrative. The novice, meanwhile, also proves willing to accept the expert's reformulation of the original narrative while actively participating in the reformulation. This kind of mutual ratification of one another's contribution to the problem-solving activity can only have a positive effect.

The Writing Conference

The uses of repetition strategies during writing conferences resemble those observed in the computer consultations. Here, too, expert and novice strive to negotiate a joint product, using repetitions and redrafts to weave the necessary cohesive ties. However, the nature of the product and the relationship between the parties is different. That difference can be seen in the discourse strategies they deploy. While the solution to a computer problem either fails or succeeds and finally concerns only the person experiencing the problem, such is not the case in the acquisition of academic writing skills, which involve graded activities in which the teacher, the student, and the entire institution take an interest.

The segment below was chosen because it is especially illustrative of the uses of repetition strategies used during conferencing. A variety of concerns were addressed during the conferences, each usually the topic of a distinguishable episode. The sample below is typical of one such episode. It starts when the teacher begins giving the student feedback on his in-class writing, feedback which the student has been soliciting. In line 17, the teacher notes that the student might benefit from increased speed. The student seizes on this aside and, with some persistence, draws the teacher out on exactly how fast he ought to be writing in class.

STRATEGY	UTT.	SPEAKER	
	15	S	can you see any fundamental problems?
	16		where

Assessment 1	17	T	uhm, you're gonna have to speed up,
	18		I mean although I think you came in late [right?]
	19	S	[yeah.]
Redraft of Ass. 1	20	T	so you didn't have very much time at all
	21	S	so given, what did we have, <u>forty minutes</u>?
	22	T	yeah
Rep-Expansion of 21	23	S	how much would you expect <u>in forty minutes</u>, [how many pages,
Echoing of 23	24	T	[in forty minutes,
	25		okay, let me give you an example from my past
	26		I had students, uh, a year ago, that started out, writing two pages max,
	27	S	uh-huh,
Rep of 24	28	T	<u>in forty minutes</u>, and ended up writing between eight and ten pages,
	29	S	great
	30	T	at the end of the course
	31		you know, I did that,
	32		we did that systematically because we determined that they needed to write <u>faster</u>
	33		so I'm gonna start, on Tuesday with speedwritings,
	34	S	hm,
	35	T	and you'll, they're fun,
	36		[you'll get to see that yes]
	37	S	[really?] fantastic
Assessment 2	38	T	uhm, but for you, you know,
	39		I mean the thing about you especially is
(Redraft of Ass 1)			that you need to be able to get it down on paper <u>faster</u>, uhm,
	40		because your thinking <u>needs development</u> on the page
	41		at least that's the way it reads,
	42		and that's good, that's very good,
Redraft of 1 of Ass 2	43		you know cause I mean [you've got]
Echoing of 40	44	S	[needs development?]
Redraft of 2 of Ass 2	45	T	no no it has it, I mean
	46	S	oh okay

Redraft 3 of Ass 2	47	T	but, you know, it's time consuming,
	48	S	right
Redraft 3 cont.	49	T	to develop something that thoroughly on the <u>page</u>, uhm,
	50		that's wonderful,
	51		because a lot of people don't have that,
	52		but you need to learn how to do it <u>faster</u>

During this episode, several key terms and phrases—*faster, in forty minutes,* and *needs development*—are used repeatedly by both teacher and student to negotiate a mutual understanding of the class requirements. Forms of the verb *need* are used repeatedly, tying the past to the currently perceived problem via the proposed instructional solution.

Other repetition strategies are also in evidence. Allo-repetition or echoing is used by the teacher to ratify the new topic (line 24) and by the student to challenge the teacher and draw her out (line 44). Redrafts are used extensively by the teacher to negotiate her assessment of the student's competence and needs and to link these assessed needs to proposed instructional solutions (lines 17, 39, and 42). Lexical repetition, echoing, and redrafts combined yield the specific information the student seeks and allow the teacher to drive home an instructional point. The two motives are brought together and linked, if not reconciled, in this adroit negotiation between the two participants. In such a manner, a zone of proximal development emerges.

Again, the repetitions permeating the interaction appear redundant but accomplish a great deal of communicative work. Conferencing entails student assessment on the part of the teacher. That assessment guides instructional choices, but at the same time, sooner or later enters the intrainstitutional information exchange that will make (or break) the student's academic career. In this manner, conferencing touches on sensitive issues. The teacher must therefore balance instructional and institutional requirements while ensuring at least minimal student acquiescence. By turning her assessment into a negotiable matter, the teacher is signalling the possibility of future improvement while at the same time tying such improvement to her instructional goals at both the individual and institutional levels. In the affective domain, she softens potential challenges and secures at least the surface manifestations of student agreement.

The Bilingual Reading Lesson

The bilingual reading lesson likewise illustrates a teacher "scaffolding" (Bruner, 1983) the comprehension of her students. In this interaction, the teacher sits at a small desk surrounded by three of her third-grade students. The teacher or a selected student reads a short passage of the story, and the teacher initiates discussion. The reading of the story itself involves much repetition at both the sound and syllable level as well as at the word and phrase level as the students learn to decode as well as grasp the story line.

The segment which follows is dominated by redraft. In this segment, the teacher repeats both her own and the students' words and phrases. Third graders are naive, not fully developed learners. Therefore, the task at hand is not only mastering the information but also learning how to access that information; the students are acquiring, not only data, but ways of looking at, thinking about, and reacting to it.

In this excerpt, the teacher asks what the students would do in a dangerous situation. The question itself echoes the scenario of the story being read, in which a coyote goes sliding on some rocks (against the advice of sliding lizards) and hurts himself. The lizards must then decide whether to help the coyote, who is a potential enemy and who has brought his misfortune on himself.

STRATEGY	UTT.	SPEAKER	
	01	T	si algo es peligroso
	02		que puedan hacer ustedes?
			(if something is dangerous what can you do?)
	03	S1	( )
	04	T	huh?
	05	S1	no me subiera
			(I wouldn't go up)
Echoing of 05	06	T	no se subiera
			(you wouldn't go up)
	07		otras cosas
			(other things)
Redraft of 01-02	08		si usted ve algo peligroso
	09		que hace?
			(if you see something dangerous what do you do?)
	10	S2	yo me lo mataba
			(I would kill it)

Parallelism in Ss' answers	11	S3	yo ( ) usted (I . . . . you)
	12		los veo (I see them)
	13		y ya me voy (and I'd go away)
	14		mama (mama)
	15	S1	y solo (and alone)

Redraft of 01-02
and 08–09
	16
	17
		T	que si ya se ve algo peligroso ustedes
			    se van a meter?
			(and if there is something dangerous
			    are you going to get involved?)

	18	S1	nooooo (nooooo)
Redraft of 09	19	T	que van a hacer? (what are you going to do?)
	20	S2	yo si (me, yes)
Parallelism in Ss' answers	21	S1	yo no (me, no)

Redraft of 01-02,
08-09, and
16-17
	22	T	que le, que le van a hacer si se ve
			    algo peligroso?
			(what are you going to do if there is
			    something dangerous?)

	24	S1	decirle a alguien (tell someone about it)

Rep-Expansion of
24
	25	T	decirle a alguien que para ayudar a la
			    otra persona
			(tell someone about it in order to
			    help the other person)

Note that the teacher redrafts her initial question (lines 01–02) three times. Each redraft retains the key notions of "being in a dangerous (peligroso) situation" and "what to do in that situation." The question constitutes an application of the story scenario to the students' lives rather than a mere repetition of what has happened in the story and calls attention to the fact that dangerous situations occur in everyone's life. The teacher's repeated question serves to contribute to possible lessons suggested by the story—perhaps "Don't take foolish chances" or "Be careful about whom you help." Cognitively, such extensive repetition signals that the question is a timely one worthy of the teacher's attention and the students' consideration.

Repetition occurs simultaneously in another dimension as well. The teacher's question is repeated with minimal intonation, creating the effect of "flat affect." In contrast, the students' answers exhibit exaggerated but parallel intonation. The result is an almost chantlike exchange, with the teacher setting a stable background rhythm and the students' punctuating with interjection-like answers as they alternately chime in. The teacher's repetition serves to encourage these answers.

The goal of the teacher's repetition appears not to be the discovery of the "right answer," but rather the elicitation of a range of possible answers reflective of both the universe of possibilities and the students' individual personalities and social roles. For instance, S1 is a girl whose answers in lines 06 and 18 tend to reflect a flight role, while S2 is a boy whose answers in lines 10 and 20 suggest a fight role. The teacher's sequential redrafts allow both of these reactions and responses to emerge with equal weight.

In the affective domain, the teacher's redrafting provides a familiar framework within which the students are licensed to vary their responses. The parallelism in the students' replies signals an awareness on some level of the opportunities afforded by such generous repetition. If the question had been asked just once and an answer ratified or rejected, the lesson would have taken on a more judgmental tone. That is, the rules of the game would have changed, operating rather to select out the best answer.

In line 06 the teacher uses repetition as an evaluation move rather than saying "good" (bien), or "no," or making other such evaluative remarks. In line 25 the teacher echoes and expands the student's utterance in yet another evaluation move, indicating the teacher's approval while demonstrating what a longer, more complete answer might sound like. By adopting and repeating the student's words, the teacher supports the student's language and information choices, a move particularly supportive of young learners developing linguistic expertise in literacy-related tasks.

PATTERNS OF DISTRIBUTION

Quantitative analysis of the data in the three settings reveals three generalizations regarding the distribution of repetition strategies:

1. Experts made much more extensive use of redrafting, especially of their own utterances;

2. Novices made much greater use of allo-repetitions, especially allo-repetition reductions, through which they "echoed" the experts, and;
3. Self-repetitions and self-redrafts tended to occur in competitive frames in which participants failed to ratify each other's goals; allo-repetitions and redrafts helped index a cooperative orientation between participants.

Though a complete discussion of these results is beyond the scope of this chapter, these patterns can be observed in the samples above. The fact that they hold across contexts suggests that the form–function relationships noted are not random. That is, repetition strategies are deployed differentially to create varying effects and serve varying ends within the discourse of the instructional setting.

DISCUSSION AND CONCLUSION

Some of the more salient functions of the repetition strategies we have described are as follows: In the computer lab, the expert (consultant) attempted to clarify the problem by redrafting and repairing the novice's initial narrative, while, through echoing this redraft, the novice was able to acknowledge the expert's repair. When the expert finally answered the question posed, the novice made use of repetition to reinforce the reply.

In the writing conference, the novice (student) used repetition to focus, or seize, on one aspect of what the expert was saying, thus diverting the expert's attention to the novice's specific concern. This function foregrounds the attention-getting aspect of repetition. Subsequently, the expert used repetition to acknowledge the novice's topic of concern. Repetition was further used by the novice to challenge the expert and to elicit her input on a specific point.

In the bilingual reading lesson, the expert (teacher) deployed repetition similarly; namely, to elicit an array of responses, to acknowledge possible responses, and to reinforce timely information in both her own questions and the students' responses. In the few instances where some selection did take place, the teacher used repetition with differential intonation to challenge less desirable responses and confirm or ratify more desirable ones. A crucial function of repetition in the reading situation was the teacher's use of repetition-expansion to model for the students a more thorough and complex way of displaying information.

On a somewhat more general plane, self-repetition typically affords the speaker time to assess the effect of his or her words on the hearer and to plan the next move. Allo-repetition or echoing allows the speaker to coordinate input from diverse sources and to assimilate the information conveyed by those words. Additionally, such echoing helps interlocutors accommodate to each other in linguistic, cognitive, and affective ways; that is, to adjust to each other's communication style, information base, and primary purpose in a given context—in effect, creating a type of affective "zone of proximal development" in which cognition may jointly be constructed.

What has emerged from the above descriptions of the discourse found in instructional settings and of the multifunctionality of repetition strategies across such settings is the power of repetition and redraft as communication and negotiation tools. Through their use, joint meaning is achieved among interlocutors and expertise is "packaged" for consumption while novice and expert alternately secure each other's acquiescence. In this manner, both cognitive and affective ends are served and learning progresses. One can hardly imagine learning without repetition—perhaps because, through repetition and its many functions, the work of cognition is accomplished.

REFERENCES

Bruner, J. (1983). *Child's talk: Learning to use language.* New York: W.W. Norton Co.

Ferris, D., Ferris, R., Hared, M., Kowall, K., & Patthey, G. G. (1989, April). *The influence of conferencing revision.* Paper presented at TESOL 89, San Antonio, Texas.

Merritt, M., Cleghorn, A., & Abagi, J. O. (1988). Dual translation and cultural congruence: Exemplary teacher practices using English, Swahili, and mother-tongue in three Kenyan primary schools. In K. Ferrara, B. Brown, K. Walters, & J. Baugh (Eds.), *Linguistic change and contact* (pp. 232–239). Austin, TX: Department of Linguistics, University of Texas (Vol. 30 of *Texas Linguistic Forum*).

Ochs, E., Taylor, C., Rudolph, D., & Smith, R. (1989). *Narrative activity as a medium for theory building.* Unpublished manuscript, University of Southern California.

Patthey, G. G. (1991). *The language of problem solving in a computer lab.* Unpublished doctoral dissertation, University of Southern California.

Sacks, H., Schegloff, E., & Jefferson, G. (1974). A simplest systematics for the organization of turn-taking in conversation. *Language, 50,* 696–735.

Tannen, D. (1987). Repetition in conversation: Toward a poetics of talk. *Language, 63*(3), 574–605.

Tannen, D. (1989). *Talking voices: Repetition, dialogue and imagery in conversational discourse.* New York: Cambridge University Press.

Vygotsky, L. S. (1978). *Mind in society. The development of higher psychological processes.* Cambridge, MA: Harvard University Press.

Chapter 15
Grammaticalization and Discourse Functions of Repetition

Susan C. Shepherd

Department of English
Indiana University at Indianapolis

Many studies of repetition focus on conversational meanings, paying particular attention to cohesive functions and relatively little attention to sentence syntax and semantics. On the other hand, codified forms of repetition, such as reduplication, have been dealt with primarily at the morphological or lexical level, with little attention paid to the discourse of which the repeated element is a part. This chapter explores relationships between the uses of repetition as a discourse process and as a grammatical process. Givon (1979), Traugott (1982, 1989), Heine and Reh (1984), Bybee and Pagliuca (1985), Sweetser (1988), and Traugott and König (forthcoming), among others, have explored the process of grammaticalization. Their work suggests that, in using old forms for new functions, the direction of meaning change is from concrete to abstract. Givon (1979, p. 209) has proposed that the process involves cyclic waves, characterized as:

$$\text{Discourse} \rightarrow \text{Syntax} \rightarrow \text{Morphology} \rightarrow$$
$$\text{Morphophonemics} \rightarrow \text{Zero}$$

He concentrates on the first two steps, from discourse to syntax and from syntax to morphology—the levels at which repetition also happens to be most actively employed. Traugott and König (forthcoming) have considered "pragmatic meanings that are conventionalized . . . and those that are inferred in context, largely through conversational processes of meaning specification." The grammaticalization of repetition supports their findings, providing evidence of specification of meaning (rather than bleaching). As will be shown, the functions which seem to me to be most concrete— emphasis and intensification—are the meanings most likely to be codified or grammaticalized.

The data to be discussed here come from language varieties in which the functions served by repetition are both conversational and grammatical. This chapter will explore the use of self-repetition in Antiguan Creole, an English-based West Indian creole, and in child language acquisition in American English, with particular consideration of grammaticalization or codification and the directionality of change.

In Antiguan Creole repetition is pervasive, occurring phonologically, morphologically, syntactically, and on the level of discourse, and serving related but different functions on each level (Shepherd, 1985). Repetition for the purposes of emphasis, intensification, and iteration is codified in the form of reduplication (examples 1–4).

Reduplication

intensive-emphatic:
1. Me swim fas-fas an far-far.
   "I swam very fast and very far."
2. De gyaal crazy-crazy.
   "The girl is really crazy."

iterative-habitual:
3. De pikny sicky-sicky.
   "The child is always getting sick." ("The child is sickly.")
4. She a wok-wok.
   "She is always working."

Similarly, topicalization involves the codified use of repetition in Antiguan Creole. Topicalized sentences require the repetition of a key adjective or verb. The element focused upon occurs at the beginning of the sentence, and again at its normal position in the sentence, as illustrated in examples 5–7. (Topicalized adverbs and nouns are not repeated.)

Topicalization

5. A emty de cup emty.
   "The cup is *empty!*"
6. A tiif me tiif?! A borrow me borrow.
   "I *stole* it?! (No,) I *borrowed* it.
7. A rongo me rongo. Me na min tap long.
   "I hurried! I didn't stay long."

Repetition at the sentence level also occurs for the purposes of iteration (as in 8, and possibly 9) and emphasis (9 and 10). The main clause is repeated at the end of the sentence, sometimes with additional information included.

8. i tek smell tek smell, i tek smell.
   "He kept sniffing, he sniffed."
9. Dat time drum play, ya know drum, drum play.
   "At that time drums played, you know drums played."
10. Dey don even serve notice, dey don even serve. Come now masquerade, don even serve come roun now an play.
    "They don't even notice, they don't even notice. Now when the masqueraders come, they don't even notice when they come around now and play."

The discourse functions of cohesion, argument, and humor are also conveyed through repetition—usually exact phrasal repetition, occurring throughout the discourse unit. The functions of repetition in conversational and narrative discourse are discussed in detail in Shepherd (1990), but a few examples will be given here. In example 11, the expression "i na get none, co i go late" was not responded to by the listeners. The speaker (PH) regains the floor, and the attention of the others, through her repetition of "Ya na min hear me. . .", and then repeats her previous utterance to close this portion of the conversation. LT also uses repetition, "watch Dee, watch Dee, watch Dee. . .", to gain the floor.

11.	PH:	i na get none, co i go late.	"He didn't get any because he went late."
	LT:	watch Dee, watch Dee, watch Dee.	"Look at Dee. Look at Dee. Look at Dee."
		. . .	. . .
	PH:	ya na min hear me tell Dee when he come in me ha subm fuh tell i? ya ya na min hear me a gon tell i?	"Didn't you hear me tell Dee when I came in that I had something to tell him? Didn't you hear that I was going to tell him (something)?

LT:	tal	"Not at all."
PH:	i na get none co i go late.	"He didn't get any because he went late."

Topic control in Antiguan Creole conversations is often determined through the skillful use of repetition. In example 12, the
5-year-old speaker is attempting to regain control of the activities of
a group of children. Her anger at not being allowed to determine the
course of their play is expressed and then defused through repetition of and "me na wan na noise on muh head" and "me serious."
Eventually the other children draw her into their game, but do not
allow her to take control.

12. (age 5)

KE: I don wan noise in muh head.

"I don't want any noise in my head."

. . .

me na wan na noise on muh head . . . me na wan na noise on muh head

"on my head . . . I don't want any noise in my head."

. . .

na wan na noise on muh—an you not readin nuttin ya dus turn de page to look an /chups/

"I don't want any noise in my—you're not reading anything. You just turn the pages to look, and /chups/ (an expression of disgust)"

. . .

paper ya wan? me na wan na noise in my head naa

"You want paper? I don't want any noise in my head you know."

. . .

a wonder if ya- wonder if muh s- ya- ya know muh serious.

"I wonder if you-wonder if I-you know I'm serious."

. . .

muh say muh na wan na noise in muh head

"I said I don't want any noise in my head."

. . .

a ya mosa gon play we de sudn, muh na. . .

"All of you have to go play with the thing. I don't. . ."

. . .

wonder if aya na know muh serious. wonder if aya na know me serious serious. me serious serious.

"I wonder if all you don't know I'm serious. I wonder if all you don't know I'm very serious. I'm very serious."

. . .   . . .

me serious serious serious	I'm very very serious."
. . .	. . .
muh serious. me na wan na noise in muh head. muh serious.	"I'm serious. I don't want any noise in my head. I'm serious."

Adults make similar uses of repetition, which if it goes on long enough, becomes humorous to both speaker and listener(s). The expression of discontent is made, usually several times. Speakers who wish to show that there are no hard feelings may continue their repetition, or bring it back into the conversation much later, usually resulting in laughter. The laughter is both an acknowledgement of the complaint and a signal that the anger has passed.

In narrative discourse, repetition is used to open and close individual episodes, much as it is used in topic control in conversational discourse:

13.   i na see de krapa. dus he an de clos. na see de krapa.
      "He didn't see the frog. Just he and the clothes (are in the
      room). He didn't see the frog."
14.   De deer trow off de boy in un river an de dog an all drop ova in
      dey too. When de boy drop ova in de river headway, de dog an all
      drop in dey too.
      "The deer threw the boy off (his head) into a river and the dog
      fell in there too. When the boy fell in the river headfirst, the dog
      fell in there too."

Repetition is also used to structure the entire narrative, through repeated mention of a key theme, as in example 15, which presents utterances which occurred at key points throughout a narrative.

15.   Nobody really know wey de krapa gone. . .
      Nobody can know where de krapa gone. . .
      Nobody na know wey de krapa gone. . .
      Nobody know wey de krapa can gone. . .
      ("Nobody knows where the frog could have gone.")

The functions served by repetition in narrative discourse—short-range and long-range cohesion—are more specific than those found in conversational discourse—negotiation, control, and attention getting (Shepherd, 1990). In Antiguan Creole child language acquisition, the conversational functions appear earlier than the narrative functions, suggesting that the direction of change is from less specific to more specific, and from emotive and interpersonal to textual. This supports Traugott's (1982) discussion of the unidirectionality of change from propositional to textual meanings, but seems to contradict her prediction (1989, p. 31) that changes from expressive to textual are highly unlikely in the history of a grammatical marker.

In child language acquisition data, self-repetition appears early, particularly in contexts involving verbal play and private speech. In addition, reduplication is a strategy used by many children as they acquire a language (Smith, 1973; Ingram, 1975), as well as being a characteristic of baby talk in many languages (Ferguson, 1977). Many significant conversational functions of repetition also develop relatively early in children. These include clarification, emphasis, attention getting, and regulation. There are striking parallels in the uses of repetition among children and creole speakers, both in terms of the wide variety of functions served and the extent to which repetition is used. In an unpublished study of repetition in the speech of one child from age 3;10 to 4;0, DeLauter (1989) found that 35% of the child's utterances at mealtime and bathtime (the times at which she recorded) consisted of self-repetition. Her analysis is based in part on functional categories discussed by Ochs (1979), Shepherd (1985), Casby (1986), and Tannen (1987). The most frequently occurring functions in her data were play (41%); regulatory (16%); attention-getting (16%); clarification or solicitation of information (6%); and emphasis (6%). As in the creole, two of the primary conversational functions of repetition are to gain and maintain control.

I would like to be able to argue that the most common uses of reduplication are relatively concrete and iconic. This is true to some extent, but does not always appear to be the case. Intensity and iteration are among the most common uses of repetition in Antiguan Creole and child language, and this process-meaning relationship seems to be fairly concrete and iconic. There is a connection between multiple occurrences and intensity, and an habitual event is one which is repeated over time. Moravcsik (1978) has identified several functions served by reduplicative constructions in a wide range of languages. These include quantity, intensity, diminution, attenuation, iteration, and continuation. Although the functions of quantity, intensity, and iteration seem to me to be linked intuitively with repetition, diminution and attenuation do not. It might be argued, however, that the basic meaning of diminution has to do with quantity (smaller than the norm), and of attenuation, intensity (less than the norm). Although the relationship between the specific meanings (diminution and attenuation) and multiple occurrences of a form is counterintuitive, there is a connection between the basic meaning components.

As pointed out by Heine and Reh (1984, p. 47), an additional characteristic of reduplication in many African languages is that it marks the transition from process to state, and may result in a change in word category. This is at least marginally true of Antiguan Creole as well. A preverbal marker *de* is used to mark habitual aspect, but reduplicated forms of some verbs and adjectives result in the same meaning, as in examples 3 and 4. The reduplicated verb in 4 can also be used as an adjective, as in "She one wok-wok girl" (She's an industrious girl). In this instance, repetition (or reduplication) clearly serves a grammatical function, by changing the grammatical category of the form. Although repetition is clearly conventionalized or codified in Antiguan Creole, this particular use seems to be the clearest instance of grammaticalization.

There are several possible sources of repetition in creole languages. It is a common feature of talk addressed to children and nonnative speakers of a language (Snow, 1972; Ferguson & DeBose, 1977; Ferguson, 1977). Reduplication occurs in child language acquisition, and also is prevalent in African languages that were involved in the process of pidginization. It appears that many of the discourse functions of repetition are universal, with, perhaps, the most concrete uses developing earliest. Textual meanings appear to grow out of meanings connected to the social structuring of conversation. In terms of the meanings expressed, there are strong connections between the grammatical and discourse functions of repetition. In each case the use of repetition is reinforced through historical origins, patterns of language development, and language universals. Thus far, I have no evidence that the morphological uses of repetition develop out of syntactic and discourse uses, but the meaning similarities may encourage continued and expanded development of repetition at all levels in the language.

In my work on repetition I have been primarily concerned with language varieties that have strong oral traditions. Repetition plays an important role in such languages, serving cohesive and focusing functions, even though it may be devalued, at least in planned oral and written discourse (Ochs, 1979), in languages that rely heavily on written traditions. Interestingly, grammaticalization or conventionalization of repetition is prevalent in oral societies. As written traditions develop, repetition may be partially replaced by other cohesive devices. This is not to say that repetition will cease to be used for such discourse functions in societies with strong written traditions—clearly that is not the case. Nevertheless, written norms may influence oral discourse patterns, which would not be the case in communities relying primarily on oral traditions. This may contribute to the negative evaluation repetition receives in many educational contexts, for example, even though it continues to be used. In cultures in which narrative structure is strongly influenced by written traditions, we can expect that repetition will play a less significant role in both written and oral discourse, than in cultures in which oral traditions predominate. If, as Traugott proposes, textual meanings develop out of propositional meanings, we should expect societies which emphasize written traditions and those which emphasize oral traditions to manifest differing paths of development and use of repetition. Languages that embrace repetition in both planned and unplanned discourse may also be more likely to employ the process of repetition grammatically.

REFERENCES

Bybee, J., & Pagliuca, W. (1985). Cross-linguistic comparison and the development of grammatical meaning. In J. Fisiak (Ed.), *Historical semantics: Historical word formation* (pp. 59–83). Berlin: Mouton de Gruyter.

Casby, M. (1986). A pragmatic perspective of repetition in child language. *Journal of Psycholinguistic Research, 15,* 127–140.

DeLauter, M. S. (1989). *A study of repetition in child language.* Unpublished manuscript, Indiana University, Indianapolis.

Ferguson, C. A. (1977). Baby talk as a simplified register. In C. E. Snow & C. A. Ferguson (Eds.), *Talking to children* (pp. 209–235). Cambridge, UK: Cambridge University Press.

Ferguson, C. A., & DeBose, C. E. (1977). Simplified registers, broken language, and pidginization. In A. Valdman (Ed.), *Pidgin and creole linguistics* (pp. 99–125). Bloomington, IN: Indiana University Press.

Givon, T. (1979). *On understanding grammar.* New York: Academic Press.

Heine, B., & Reh, M. (1984). *Grammaticalization and reanalysis in African languages.* Hamburg: Helmut Buske.

Ingram, D. (1975). Surface contrasts in children's speech. *Journal of Child Language, 1,* 233–241.

Moravscik, E. A. (1978). Reduplicative constructions. In J. H. Greenberg (Ed.), *Universals of human language* (Vol. 3, pp. 297–334). Palo Alto, CA: Stanford University Press.

Ochs, E. (1979). Planned and unplanned discourse. In T. Givon (Ed.), *Discourse and semantics* (pp. 51–80). New York: Academic Press.

Shepherd, S. (1985). On the functional development of repetition in Antiguan Creole morphology, syntax, and discourse. In J. Fisiak (Ed.), *Historical semantics: Historical word formation* (pp. 533–545). Berlin: Mouton de Gruyter.

Shepherd. S. (1990). Functions of repetition: Variation in narrative and conversational discourse. In J. A. Edmondson, C. Feagin, & P. Mühlhäusler (Eds.), *Development and diversity: Linguistic variation across time and space* (pp. 629–638). Arlington, TX: Summer Institute of Linguistics and University of Texas at Arlington.

Smith, N. V. (1973). *The acquisition of phonology: A case study.* Cambridge, UK: Cambridge University Press.

Snow, C. E. (1972). Mothers' speech to children learning language. *Child Development, 43,* 549–565.

Sweetser, E. (1988). Grammaticalization and semantic bleaching. *Berkeley Linguistics Society, Proceedings of the Fourteenth Annual Meeting* (pp. 389–405). Berkeley, CA: Berkeley Linguistics Society.

Tannen, D. (1987). Repetition in conversation: Toward a poetics of talk. *Language, 63,* 574–605.

Traugott, E. C. (1982). From propositional to textual and expressive meanings: Some semantic-pragmatic aspects of grammaticalization. In W. P. Lehmann & Y. Malkiel (Eds.), *Perspectives on historical linguistics* (pp. 245–271). Amsterdam: John Benjamins.

Traugott, E. C. (1989). On the rise of epistemic meanings in English: An example of subjectification in semantic change. *Language, 65,* 31–55.

Traugott, E. C., & König, E. (forthcoming). The semantics-pragmatics of grammaticalization revisited. In B. Heine & E. C. Traugott (Eds.), *Aspects of grammaticalization.* Amsterdam: John Benjamins.

Chapter 16

Affirming the Past and Confirming Humanness: Repetition in the Discourse of Elderly Adults

Jeutonne P. Brewer

Department of English
University of North Carolina at Greensboro

INTRODUCTION

This chapter focuses on repetition in the discourse of four elderly adults, two married couples who have known each other for more than 25 years. During the past 5 years, the couples have at times lived together in the same house so that their family could take care of their special needs.

As a participant-observer, I have tape recorded conversations between the two couples, conversations with family, and interviews with individual adults; I have also collected examples of brief exchanges when no tape recorder was present. These elderly adults were given no tasks to perform. They chose their own topics of conversation and worked out their own discourse strategies in such normal conversational settings as the dinner table. The couples are relatives of mine who permitted the recordings to be made and who knew the tape recorder was on the table or the nearby cabinet.

At the beginning of the project, the wife of Couple A was 67 years old, the husband 74 years old; the wife and husband of Couple B were the same age, 85 years old. The husband of Couple A had been diagnosed as having an advanced case of arteriosclerosis, the wife of Couple B as having Alzheimer's Disease.

A significant aspect of their conversations, as of all conversation, is the use of repetition. Tannen (1984, 1987, 1989) has shown that "repetition functions in production, comprehension, cohesion, and interaction" (1987, p. 576). In fact, "the congruence of these levels of discourse creates coherence" (p. 376) of both the message and the meanings beyond the words actually spoken. Repetition provides a framework into which speakers can place new information.

REPETITION, PARADIGMS, AND A MENTAL STUTTER

Particularly informative is the discourse of the two adults diagnosed with serious illnesses. The male of Couple A (age range during study, 74–77 years, arteriosclerosis) repeatedly relates experiences as a means of family affirmation, a means also for creating (or recreating) family myth. Although he may change details, his stories are in effect the same. He uses repetition in discourse to affirm his past, to confirm that it is there, and to maintain his claim to his place in the family. The female of Couple B (age range 85–88 years, Alzheimer's Disease) uses language primarily as a personal activity rather than as a familial/social activity. She reads aloud, is comfortable talking to herself about what she reads, and willingly talks about any subject that comes to mind. She comprehends what she reads, although she may have difficulty understanding the significance of the passage in the present context. It is as though reading is a contact with the outside world, although she no longer clearly understands that world. In this way she affirms the present, her present, using repetition in discourse to prove that she is human; talking is a human activity.

Both of these adults use episodic memory (Nebes, 1985, p. 110)— personal records of unique events, and semantic memory—knowledge of associations between words and concepts, to tell and retell their narratives. It seems, however, that their pragmatic purposes are inwardly or personally focused; more important than recognizing the intentions and purposes of other speakers is the opportunity to affirm the past and confirm humanness.

Husband A (Bill) most enjoys talking about family lore and legend. Other topics are things that disturb or upset him—insurance details, politics. For example, President Reagan receives a special measure of dislike because he cut Bill's annuity, and, according to Bill, lied about it. A recurring story relates how the Reagan government had taken the railroad/social security money, used it, and never repaid it.

With little prompting, sometimes none, he tells the stories about his own past or about his family's history. One story is about the killing of Tom, the first husband of Bill's mother. After Tom was killed, Bill's mother married Tom's brother, John, who was Bill's father. An important part of telling the story is explaining why and under what circumstances Bill's mother married the two brothers:

B: His name was Tom, and he went down to a neighbor's on the back section, quarter section of land.

J: Now was this in Oklahoma or Kansas?

B: It was in Oklahoma, I mean, no, in Kansas. Anyway, he went down to this neighbor's house in Kansas. And he went down to the neighbor's house. He made some insulting remark about Mother, called her a bitch or something. That's all he had to do, and Dad—Uncle Tom—took up for Mother. Why he took after him and went on down the road. This old boy cut through the section line, ambushed him as he came by. Just up and shot and killed him. Mother was a widow, and Dad was a widow because his wife had died. Her name was Wolcott.

Sometimes Bill adds additional details. Tom was shot in the back. Nobody was ever caught or punished for the killing.

Another story is about Bill's dad serving in the army, the 7th Cavalry, under Custer's command. His dad and several other soldiers were on leave in Oklahoma when Custer and his army were killed at the battle of Little Big Horn. When asked about who first told him the story, he replied:

B: Mom was telling me about it first, I guess. Dad was already dead and gone, and she was the first one to tell me about it. And she heard it somewhere; I don't recall the details of it; she heard it somewhere, in this book. [He had explained earlier in the interview that "there's a book about that thick about it."]

J: Oh.

B: And she was telling about her, and I think, another lady, Mrs. Henshaw, were together, staying there together, staying there, and said they could hear something running, sound like somebody was running [clapping his hands]. Running back and forth.

J: Uh hmmm.

B: [laughing] They got up the next morning and saw a big old bobtail cow.

This happened "after [Dad] left to go up there to wherever it was" to meet Custer. The women, living alone in the country, thought the sounds might be Indians. They kept the doors and windows shut tight throughout the night. The next morning they saw the cow that had made the noises during the night.

The self-repetition in these examples provides additional support for the view that these phrases are "ready-made" phrases from prior discourse (Tannen, 1989, pp. 55–56). Statements like "ambushed him," "Just up and shot and killed him," "Mother was a widow, and Dad was a widow" stress "what is memorable and reportable about this experience" (Tannen, 1989, p. 56) as the story is told and retold. In a similar way, "could hear something running," "somebody was running," and "running back and forth" underscore the notable and reportable scary night that turned into a funny happening when the fear of danger faded into a "big old bob tail cow." Although I have only a recent retelling of the stories on tape, the stories are part of family lore, retold periodically. They are examples of what Tannen calls repetition across discourses and time.

Wife B (Ruth) uses discourse in a different way. Although she sometimes discusses family and family events, she usually focuses her efforts on attempts to converse in the immediate setting. She is more likely than Bill is to talk about things in the setting—"bugs" on the tablecloth, details about people she knows or knew, for example. She also enjoys reading aloud and then talking to herself or others about what she has read. Ruth now lives in a nursing home. On one of his regular visits in December 1989, her son, Chris, decided to take Ruth downstairs for a Coke. As Ruth was getting on the elevator, she encountered other people, visitors, already in the elevator. She knew that it was appropriate to speak to them. Wanting to greet them and introduce her partner, Ruth said:

R: This is my—this is my brother.
C: [laughs] And I'm your son.
R: [Claps her hands with delight and smiles] Oh, then we're related on both sides!

On another visit during the same month, Ruth and her son were talking about Mr. Pennington from "back home." Ruth used to drive for Mr. Pennington, who had lost his right arm in an accident. In identifying Mr. Pennington, Ruth asks: "He had two arms, didn't he?" In this case Ruth remembers the driving, remembers Mr. Pennington, remembers that he had a handicap, but she is not able to ask the appropriate question that would verify what the problem was.

Ruth provides intriguing examples of repetition in discourse. Particularly disconcerting to those who suffer from Alzheimer's Disease is any change in schedule, any change in setting. In March 1988, her son had gone on vacation to Arkansas, where he could continue his work on a family history. During the first week of his absence, Ruth and I had this conversation many times:

R: Where's Chris?
J: He's gone to Arkansas.
R: He did? What'd he do that for?
J: He's visiting family and he's working on his family history.
R: What's he want to do that for?
J: He just enjoys working on it.

Silence. Brief pause.

R: Where's Chris?
J: He's gone to Arkansas.
R: He did? What'd he do that for?
J: He's visiting family and he's working on his family history.
R: What's he want to do that for?
J: He just enjoys working on it.

Silence. Brief pause. Then the cycle begins again, to be repeated three, four, or five times. The final repetition has an importantly different conclusion.

R: Where's Chris?
J: He's gone to Arkansas.
R: He did? What'd he do that for?
J: He's visiting family and he's working on his family history.
R: What's he want to do that for?
J: He just enjoys working on it.

Ruth turns to me and asks:

R: Did you go with him?

Brief pause.

J: [slowly] No, Ruth. I stayed here with you.
R: Oh yes. You did.

These repetitions are not really false starts. Nor do they produce a paradigm into which new information can be placed. The last cycle quoted above contains the only significant change that occurred during the 4 to 5 days in which the conversation repeatedly took place. The entire conversation is played to its conclusion each time. There are no overlaps in the conversation. After a brief pause, the same conversation begins again. In this example, repetition does not occur within the conversation; the entire conversation is repeated. From Ruth's point of view, each conversation is appropriate because she doesn't remember the previous conversation. She does not paraphrase or change her comments; she repeats the conversation without change in the meaning or adding to the meaning. We might call this a mental stutter.

STUDYING THE LANGUAGE OF THE ELDERLY

In order to understand the linguistic capabilities of the elderly, we need to understand the full continuum of language development. Researchers have studied language use by young children, adolescents and younger adults. To understand language development in children, researchers have studied their language use at different stages and written grammars to reflect their linguistic ability; researchers typically do not describe a child's language use in terms of deviation from an adult standard. Significant advances in our understanding of language form and use have come as a result of studying language use in typical settings.

With the exception of the Linguistic Atlas projects of the American Dialect Society, which focused primarily on the study of vocabulary in order to determine dialect boundaries, language use by elderly adults has not received much attention. The results of clinical studies of language capability tell us little about conversational ability and linguistic capability; such tests place elderly adults in strange settings in which they are given unusual tasks to perform, and describe their behavior, when it differs from that of younger adults, as deviant. Such tests and findings can tell us little about life-long language development and language loss. Cohen and Faulkner (1981, pp. 263–64), for example, reported that the memory of the elderly was impaired in the area of discourse. However, they also reported that "the experimental task in this study is considerably more demanding than conversation. A large amount of information, divorced from a situational context was presented, and the kind of speaker-hearer interaction that permits an adjustment of pacing, and of amount of redundancy, was absent" (p. 264). These points call into question the claim that the findings demonstrate memory impairment in discourse. Rather they suggest that elderly adults may not perform well in clinical testing situations. The important question is how elderly adults perform in normal conversations when they are talking about topics of interest to them.

Research has indicated that pragmatic competence is affected early in elderly adults with dementia (Bayles, 1985, p. 159). But there are no valid and reliable tests for linguistic abilities. In addition to considering possible cognitive impairment caused by dementia, researchers need to determine what is "a normal stage in the life span language development continuum" (p. 137). In one recent study, researchers concluded that, by conducting their study, they found age-related bias to be as important as their other findings; they noted the need to study "the nature and magnitude of aging changes" (Lieberman, Rigo, & Campain, 1988, p. 295).

Sociolinguistic studies generally work on the assumption that adults of middle age and older are less susceptible than younger people to social pressure to change how they use language. Adolescents are very sensitive to linguistic variation (Labov, 1972, pp. 256–258; Halliday, 1978, p. 184) and speak the most consistent vernacular (Labov, 1972, p. 257). Labov claims that "the grammars of adults seem to be permanently changed by their use of standard rules" (p. 257), although "in old age, much of the superposed variation disappears" (p. 258). More recently, Bailey and Bernstein (1989) and Bernstein (forthcoming) have found that age is the most significant factor in predicting phonological variation; younger speakers are more likely to use innovative forms than older speakers. It seems reasonable to assume that older adults may also be less constrained by the pragmatic rules imposed by society on certain social settings. Older adults decide what dialectal words and sentence structures they will retain and use regularly. It seems reasonable that older adults may decide which pragmatic and discourse rules will be important and binding for them, which rules they may adapt, deemphasize, or ignore. These decisions could affect formal testing situations. Are the pragmatics of the testing context the same for younger adults and older adults? If not, how do researchers take the difference into account?

It seems unlikely that the artificial speech events created in clinical testing will be the same for younger adults and older adults. The adult of 70 years has quite possibly been away from the formal classroom for half a century; the younger adult is closer to the classroom and formal testing, both in time and in social distance. Schools, the training ground for formal testing, have changed in many ways during the past 50 years. The present classroom and testing context are generations of social distance removed from older adults and their experience. Older adults may not respond well to the socially distant world of standardized testing, the clinic, the laboratory.

DISCOURSE PERSPECTIVES OF THE ELDERLY

As a participant-observer in this study, I learned that it was necessary to view communication from the perspective of the elderly. This seems obvious, but, as I have pointed out, many observations about language use by the elderly, particularly the demented, seem to start from the perspective that the language of the elderly should be viewed as language deviant from a standard, or at least deviant from the language of younger adults.

The four elderly adults in this study spoke frequently, fluently, and competitively in a familial, familiar setting. On the one hand, they tried to establish floors for discourse and at times effectively used turn-taking techniques to control conversation (Sacks, Schegloff, & Jefferson, 1974). On the other hand, at times they ignored or no longer appeared to control pragmatic abilities; Grice's (1967) Cooperative Principle could be irrelevant. For example, all four elderly adults could talk at the same time on different topics, a situation that disconcerted the family but did not bother them. All of these factors are important in understanding and explaining communicative competence and pragmatics—the relation between language use and its structure and content—in the language of elderly adults.

Using their linguistic repertoire, the elderly adults clearly used different pragmatic rules at times. The first inclination is to claim that their pragmatic rules have eroded. But that is too easy. The adults could talk to each other, and they could talk to others outside the family circle. It is true, however, that they played the linguistic game by their own rules at times. Their pragmatic rules have changed, whether as a result of physical ailment, the aging process, or by choice.

CONCLUSION

Researchers analyze language use by children in terms of development and change. This study indicates that researchers should also analyze language use by the elderly in terms of development and change. In other words, language is best viewed as a life-long learning process. For the elderly, pragmatic rules may change because their sense of community changes; community seems to be more restricted or constrained than in earlier periods of their lives. It is reasonable, perhaps a natural development, that they would adapt their pragmatic rules. Only in the most extreme cases, such as advanced stages of dementia, do the elderly lose their syntactic and lexical abilities. Until then, they adapt to their linguistic surroundings. This study suggests that researchers must study the language ability of the elderly in the context of language change and adaptation rather than primarily as language loss. I have illustrated this point here with reference to two elderly adults' uses of repetition. One used repeated retellings of familiar stories to affirm his central familial identity. The other repeated entire conversations, as a way of keeping talk going and remaining connected to other humans. These two uses of repetition, while unlike those of younger speakers in some ways, can be seen to serve clear pragmatic functions in their speakers' worlds.

"No serious studies" are available about how the expectations of others and discourse settings influence the "communicative styles of adults" (Ulatowska, Cannito, Hayashi, & Fleming, 1985, p. 127). As a study of how elderly adults converse with each other, with family, and with others, this project addresses these gaps in our research and knowledge. As a longitudinal study, this project will provide important data about what changes in linguistic ability occur in language form and use in the speech of the elderly.

REFERENCES

Bailey, G., & Bernstein, C. (1989). Methodology of a phonological survey of Texas. *Journal of English Linguistics, 50,* 6–16.

Bayles, K. A. (1985). Communication in dementia. In H. K. Ulatowska (Ed.), *The aging brain* (pp. 157–174). San Diego: College-Hill Press.

Bernstein, C. (forthcoming). A phonological survey of Texas: Cluster analysis of the Texas Poll data. *Proceedings of the International Congress of Dialectologists, 1990.*

Cohen, G., & Faulkner, D. (1981). Memory for discourse in old age. *Discourse Processes, 4,* 253–265.

Grice, H. P. (1967). Logic and conversation (William James Lectures, Harvard University). In P. Cole & J. Morgan (Eds.), *Syntax and semantics Vol. 3: Speech acts* (pp. 113–127). New York: Academic Press, 1975.

Halliday, M. A. K. (1978). Language and social structure. In *Language as social semiotic* (pp. 183–192). London: Edward Arnold.

Labov, W. (1972). The linguistic consequences of being a lame. In *Language in the inner city: Studies in the black English vernacular* (pp. 255–292). Philadelphia: University of Pennsylvania Press.

Lieberman, D. A., Rigo, T. G., & Campain, R. F. (1988). Age-related differences in nonverbal decoding ability. *Communication Quarterly* *36*, 290–297.

Nebes, R. D. (1985). Preservation of semantic structure in dementia. In H. K. Ulatowska (Ed.), *The aging brain* (pp. 109–122). San Diego: College-Hill Press.

Sacks, H., Schegloff, E., & Jefferson, G. (1974). Towards a simplest systematics for the organization of turn-taking for conversation. *Language*, *50*, 696–735.

Tannen, D. (1984). *Conversational style: Analyzing talk among friends.* Norwood, NJ: Ablex Publishing Corp.

Tannen, D. (1987). Repetition in conversation: Toward a poetics of talk. *Language*, *63*, 574–605.

Tannen, D. (1989). *Talking voices.* Cambridge, UK: Cambridge University Press.

Ulatowska, H. K., Cannito, M. P., Hayashi, M. M., & Fleming, S. G. (1985). Language abilities in the elderly. In H. K. Ulatowska (Ed.), *The aging brain* (pp. 125–140). San Diego: College-Hill Press.

Author Index

Subject Index